The Thunder of Captains

The Thunder
of Captains

Dan Lynch

Three Lakes Publishing
Clifton Park, NY
2010

Library of Congress Control Number 2009941760

ISBN 0-9843430-0-3

Printed in the United States of America

For Pam

To the Reader

About thirty miles north of the red-roofed New York State Capitol building in Albany, on the western bank of the Hudson River, a series of broad, rolling hills rise up from the shoreline to form a vast plateau. In that place, the river is a dull, greenish-gray even in glittering sunlight. Atop those hills beside that river, as an early fall chill set leaves aflame in 1777, a momentous conflict occurred. Historians have characterized the battle that took place there as "the military clash of the millennium."

Some months earlier, an English army had set off from Canada in a vast armada of boats, large and small, to crush the colonial uprising. The route of the invasion was south — down the vast expanse of Lake Champlain, then overland toward Albany on the Hudson's western shore.

What followed that departure from Canada were months of bitter, bloody warfare culminating in the Battle of Saratoga — or, more precisely, in the two battles of Saratoga. In the aftermath of what turned out to be the most crucial clash of the American Revolution — and, in the view of many experts, the most consequential battle ever fought on North American soil — a great nation was born. The outcome of that confrontation was determined far less by external factors like weather and topography than by the complex passions and personalities of the men and women involved.

Yes, women. In those days women played active roles in military campaigns and constituted a critical influence on the men who fought them. Several women played key roles in the Battle of Saratoga, and they play key roles in this novel as well.

The essential lesson of history is that human events are shaped by temperament and personality. So it was with Saratoga. What happened there and what happened to the world as a consequence was the result of unique people with unique traits reacting to events in their own individual ways. Each significant character in this novel actually existed. With only minor compression of events for simplicity of narrative, the story occurred pretty much the way it's presented in this book. In all relevant respects, this novel is a faithful account of a hugely important occurrence that altered the course of history.

The events recounted here in fictional form – fiction because most conversations and other personal interactions between the participants can only be inferred from historical sources — unfolded against a complex global backdrop. In 1777 — the "Bloody Sevens," as the year came to be called — the English Empire was ruled by George III, a profoundly difficult man who had been schooled from birth that his primary duty as monarch, towering above all other obligations, was to preserve the Empire. England's world dominance was threatened by a sustained period of warfare with France that had left the Empire deeply in debt. To finance its worldwide ambitions, the English Empire turned to its prosperous colonies in North America, which were booming in population. As tax after tax was levied, colonial resistance intensified to paying the bills for the Empire's foreign adventures. At first, that resistance crystallized in the colonies' merchant and legal classes, but it finally began to spread throughout a largely rural citizenry, especially among the more affluent farmers.

At no time did the desire to break away from the Empire take root in a majority of colonial citizens. No more than a third of colonists supported independence. Another third were fierce loyalists.

Members of the final third were either undecided or unconcerned. The desire for independence did, however, develop a widespread following among the colonies' ruling and intellectual classes. That happened for financial reasons and because of a growing devotion to the democratic principles of a dead English philosopher, John Locke, who had rejected the rule of royalty in favor of the rule of the common man.

Once the rebellion began in earnest with an exchange of gunfire between colonists and British troops at Concord, the colonists begged the French king for financing to continue their quest for independence. Only if you show me you can win, Louis XVI told them. As Benjamin Franklin groveled for cash in Paris, the French settled back to determine if the colonists really could defeat what was universally viewed as the planet's finest military organization.

At the same time, King George urged his ministers to put down the uprising with dispatch and without mercy. The rebel army was a shabby, poorly equipped collection of disgruntled former English officers leading untrained tradesmen, farmers and backwoods squirrel hunters. Surely, it could be no match for His Majesty's Royal Army. Even the rebel army's commander-in-chief, a stoic Virginia planter and land baron named George Washington, had only limited military experience. As he employed tentative, hit-and-run tactics in steadfast retreat, Washington also studied military tactics by candlelight in his tent, hoping to teach himself how to wage a war.

As the rebellion continued, denying the empire crucial tax revenues, English politicians came to understand that he who engineered a swift and decisive victory for the Crown would enjoy the brightest of futures. Those whose efforts bore no fruit would fall by the political wayside. It was in this environment that Major General

John Burgoyne, a member of Parliament and a vaunted English field commander, convinced the king to bankroll an ambitious invasion from the north. The campaign would be commanded, of course, by Burgoyne himself.

When Burgoyne sailed from England with a force composed of English regular soldiers and a contingent of German mercenaries, he left behind a determined corps of political opponents bent on undermining what Burgoyne referred to as The Grand Strategy. As Burgoyne set sail on Lake Champlain the following June to begin his campaign, the rebel army led by Washington was a hapless shambles. It had failed in the field against the English on Long Island and in New York City. It was badly outnumbered. For the most part, its commanders were inexperienced, undisciplined and often at odds with one another. Its troops were outgunned, underfed, riddled with disease and suffering from morale so low that it bordered on despair. Both the rebellion and the raucous central government it sought to preserve lacked popular support from the citizen/soldier membership of colonial militias.

How could the rebels derail Burgoyne's Grand Strategy? How could the untrained and under-supplied Army of the United States withstand his assault? Could colonial citizens be persuaded finally to rise to defend their homes against invasion by the Crown? Could the rebel army's fractious commanders manage to bury their own bitter animosities to stand successfully against the fiercest fighting machine the world had ever known?

That's what this novel is all about.

Key Characters

The Men

English Major General John Burgoyne: Born into a middle-class British family, Burgoyne began his political and military rise with a fortuitous marriage to the daughter of a wealthy nobleman. His election to the House of Commons has made him a major player in London politics and fueled his lust for a higher station in life.

Rebel General Philip Schuyler: The scion of a wealthy family of Dutch settlers, Schuyler was a colonial aristocrat determined to see the colonies shake off the chokehold of British royalty.

Rebel General Horatio Gates: A highly experienced former English officer frustrated by the rigid class structure of the Royal Army, Gates was a cautious, deliberate man eager to rise in the New World.

English General Simon Fraser: Viewed by superiors and subordinates alike as a soldier's soldier, Fraser was an engaging Scot who led Burgoyne's advance troops. He commanded universal respect from comrades and enemies alike.

Rebel General Benedict Arnold: Fearless and alive with energy, Arnold was a new widower in his mid-thirties who channeled his chronic depression and relentless anger into dramatic action on the battlefield.

Baron Friedrich Adolf von Riedesel: The austere commander of Burgoyne's German mercenaries, General Riedesel was a skilled professional soldier who viewed war as a serious business too seldom conducted by serious men.

Sir Francis Clerke: Burgoyne's chief aide.

Colonel James Wilkinson: Chief aide to Army of the United States General Horatio Gates.

Colonel Daniel Morgan: Commander of Morgan's Rangers, a special unit of the Army of the United States

Benjamin Franklin: The new American government's representative to the French government in Paris.

Major Richard (Dirk) Varick: General Benedict Arnold's key aide.

The Women

Babette LeDoux: The central female character in the novel, Babette was beautiful and charming and determined in her desire to become a lady of quality.

Baroness Frederika von Riedesel: The daughter and wife of generals, the baroness was a devoted spouse and mother and a woman of towering fortitude. Where her husband went, she went, whatever the hardship involved.

Jane McCrea: Young and beautiful, Jane was a woman deeply in love and reckless in her determination to satisfy her desires, whatever the cost.

Frederick and George. 1781

Through the window of his carriage on the dirt road below the crest of the hill, he could see the tents higher up. Dark morning clouds were massed behind them, and the sun peeking up over the Thames made those clouds luminous. The light was pallid -- an early November sun battling vainly against Britain's characteristic morning mist.

Frederick thumped the inside of the carriage's roof with the brass head of his walking stick. The coachman, flawlessly trained, immediately pulled the team to a halt.

Frederick fumbled in his pocket for the summons he'd received in London the night before. His fingers closed on the stiff bit of parchment. He pulled out his steel-rimmed spectacles and adjusted them atop his bulbous nose. At nearly fifty, Frederick was now a slave to his eyeglasses. The vision from his somewhat bulging eyes grew dimmer by the day. He could read no document without the aid of the spectacles. This one, in the spidery calligraphy of the king's personal secretary beneath the embossed royal seal, was especially difficult to decipher. Frederick studied it once again.

By order of His Majesty, George Rex III, you are commanded to appear upon the dawning at the Royal Tent at Strathmont on Thames for consultation.

Just that, no more, and no way to avoid it. Frederick sighed silently and returned the summons to his coat. He removed the hated spectacles and stowed them away. He knew what this was about -- what it had to be about. In his mind, he was rehearsing. He'd learned long ago that a man who rehearsed for what he knew would be a trying encounter was a man likely to emerge from that encounter with no worse than a stalemate. He who planned strategies and carried them out diligently always had the edge over he who simply blundered along, as this king tended to do. Bolstered by experience, Frederick hoped to emerge from this encounter not only unharmed but perhaps even with some small advantage gained from the occasion. Still, this would not be a pleasant day. No day in the service of this monarch had been pleasant for seven long years now, ever since Frederick had ascended to the post of first minister. Frederick consoled himself with the knowledge that the days were gone when a man in his position might be greeted atop this hill by a headsman. The brass handle of the walking stick slammed again into the carriage roof. Frederick heard the crack of the coachman's whip in the crisp morning air. With a jolt, the team lunged into action, and the carriage resumed its bumpy climb.

The tents, a good dozen of them, sprawled across the hill's crest, looking down on the steam rising in filmy wisps from the water below, swirling in the sickly sunlight. As Frederick's carriage pulled up in front of the largest tent, the one adorned with the royal pennant, the king emerged. The red-coated guards at the tent's entrance clicked their heels. His Majesty was a thick set man nearing forty years of age with a cleft in his chin and a receding hairline above a high forehead. He was clad in a nightgown and robe, his thinning hair sticking out at all angles and a delicate china teacup suspended from his thick right index finger. Frederick climbed down from the carriage and bowed.

"Good of you to come," said King George III. "Join me inside, please. We have tea."

Silently, the short, pudgy Frederick bowed slightly at the waist and then followed the king into the spacious tent. Inside the silk-lined pavilion, the grass and dirt were hidden beneath lavish Persian rugs, and atop the rugs sat dozens of pieces of heavy, ornate furniture. Toward the rear of the tent was a gigantic, canopied bed, its curtains drawn. Off in one corner of the huge tent, a huge mastiff lay on its stomach, blissfully gnawing on a bloody beef bone. Servants scurried about. When His Majesty escaped the gilded cage of his palaces to go camping, as he often did when his mood grew dark, he went in a style befitting his rank; the riches of the royal palace went with him. Several steel stoves around the tent radiated welcome warmth. As Frederick settled into a high-backed chair with silk cushions, the king took his own thickly cushioned seat and motioned for a liveried servant to provide Frederick with tea.

"A crumpet, my Lord?" the servant inquired.

Frederick, Lord North, prime minister of Great Britain and the English Empire, shook his head. "Just the tea, thank you."

"You should take nourishment," the king said. "I most assuredly would were I able."

"The stomach pains again, your Majesty?"

"And the aches in the arms and legs," the king muttered. "And the urine the color of port. The physicians are monumentally useless, Frederick. Whatever this ailment is will surely kill me at some point."

At least that'll end the evil humors, Frederick thought. And the arrogance and the deplorable judgment.

"Your Majesty is a number of years my junior," the prime minister said. "Surely your reign over the empire will endure for many years to come."

King George frowned. "Such as the empire is at this juncture. You've studied the message from Cornwallis at Yorktown?"

Lord North gazed down at the richly patterned rug. "I have, your Majesty. A full report has been delivered to St. James Palace and awaits your attention. The French navy played an active role on behalf of the opposition, you should know."

"I've been here since your initial communication reached me," King George said in a low voice. "I required solitude and reflection. Total defeat, Frederick -- the colonies lost forever. God save the empire."

"Not necessarily," the prime minister responded. "Infant nations suffer high mortality rates. If we're patient, another opportunity might arise."

"There must be hearings in Parliament," the king snapped. "We must understand thoroughly what happened at Yorktown -- and why it happened."

"And so there shall be," Frederick replied. "Have no doubt that we'll investigate this assiduously."

"Any number of my predecessors would have had the head of Cornwallis on a pike and then made inquiries of his subordinates after the fact."

"Most assuredly, your Majesty, but I submit that the head of Cornwallis attached to the rest of him will be more useful to us for now, at least. Eventually, we can ship him off to deal with the ruffians of Ireland as a punishment, but first we must determine what happened at Yorktown."

"Better than we did with Saratoga, I hope," George III said.

There it is, Frederick thought. This particular bug has been up his arse for four long years now.

"That was the turning point, Frederick." the king said sullenly. "Looking back, it's clear now that was the vital moment. And the investigation was laughable beyond imagination. Jack made fools of you all. I nearly made him a Knight of the Bath, you know, almost a year before all that happened. He told me no -- that he could not accept a knighthood until he'd had the opportunity to earn it by putting down the rebellion."

"I didn't know that," Frederick said. "Typical of Jack, though. That would have been a persuasive argument designed to entice you into financing the effort and to place him in command of it. Jack has always been a uniquely persuasive fellow, as you know."

"And what, might I ask, is he up to now?"

"Oh, he's becoming quite the darling of the London stage. He's writing plays. Jack was always a uniquely creative chap as well."

"Yes," the king mumbled. "A consummate showman, Jack is."

For a long moment, there was silence between the two men. The king sipped his tea and gazed off into space, frowning deeply. This was not over, Frederick knew. He had rehearsed in his mind what he would do if pressed. He was prepared, if absolutely necessary, to resort to the truth.

"Will we ever know about Saratoga?" George III asked at long last.

"The formal investigation was botched," Lord North admitted, surrendering to the unaccustomed need to abandon subterfuge and obfuscation. "I have, however, looked into it privately, your Majesty, for the sake of my own curiosity -- and, of course, for the benefit of the Crown. I've had detailed inquiries made both amongst the military and in the colonies, assuring all who would cooperate total anonymity. The stories have been taken down and delivered to me. I've read everything, committed it to memory and destroyed the documents. You're quite correct; Jack managed to charm all my blithering colleagues in Commons, many of whom are his friends to begin with. The full truth never came out."

The king sat up straight in his high-backed chair. "Yes?" he said, his eyebrows climbing halfway up his brow.

Frederick recognized that it was now time for candor. Lord North felt no affection for this king, did not respect him as a man. King George III was an inept politician, a monarch utterly lacking in the magnetism a leader needs to pull followers along with him, rather than merely pushing them. The king also was a meddling fusspot with a distressing tendency toward bluster. He had permitted Lord George Grenville, as the king's chief minister, to goad the colonies again and again with taxes and other laws that the more prosperous colonists found uniquely onerous. By the time Frederick had assumed power, after years of ineptitude on the part of Grenville and his successor, the maddening "Champagne Charlie" Townshend, the damage had been done. Revolution was bubbling fiercely across the Atlantic, particularly in Massachusetts, which the king regarded as a particularly insidious hotbed of sedition. In no way could England permit its North American colonists to break away, but there was little Frederick had been able to do to deter the king from policies virtually certain to incite the pot to boil over.

The prime minister understood, however, that he was obliged to inform and advise. As a matter of policy, since the king was uniquely mercurial, Lord North had been generous with advice but stingy with information. Still, since it was now too late for George III to further muck up matters, the king was entitled to understand the bizarre sequence of events that had cost the English Empire its most lucrative colonies.

He said, "It's a complex story, your Majesty."

"We have the time, Frederick," the king said evenly as he sat back in his chair. "We will not be disturbed here; I've seen to it. You were summoned specifically, as I'm sure you now understand, not merely to excuse Yorktown to me with reference to the French navy, but to explain Saratoga as well. The truth, Frederick. As your king, that's all I ask."

Lord North nodded, pursed his lips and gathered his thoughts. For a long moment, he arranged the sequence of events in his mind.

Then, slowly, he said, "Well, your Majesty, it seems that there was a woman ..."

Babette: Before it all began

On a crisp, fall afternoon, as the sun began to glow red over the western treetops of the thick northern forest, the red-coated officer reined in his mount. He sat in his army-issue saddle atop a rise on the muddy dirt road that led from Quebec to the garrison town of St.-Jean-sur-Richelieu. He gazed down through the trees at a small, rude log cabin on the banks of the slim, babbling stream below. The smell of wood smoke rising in a towering plume from the cabin's stone chimney had drawn the officer's attention. Now that he was closer, another aroma filled his nostrils -- the tantalizing odor of meat roasting on a spit inside the log cabin's fireplace.

Two days of heavy rain had dragged out his journey, made for the purpose of purchasing several tons of flour from the grasping, French-babbling millers of Quebec. With only his horse for company, the officer had spent the downpour in a damp but spacious cave, consuming the last of the salt pork and hardtack he'd brought with him and shivering in the dankness of his rock shelter. Now, the hunger in his belly almost a physical pain, he dug his spurs into his mount's sides and galloped the animal down the gentle slope until he reached the cabin's door.

The woman emerged with a musket in her hands.

"Good afternoon, Madame," the officer said, smiling and doffing his hat with a gallant flourish.

She made no response, other than to glower at him from behind her rusted Brown Bess musket -- Royal Army issue, the officer noted. He wondered where she'd stolen it. She was young -- a touch more than twenty, he guessed, and even through the grime on her face she was incomparably lovely. The girl, and that's what she was to a man of thirty-eight, was tiny and delicate. Her hair was as black as a moonless night in the Canadian forest. It framed a heart-shaped face. Her large, expressive eyes were the color of robins eggs. The eyes betrayed only a careful appraisal of the scarlet-coated rider before her.

"Do you speak English?" he asked.

She remained silent. The blue eyes betrayed no fear. The officer spied in them something that impressed him -- curiosity, assessment, intellect. As the officer began to address her in French, an aged Indian in homespun shirt and buckskin pants appeared in the doorway beside her, a tomahawk clutched and poised in his hand. He was shaking with excitement.

"Go 'way," the Indian muttered in heavily accented French. "Maitre Ettiene say no one stop here."

"I'm harmless, I assure you," the officer said, smiling. "I seek only some foo-"

"--Go 'way!" The old Indian snapped, stepping around the woman and in front of her, raising the tomahawk higher.

By then, however, the officer had already swung down from his horse, moving easily and without haste. Almost casually, he drew his saber. He still smiled, but now the smile was cold and more than a trifle threatening. The woman could see his eyes glitter in the fading sunlight. She discerned in them not just willingness for combat but an actual desire for it. The Indian, moving toward the English officer, immediately stopped, an expression of uncertainty settling on his face. He glanced at the woman from the corner of his eye.

"Do not harm the old one," she urged the officer in French-accented English.

"Unless he drops the tomahawk," the officer replied quietly, "I'll be forced to kill him. I mean you no harm, Madame, but neither will I permit myself to be harmed. I promise you, I'll run this bugger through if need be."

"My father," she said. "He ordered this man to protect me against strangers."

The officer raised his saber to fighting position, swirling its tip in tight little circles. The old Indian glared at the officer, then dropped the tomahawk and retreated quickly into the house. The officer returned his saber to its scabbard.

"Tell him to come back out here," he ordered the woman.

"To do him harm," she said, tightening her grip on the musket, "you will first have to kill me. You might find that something of a chore, Monsieur."

The officer eyed her for only a moment. Then, moving with the speed of a striking rattlesnake, his hand shot out and closed over the musket barrel. In one swift burst of movement, he wrenched the weapon from her grasp and tossed it to the ground in front of his horse. The woman moved back and froze against the log wall of the cabin. Her expression radiated no fear, only caution. And a smoldering rage.

"I'll not harm him," he officer said softly. "Call him -- now, Madame."

The robins-egg-blue eyes searched the officer's face. Then she turned and called through the door in a tongue the officer couldn't decipher. From inside, the old man responded in the same guttural language. Again, she spoke to him, only now in a harsher, louder tone. The aged Indian appeared in the doorway, clearly terrified. The officer stepped forward, grabbed the old man's ragged shirt of homespun and dragged him out of the little building. The English officer was a big man, and powerful. The old Indian was smallish. The officer held him up until the smaller man was standing only on his toes. Then the officer leaned close to the Indian, his face only inches away from the old man's.

"Never threaten a soldier of the Royal Army," he said softly in French. "Never again threaten any white man -- no matter who tells you to do so. Do you understand?"

The Indian nodded vigorously, his eyes wide. The officer released him roughly and pushed him away. The old man staggered backward, fought for his balance and eventually managed to retain his feet. Immediately, he spun about and fled into the woods.

"He's going back to his people," the woman said softly. "He might come back with younger men to help him."

"If he does, then so be it. He has, however, left you alone, Madame -- to my tender mercies."

Now, finally, he could see the fear in her face.

"Have no concern," the officer said. "I seek only some nourishment and shelter for the night. I'll not harm you, I assure you -- although you and your pet savage clearly were about to harm me."

"You are a stranger," she explained. "Only a fool presumes that all people are what they ought to be."

"A stranger no longer," he said, smiling and bowing. "Captain Peter Loescher of His Majesty's Commissary Corps, at your service. And you, Madame?"

"Babette LeDoux. My father is Ettiene LeDoux."

"And where might he be?"

"In Quebec, trading furs."

"He left you alone here?"

"He left me with him whom you just chased away."

Loeschler felt his stomach rumble. He stepped forward and put his hand on her elbow, steering her toward the cabin door "The food, Madame, if you will."

Inside the cabin, the woman removed a venison haunch from the fire. Loeschler sat silently at a crude, wooden table in the filthy, dirt-floored cabin, studying her. A goddess, he realized -- a goddess in the rough. As she sliced at the meat with a long knife, he ran his eyes over her with intensifying interest. Then he rose and moved around the table to stand behind her. She sensed his presence and spun about with the knife. A strong hand grasped her wrist. Another whipped around her and settled at the small of her back. He drew her near, felt her pressing unwillingly against him. She gazed up into his face. Strangely, Loescher could discern no overt fear on her features. Slowly, he lowered his head, and her features became a blur. He could smell wood smoke and a soft, warm, intensely womanly fragrance.

"You said you wouldn't harm me," she whispered.

"Nor shall I," Peter Loescher said, gently pressing his lips to hers, blotting out what was left of the failing light falling in through the cabin door.

When he lifted his head and the pallid light fell across her face once again, Babette said, "My father, he would kill you."

Loescher let her go then. He strode back to the table and settled back into the chair.

"We'll do that again later," he said. "For now, however, I am a uniquely famished man."

Babette gazed at him carefully for a long moment. Then she realized that she still held the knife in her hand -- had been holding it throughout the long, unexpectedly tender kiss. She turned her back to him once more and began to slice the venison roast. She could feel his eyes on her. Then, as she pulled boiled potatoes and carrots from a steel pot over the fire and prepared the steel plates, her hands began to shake in the silence of the cabin. As darkness fell, the only light in the tiny building emanated from the blaze in the fireplace. As she placed the food on the table, along with eating implements that the officer recognized as equipment from some stolen military mess kit, he rose and approached her once again.

"A lonely place, this," Peter Loescher said, turning her around and taking her hands in his, "The solitude must be burdensome. A fetching little creature like you would find life much more agreeable, I imagine, in a settlement like St.-Jean."

Babette felt the roughness of his big hand on her tiny one. In just a heartbeat, she pondered the circumstance, the offer. She considered the bleak past, the tormented present, the foggy promise of a more acceptable future.

Then she said, "I might."

Ticonderoga. 1777

Except in the deepest pit of winter, when the snow-shrouded stillness could inspire an almost terrifying awe, the forest was never silent. It seethed with a startling abundance of life and death, and a vast multitude of things being born, growing, dying and decaying.

Panther was lying on his stomach atop a patch of ragged spring grass and dead, rotting leaves from the previous fall. In the thick, leafy canopy of tree branches above him, birds sang a shrill, staccato symphony while gray squirrels chattered like old women. Off to his left, in a tangle of underbrush, he could hear an intermittent, muffled rustling. Perhaps a rabbit or a fox — petrified prey or determined predator. Slowly and with great care, he raised his head and sniffed the wind wafting gently over him from that direction. His sensitive nostrils caught the pungent stink of what he recognized as fox urine.

His lips curled in a slight smile. Another hunter on the hillside. Today, however, Panther knew he was the deadliest hunter prowling this heavily wooded mountain, and his mind was intently focused on the steep, tree-studded incline before him, the last such slope before the summit. As midday sunlight poured like liquid gold through the lattice work of branches above, the only sound Panther generated was the thump, thump, thump of his vigorous heart pushing blood past his ears with a rush that only he could hear. He knew he smelled human – redolent of wood smoke and sweat and the grease of roasted meat, but he'd methodically rolled in a pile of deer dung to cloak his scent before beginning his climb up this mountain. It was the habit of a lifetime, a chore undertaken before any hunt. He was reassured, however, by the certain knowledge that his prey had no nose. These pale people had no talent for reading the wind. As the thought came to him, the breeze suddenly shifted and brought Panther the faint sound of voices up ahead. His prey beckoned to him through the trees to the front and right.

He moved then, for the first time in many minutes. He slid forward on his stomach over the grass and crumpled leaf fragments, his head only slightly elevated, ears and nose alert and soft, amber eyes directed toward the sound. After he'd crawled forward perhaps a hundred feet and properly gauged the distance to the sound's source, he realized that he could stand and move on his feet without being detected. So, Panther rose slowly, moist copper skin glistening in the crisp June air. Then, as stealthily as any fox, the big Ottawa warrior glided forward, up the slope, leaning forward in his moccasins, ascending the sharpening incline effortlessly without the use of his hands on the trees for support. Panther's legs were strong enough for the climb, and his hands bore his weapons — his bow and his steel-headed hatchet. The distant voices strengthened in his ears.

As he moved toward them.

There were two of them, he noted as he drew nearer — two distinct voices, each male, each relaxed in tone, although Panther could not decipher their conversation. He could speak the lyrical language of his mother's people, and French, the vile tongue of his vile, dead father. He could not fathom the gibberish of English and had no urge to master it. Panther dropped back to the ground and crawled silently through the brush, sampling the wind with his hunter's nose as he went. The wind brought him news of weak, pale perspiration, of tobacco smoke, leather and gunpowder. Soon, crawling silently, he finally spotted them through the trees — two men in homespun cloth and leather shoes beneath floppy hats, only yards away.

And bearing muskets, too. Panther rejoiced. He very much wanted his own musket. Now he would have two — one for hunting and war and one to trade for treasure.

For a long while, Panther lay immobile in the brush, spying through the trees. There were only these two, he decided finally, and they chattered like the squirrels. They sat cross-legged beneath a towering pine, smoking corn cob pipes and oblivious to all around them. Sentries, they were supposed to be — sentinels who saw and heard nothing, he noted. One was youngish, about Panther's age. The other was a man of middle age. These were farmers, not trained warriors, easy prey for a hunter/warrior of Panther's powers. As he studied them, he pondered the mechanics of his attack. Speed was crucial here, since they had muskets and he did not. He would take one down with the bow and rush the other as he scrambled to his feet in panic. In his mind, Panther measured the distance. No more than a dozen yards. Even moving uphill, he could cover that in only a few bounds.

Slowly, and with great care, Panther fitted an arrow in his bow. Sighting through the trees and in a single fluid motion, he stood straight up and let the arrow fly. The maneuver took less than a full second. The razor-sharp steel arrowhead caught the older man squarely in the throat, passing fully through his neck and pinning his head to the tree bole against which he was leaning. The man's hands flew to the arrow, clutching wildly at it as he issued a weak, gurgling scream. By then Panther had dropped the bow, reached for his hatchet and was moving as a blur darting through the trees. The younger man sat unmoving for only a moment, staring in disbelief at his stricken comrade. Then he scrambled to his feet just as Panther reached him, grabbed him roughly by the shoulder and planted the hatchet's blade squarely between the man's eyes.

As the younger man fell, Panther turned to the older one, pinned tightly against the tree trunk with his eyes rolling wildly. Blood gushed like a fountain around the arrow's shaft, drowning the older man's choked cries. With his left hand, Panther grabbed the brim of the man's hat and tossed it aside. He clutched the graying hair firmly in strong fingers. With his right, Panther replaced his hatchet in his belt, unsheathed his knife and moved to the man's side to casually saw the scalp off the top of his skull. By the time Panther had completed his task, the older man had stopped screaming and struggling and sat impaled to the tree by the arrow, eyes staring blankly ahead, silent forevermore as the birds made music in the trees overhead.

Panther then turned his attention to the younger man, who was just beginning to move his limbs in feeble gestures. Panther bent over, neatly sliced open the man's throat and sawed off his scalp as well — a quick, circular cut around the top of the head, followed by a powerful yank of the hair that tore the flesh away from the skull with a sharp pop! Panther jammed the bloody shreds of skin and hair into the leather bag that hung from his belt. Later, they would be scraped of stray bits of flesh and dried in the sun as trophies. He gathered up the two muskets along with the powder horns and bags of lead balls the sentries had worn from straps over their shoulders. Then, without a backward glance at his victims, Panther started back down the mountain. He'd been part of a party of scouts moving like ghosts over the entire mountainside all morning, killing sentries where they found them, before finally Panther finally had happened upon these two final, careless guards. The path to the mountain's summit was clear.

Now Panther had to rejoin his brother warriors and move back down the mountain to inform Le Loup.

୫୬

The sun had moved past its midpoint when William Phillips reached the bottom of the mountain with his regiment of infantrymen, his gunners, his twelve-pounders, his cart of shovels, axes and saws and his teams of lowing oxen. He found Le Loup lounging at the foot of the slope with his scouting crew of a half dozen savages. As usual, the Indians were antagonistic in manner, silently eyeing the English with open animosity. As usual, the hulking old Frenchman with the white scalp lock and the black eye patch was all greasy buckskin, mendacious grin and reeking of rum.

"The way to the top is open, mon General," he told Phillips through a toothless smile. "My children have purified this mountain."

General William Phillips, resplendent in the blue coat, red facings and gold braid of a royal artillery officer, glanced past the knot of brooding savages to the mountainside. He gazed up the steep wooded incline and raised his eyes until he could see the mountain's crest. A hard afternoon's work ahead, the general concluded. In three decades as an officer of artillery, he'd dragged big guns over difficult territory before, but he'd seldom encountered an obstacle quite this daunting. The general swung down from his mount and motioned for young Lieutenant Twiss to join him.

"Well, Lieutenant," the general said, "you're the engineering officer. Now, engineer for me a path up this mountainside for my guns."

"There's the most suitable route, there," the lieutenant said, gesturing with a red-clad arm toward the gentlest part of the slope. "The trees must be felled low to the ground, Sir, so the oxen can get over the stumps and to keep the guns from getting hung up. We might also have to use the tree trunks tied together with rope to construct some ramps as we go up, and we'll have to do some digging to properly grade the pathway. I'll know precisely how much grading we'll have to do as we climb higher."

Phillips surveyed the slope and nodded. "Get it done, then, Lieutenant. Speed is crucial."

"Yes, Sir," Twiss replied. He turned and shouted orders to his infantrymen. Muskets were set aside and tools were pulled from the ox cart as Twiss moved off with the workmen.

"Your men, too," the general snapped at Le Loup. "This path must be cleared and the guns atop the mountain's crest by nightfall."

Le Loup's grin faded, replaced by a distinct expression of alarm. "My children are not ax men, mon General. Let them move into the forest to stand guard."

Phillips frowned. In his gleaming black boots, he strode to the cart and pulled out an ax. He marched smartly to the knot of Indians and held out the tool toward them at arm's length. A particularly menacing looking savage, naked to the waist and rippling with hard, knotted cords of muscle, glared at the officer in open defiance. Slowly, he spat on the ground and turned away. Instantly, Le Loup was at the general's side as the sound of axes biting into hardwood rang in the forest behind them.

"Please, mon General," the Frenchman pleaded. "Do not insist."

Phillips was furious. He fixed a firm gaze on the back of the Indian who'd turned his back on him.

"Who is this man?" he demanded of Le Loup.

"He is Wyandot Panther," the Frenchman said. "He is a loyal servant of his great and royal Majesty, King George. He is eager to kill enemies of the English."

"Then let him help us clear the way. If he'll work, then the others will work as well."

"This is not the work they came for, mon General," Le Loup said.

"What sort of bloody name is Wyandot Panther?" the general demanded.

"Panther is the English version of his Ottawa name. Marcel Wyandot was his father, a fine friend of mine from Marseilles. When Panther was fourteen, he killed him. Like my other children, mon General, Panther came here to take scalps and treasure, not to down trees. I urge you; please leave them to me."

His brow furrowed, Phillips turned away. He had but a single afternoon to clear a narrow path and to drag these guns to the mountain's summit. This task was the key to a swift victory at this place — to avoiding a long, drawn-out siege — and he needed all the manpower he could muster. There had, however, been something in Wyandot Panther's eyes ... Will Phillips was both a general and a member of Parliament, accustomed to a certain degree of deference from all he encountered. Moreover, he was no coward. As a professional soldier, he felt no entitlement to living to see the sunset on any given day. He also was trained, however, in the realistic assessment of risk. He deemed it unlikely, though hardly impossible, that a decision to press on this issue could result in someone's death, perhaps his own. The gain was worth neither the peril nor the fuss. His own troops could clear the path.

Phillips frowned deeply as he reflected on how much he despised these surly savages reeking of blood, manure and bear fat. Futilely, he'd counseled the commanding general against bringing them. They would be more trouble than they were worth, he'd argued, and they already had been. They openly disregarded direct orders, even from generals like himself. The very sight of them inspired terror, and justifiably so, in the several hundred women and children who accompanied the army.

Nonetheless, here they were, four hundred of them — Mohawks and Algonquins from Quebec, Ottawas and Chippewas whose fathers had fought for the French in the last war, Hurons, Fox, Sac and Winnebagoes from the west. All out for booty and gore-soaked bits of skin and human hair. All speaking different languages and unable to communicate, even with one another, except through sign language and broken French. All under the tenuous command of this bizarre old French renegade, who cautiously herded them like cattle and clearly regarded them as little more than wild beasts, which was Phillips' view as well.

"Put them on guard duty, then," the general snapped over his shoulder to Le Loup. "And keep the bloody bastards out of the way."

"My children salute your compassion, mon General," the Frenchman said through that toothless grin.

ઠ૭

Near the mountain's crest, as the red-coated men downed trees and the oxen strained to haul the big guns almost straight uphill, Panther ranged ahead in the forest. Higher on the slope, he happened across a copper-colored fawn, its downy coat speckled with patches of white. It was nestled in bushes as protection from predators. He killed it with a single swing of his hatchet and carried the limp, bleeding carcass to the top of the mountain.

As the sounds of sweating, swearing men hard at work drew nearer on the mountainside in the gathering gloom of night, Panther skinned and butchered the fawn with his scalping knife and gathered wood for a fire. He ignited the blaze with sparks from the knife's blade and a chunk of flint he carried in his leather bag. Then, as the shroud of darkness settled over the mountain top, he impaled chunks of tender meat on sharpened sticks and placed them directly in the flames. Panther was sitting cross-legged in the grass before his fire, dining on the charred, dripping flesh as the first party of redcoats came up over the edge of the slope in the darkness driving two straining oxen hauling a cannon behind them.

"By God, smell that wonderful, bloomin' meat," said one foot soldier.

Panther ignored them. This was his meal, not theirs. Panther had no use for pale people. He liked neither their looks nor the noise they made. He found their odor repellent. Neither did he care for their food — mainly salt pork, oatmeal and hardtack, except when they could steal better from local farmers. Panther had downed several chunks of blackened, half-roasted venison when General Phillips' black boots appeared in his line of vision, stamping out his fire. In an eye blink, Panther was on his feet, knife in hand, as the gigantic Le Loup moved in on him from the rear and clutched him in a firm embrace. Panther was a powerful man. Despite his advanced age, however, the enormous, rawboned Le Loup was more powerful.

"We'll have no fires here," the general barked out to the group, paying Panther no particular attention. "Inform your savages of that, Le Loup. Let the rebels learn of our presence on this mountaintop only in the morning, when we open fire on them."

"Caution, my son," Le Loup hissed in Panther's ear in French as the younger man squirmed in the old Frenchman's grasp.

"I should find pleasure in taking this one's hair now," Panther muttered over his shoulder in Ottawa.

"No, not this one," the Frenchman replied in Ottawa, loosening his grip slowly and with vigilance. "There will be scalps enough — and treasure as well. Are you not now the owner of two fine muskets?"

Panther returned his knife to its leather sheath. Silently, he slipped off into the darkness.

"A disorderly man," Phillips observed to the Frenchman. "Remember, it's your obligation to keep him under control."

"All my children are firmly under my control, mon General."

In response, Phillips merely snorted — a sound that only the English could make with just the proper note of derision, Le Loup noted.

Which was only one of the reasons he despised them, too.

∞

As he dozed at his desk, his brain danced with memories of the Highlands — of bonnie blue flowers amid the high, golden grass, of black water gushing in fierce torrents down the rocky streambeds to blend into the lochs. Gone from Scotland for decades, Arthur St. Clair's unconscious thoughts often transported him back home. The burr had never left his speech; the Highlands had never left his heart.

The rap on the door shook him free, bringing him instantly to full wakefulness.

"General," Wilkinson was shouting as he knocked. "You need to come see this."

St. Clair rose from the desk where he'd slipped off to sleep as he'd been composing a message to headquarters in Albany. He reached the door in two strides, throwing it open. Even in the dim candlelight, he could see the high, ruddy flush in young Wilkinson's cheeks.

"And what d'ya wanna show me, Major?" St. Clair demanded.

"Over here, Sir," Wilkinson said, moving away from the door of the commander's office, obviously expecting him to follow. St. Clair did. Without his uniform coat, but still wearing the pink sash that proclaimed his rank, he stepped out into the night darkness of Ticonderoga and followed briskly along the battlement behind the junior officer. James Wilkinson was all of twenty-one, the son of a prosperous Maryland farmer. He'd already served eighteen months as a staff officer in the rebel army. Wilkinson was dependable and capable but still tended toward excess exuberance. St. Clair had overcome his own youthful exuberance decades earlier, during his first, blood-soaked engagements in the French and Indian War. Since then, war had failed to excite Arthur St. Clair. It had saddened him, puzzled him and challenged both his judgment and energy. He now regarded waging war as a distasteful task to be performed, as a job to be done. The only excitement he felt at the moment stemmed from his certainty that he could not wage war successfully from Ticonderoga for any length of time.

Erected more than two decades earlier to guard against the French and the Indians, and given a Mohawk name meaning "Between the Two Great Waters," the stone fortress had fallen into disrepair. It had been taken early in the revolt by the forces of Ethan Allen and Benedict Arnold, who'd caught the English sleeping and ejected them at gunpoint. Surrounded by log fortifications and earthen walls, the star-shaped fort itself was a veritable city of carved, gray rock nestled among heavily forested mountains on three sides and Lake Champlain on the fourth. The fort occupied a bluff high on the west bank of the lake's southern end, its cannon barring the passage of troops and supplies to the south. It was, however, dank, gloomy and, given the ravages of sickness among St. Clair's command, a stinking, festering cauldron of disease.

Still, no vessel could survive under the guns of Ticonderoga, and St. Clair knew that English boats were on the lake. A British invasion from Canada the year before had been effectively repelled here at Champlain's lower end. Now, news of another British invasion was already weeks old as word had leaked out of Canada through scattered loyalists returning home. Scouts and spies had arrived in recent days with reports of flatboats, whaleboats, sloops, schooners and bateaux — five hundred of them moving out of the mud brown Richelieu River at the lake's northern end in Quebec not quite two weeks earlier. Now the English vessels lay at anchor in the narrow neck of water off the abandoned log fort at Crown Point, a dozen miles to the north, while English and hired German troops flooded overland down both eastern and western shores to converge on Ticonderoga for what St. Clair was certain would be a siege of no more than a few weeks.

St. Clair had nearly four thousand men stretching north and east from Fort Edward on the Hudson's eastern shore. Most were concentrated inside the stone walls of Ticonderoga and at various fortifications around Champlain's southern tip. Some were Army of the United States regulars, but most were members of various militias, due to return home soon for a summer's work in the fields. St. Clair's estimate of the English forces, based on scouting reports — roughly ten thousand troops. St. Clair lacked sufficient manpower to meet them in the field even if he'd dared try, and the manpower he did have was too weak for any such task. Smallpox, fever and dysentery had decimated his troops. Those healthy enough to fight were short of food, powder and shot. Many were barefoot.

Unless he received help from the south, the English could starve him out. The outcome of any such siege was not in doubt. St. Clair had known it when he'd taken command of Ticonderoga. Now, thanks to a flurry of messages from St. Clair to Albany, General Philip Schuyler, commander of the Army of the United States Northern Department, understood it as well. Still, however, St. Clair had received no direct orders from Albany except to hold Ticonderoga if possible and to keep the army intact at all costs. And no promise of assistance, either, since Schuyler had only a few thousand men of his own.

What folly this rebellion was, St. Clair thought for the hundredth time that week. Fighting the Royal Army with a pallid force of farmers and red-cheeked children like Wilkinson. What a fool he'd been for agreeing to take part in it. St. Clair, however, had a rich wife and a fine life in this new land to which he'd come as a royal soldier decades earlier. Moreover, the lure of rebellion against English kings could never be resisted by any true Scot — from William Wallace to Robert the Bruce and now, Arthur St. Clair himself. He was bound by duty to this land and by blood to the spirit of revolution against the English. If only he had more and better trained men. If only he had food with which to fill their bellies during the coming siege.

He followed Wilkinson along the ramparts, past cannon aimed out on the black velvet expanse of the water. St. Clair strode past torch-lit sentry posts manned by militia in mud-colored homespun and floppy farmers' hats. At the fort's southwestern corner, Wilkinson suddenly stopped and pointed.

"There, Sir — up on Sugar Loaf. It showed up only a moment ago."

St. Clair gazed out into the growing darkness — at the hulking, shadowy shape of the mountain, inky black against the deep, dark gray of the evening sky.

"Do you see it, Sir?" Wilkinson demanded, pointing again.

Then St. Clair did see it. At the top of the mountain, on its crest, he spotted a glimmer of light — a campfire, perhaps, to serve as protection against the night chill. As he observed it, St. Clair saw the light suddenly extinguish. All his hopes for successfully defending this fort, never robust to begin with, died with the fire. "Might be ours," St. Clair said, not really believing it.

"No, Sir," Wilkinson said. "I've ordered the sentries; there are to be no fires at night outside the fort. If the English have Indians scouting ahead of them, then the fires will only guide them in for the kill."

"Well," St. Clair said thoughtfully, "that one was smothered in a hurry, but there's no point in any of our sentries bein' atop Sugar Loaf at night. They'd have no need to climb so high. I suspect that means, Major, that we have no more sentries around that mountain. It means the English have command of that high ground above the fort."

"There's not much they can do from there, is there, Sir?"

St. Clair frowned. "What, d'ya imagine, would be involved in draggin' big guns all the way up to the crest of Sugar Loaf? Could you do it with horse or oxen, if ya first cleared a path with axes?"

"I don't know, General,' Wilkinson said. "General Arnold warned that the British might do that, but General Gates said it wasn't possible. Sugar Loaf's summit is nearly a thousand feet from the bottom."

"Aye," St. Clair said. "T'would be hard, Major, but I dinna think t'would be an impossibility. T'is what I would do could I manage it. I'd place the guns up there, to fire down on us here inside the walls, and us no more than fish in a barrel as the grapeshot rains down. T'was the mistake the English made at Breed's Hill. They dinna use their big guns as they should've. They know it. T'is not a mistake they would make here as well."

Wilkinson gazed up at the darkened shadow of the mountain. "Then what do we do?"

"We abandon the fort under cover of darkness and retreat into the woods south of the lake," St. Clair said. "If they have big guns atop Sugar Loaf, Major — and they surely do — then we've lost already. They'll be firin' down on us at day's dawnin', and then t'will be too late to run."

Wilkinson's already flushed face burned bright red in the torchlight. "Sir, we can't let them take Ticonderoga before a shot is even fired."

St. Clair said, "This fort was never defensible from the land side against a superior force with big guns. The best we could hope for was to delay the landing of their boats, and now we canna do that. I canna lose four thousand troops, Major. I canna lose the army itself. My duty now is to slow the English land advance south of the lake. That we'll surely do. They'll pay in blood for every foot of ground they gain in coming days."

Wilkinson shook his head wearily. "I'll gather the officers and make ready the evacuation."

"Gather the officers in my headquarters, but then be gone y'self to the south to inform Schuyler of what I've done. And only General

Schuyler, lad, none other. Tell him that the English are clearly headin' to the Hudson River, then down to Albany. And God knows what they've got in their bleedin' minds after that."

"Yes, Sir. I'll leave immediately, as soon as I find a horse."

Arthur St. Clair sighed deeply. "I'll worry the bastards in the woods all the way to the Hudson, and kill of them what I can, but I canna stop a force this size with the troops I have. That, Major Wilkinson, General Schuyler must appreciate."

Jane. 1777

She was a tall, statuesque woman of twenty-three whose luminous, copper-colored hair cascaded down her back to a point just short of her heels. David's loving nickname for her was Rapunzel. He loved her hair — the fiery waterfall, he called it. Jane McCrea couldn't think of anything about David Jones she didn't love, even though their affair had infuriated her family.

"He's a royalist son of a whore," Jane's brother, John, had raged. "He'd kiss the king's fat arse in the hamlet square if he could."

Now, John, a colonel in the local militia, was rushing through the woods with his wife and children to the shelter of Albany and to service with General Schuyler. Alarmed by news of the English conquest of Ticonderoga, he'd packed up his musket, powder and ball the night before and had marched off to fight. Jane had insisted on staying. Reluctantly, John had left his headstrong younger sister with firm instructions to stay near their cabin and to remain out of harm's way. Now Jane, the fiery waterfall flying behind her like

a silken banner, was moving at a dead run along the road toward
Fort Edward from the little streamside cabin she shared with John
and his brood. She'd been up at dawn, her meager store of personal
possessions tucked in a bag of homespun, which hung from her
shoulder as she ran barefoot in the dirt.

It was a soft, green morning, a day adorned with glittering spangles
of sunlight. Jane McCrea had been running for several hours, pausing
only rarely to catch her breath and to drink from the stream beside
the road — Moses Kill, it was called, an old Dutch name. Now, as
the stream flowed to join the Hudson, Fort Edward was only a few
hundred yards ahead. Jane quickened her pace toward the wooden
stockade and the scattered assemblage of cabins that surrounded it.
She knew who to see here. She knew where David would look for
her. They'd made the arrangements the previous fall, when he'd fled
to Canada to escape the abuse of rebel fanatics like Jane's brother.
That had been when David had pledged to return to take Jane as his
bride.

A knot of soldiers was clustered outside the fort, both regulars in
blue and buff with red facings and militia in buckskin and homespun.
Pickets, Jane realized — a shabby, paper thin line of defense against
the English professionals. They would be on the run soon enough,
Jane knew. As the English approached and the first shots rang out,
the Army of the United States would flee across the river and run
south along the western shore. She could see the small boats at the
water's edge, already loaded with supplies from the ramshackle log
fort.

The enormous mound of flesh that was Sarah McNeil was sitting on a stool, churning butter, as Jane arrived outside the older woman's cabin. A pair of sway-backed old horses grazed in a pasture behind the cabin. As Jane raced up to her, the older woman glanced up at the flurry of flying skirts and fluttering hair and breathless excitement.

"They're coming," Jane gasped out to Mrs. McNeil as she fought for breath. "And Colonel Skene will be with them. That means David will be with them, too."

Sarah McNeil was a thickset boulder of a woman, round and solid and twice Jane's age. Now a widow, she was the battle scarred veteran of a trying marriage and past the point in life where she fancied romance in any form. She frowned at the goddess-like creature before her. She knew David Jones well. She knew Jane only slightly, liked her well enough and pitied the girl her infatuation. Jane would learn soon enough, Sarah McNeil supposed. Men were worthless, every one — all the ones Sarah McNeil had ever known, at any rate.

"Aye," Mrs. McNeil said, Scotland thick in her speech, "they're coming, all right. Thousands of them, is what the word is — redcoats and Germans alike. And Indians, too, Jane. It's too bad that they brought those damned red barbarians with them. In any event, they'll chase these traitorous bluecoats out of here soon enough, and God save the king, is what I say."

Jane sank to her knees, struggling to catch her breath. "You can have the king, Mrs. McNeil. You can have the Continental Congress, too. All I want is my David, and now he'll be back. They'll be here at Fort Edward in another day or two. Can I stay with you until they arrive?"

"And then what?" Mrs. McNeil demanded. "You're going with them? A camp follower? Is that your intent?"

Jane shook her head. "My only intent is to be with David again. It's been two years since he asked me to marry him, and a nearly year since he was forced to flee to Canada. Do you know how long a year is, Mrs. McNeil?"

The older woman smiled suddenly. "Years grow shorter as a person grows wiser. Of course, girl, stay with me until they arrive. You're right; they'll be along directly. My cousin, Simon, is with them. We've not seen one another in years now. He's a general, Simon is. It's hard to imagine gentle, laughing Simon as a leader of fighting men. Then again, how we turn out is God's business. He seems to possess a perverse sense of humor, God does."

"Thank you," said Jane McCrea, swinging her waterfall of hair over one shoulder, leaning back against the rough log wall of the cabin and struggling to catch her breath. "I can't believe that David is coming — finally."

Sarah McNeil studied the younger woman closely as she methodically churned her butter. She remembered love, and marriage, too. A woman was happiest when she was in love, Mrs. McNeil supposed, which was why no woman as pretty as Jane should ever marry.

If a woman looked like Jane, what advantage lay in exchanging the attentions of many men for the eventual inattention of only one?

Schuyler. 1777

Beginning his trek in stygian darkness, Wilkinson rode hard from Ticonderoga. Carefully, he negotiated his mount in utter darkness along the narrow, treacherous forest road from Champlain, along the swampy shores of Wood Creek, the lake's outlet, past the ramshackle stockade at Fort Ann and on to the Hudson. By dawn, he'd reached the sagging log walls of Fort Edward on the river's eastern bank . After swimming his horse across the Hudson in a ferocious summer rainstorm, he reached an Army of the United States encampment at Saratoga by late afternoon. This was an advance camp established in the fields of a few small farms. It was no more than a collection of a several dozen scattered tents beside the river. Most of the Army of the United States' Northern Department force, Wilkinson knew, remained headquartered in the fragile old fort at Albany, awaiting the arrival of war.

At Saratoga, after being told that Schuyler was not in camp, Wilkinson was ushered into the tent of the ranking officer — a short, swarthy, powerfully built man with a hawklike face. At age thirty-six, General Benedict Arnold was second in command of the Army's Northern Department. Briefly, after Washington had sent Arnold north to serve as Schuyler's combat commander, Wilkinson had served Arnold as one of the general's personal aides before being sent to Ticonderoga to report to St. Clair. Benedict Arnold had eyes as blue as the porcelain of a Ming vase and radiated a constant air of loosely controlled anger. He'd always made Wilkinson nervous, but Wilkinson possessed an inborn gift both for deference and impassiveness.

"I had word from a scout," Arnold said as he sat, almost quivering with inner tension, as his collapsible field desk. "The bastards are closing in on us, aren't they?"

"Yes, Sir," Wilkinson said.

"Well, what's St. Clair doing about it?"

"I'm to report directly to General Schuyler, Sir," Wilkinson said. "Those were my orders from General St. Clair."

"Schuyler is at his town house in Albany," said Arnold, who struck Wilkinson as more than a little drunk — a not unusual circumstance, Wilkinson knew from experience. "Tell him I'm ready to move forward in an instant with any force he'll give me."

Wilkinson remounted and continued south. At the Mohawk River, he took a ferry across and entered Albany from the north. Wilkinson found the general in civilian clothes in the study of his Albany mansion. The great, gabled, brick house — surrounded by stables, a cooking house and gardens for both flowers and vegetables — occupied the crest of a high hill on the Hudson's west bank, south of Albany's bustling commercial district. The general was at a table in a high ceilinged room with a floor tiled in black and white squares of marble. He was engaged in correspondence.

Philip Schuyler was a tall, slender, red-faced man of forty four with a curly shock of dark brown hair, a prominent, hooked nose and piercing eyes. Wilkinson had served as one of Schuyler's many staff aides but had never directly addressed the commanding general. Wilkinson immediately discerned in Schuyler both an air of confident superiority and the aura of serene, studied, diffident graciousness that tended to accompany old money. For Schuyler, money was like the air; it was always there. And, while life without it might have been burdensome, it was not a topic of concern. Wealth had always existed for him in such abundance.

Wilkinson had ridden for sixteen straight hours. In the candlelight of the elegant study he was a sorry, soggy sight — muddied, exhausted, his blue and buff uniform stained and torn. Schuyler offered him a chair, some tea, a pair of roasted chicken legs and the commanding general's rapt, undivided attention.

"General St. Clair's compliments, General Schuyler," Wilkinson said. "The English have taken control of Fort Ticonderoga. General St. Clair has moved his forces into the forest south of Lake Champlain to slow further advance by the enemy, but he ordered me to report that he cannot prevent them from coming forward and plans to move the bulk of his army south and east."

"Yes," Schuyler said. "Go on."

Wilkinson recounted the events leading up to St. Clair's decision to abandon the fort. Also, attentive to the fact that he was in the presence of an influential man whose judgment of him could affect his own future, Wilkinson made a point of gently expressing his own reservations about St. Clair's decision.

"Well, he was right, Major," Schuyler said curtly, his English tinged with the Dutch he'd spoken at home as a child. "We'll need those four thousand men vastly more than we need possession of that pile of rock on the lake shore. You should know that not only are the English coming at us from the north, I received a message last week that they're coming at us from the west as well. A large force under the command of an English officer named St. Leger crossed Lake Ontario and is now moving east along the Mohawk to get behind us if we move north to meet the English coming down from Champlain. If that eastbound force gets past the garrison at Fort Stanwix, then we'll have separate English armies gnawing on us from two directions. We'll be forced to drop back and defend Albany at the town's northern border, and our fort here lacks even a single cannon. It's my belief, Major, that acceptable defensive ground can be located between here and Fort Edward. I own property up there; I know the territory. The ground here at Albany is less than ideal. Huddled along the river's edge as we are, at the bottom of this steep bank, we'd be below the English as they came, and we'd have the river at our rear, making any strategic retreat impossible."

"We'd had no word at Fort Ticonderoga on that eastbound force, Sir," Wilkinson said.

"Oh, St. Clair knows. I sent him word by courier as soon as I learned. I ordered him to hold Ticonderoga if he could but to avoid risking surrender of the army at all costs."

"General St. Clair failed to inform me, Sir," Wilkinson said.

"You had no need to know, Major," the commanding general explained with a slight smile.

"Might I inquire, Sir, as to why you're informing me now?"

"Because I'll need another senior personal aide in the trying months to come. You're a resourceful and determined young man. You demonstrated that by reaching me so quickly with this news, and in the face of considerable hardship in so doing. Also, General St. Clair recommended you for this post. He speaks highly of you.

Moreover, Major, you strike me as an ambitious fellow."

Senior aide to the commanding general? Weary as he was, Wilkinson flushed at the very prospect. Still, was this Schuyler's way of questioning Wilkinson's loyalty to his current commander?

"My only ambition is to render faithful service, Sir," Wilkinson said carefully.

"Were you not ambitious," Schuyler said, "you'd have reported General St. Clair's decision to abandon Ticonderoga without personal comment on the decision's merit or lack thereof. Don't fret at being judged ambitious, Major. Ambition can be the father of extraordinary performance. Would you welcome duty as my senior aide?"

"I would be deeply honored, Sir."

"All right, then. I have a chore for you to perform."

Taking a quill pen from its inkwell, Schuyler scribbled a few lines on cloth paper, waved it dry, rolled it up and sealed it with wax. He handed it to the younger man. "Take this back to General Arnold at Saratoga. This is his order to return here, form up and then lead a brigade to Fort Stanwix to augment the militia as I move the remainder of our forces here in Albany northward. He's to repel the English along the Mohawk and then return to Saratoga as quickly as possible."

Wilkinson rose to his feet and saluted stiffly. "Very good, Sir."

"Once the order is delivered to General Arnold, return here," the commanding general instructed. "We'll have a warm bed and dry uniform for you when you arrive. And Major, the dry uniform you'll receive will bear a colonel's insignia. My senior aides must carry a field grade officer's rank."

Despite his weariness, Wilkinson beamed. "I'm greatly honored, Sir. You have my undying gratitude, General."

"For my part, Colonel, you have my pledge that I'll work you like a galley slave. Now, be off with you."

℘

At midnight, in the cooling mist of his garden, Schuyler sat and thought. It was his habit when he was home and the harsh Albany weather was sufficiently gentle to permit the ritual. With his wife, Kitty, and two daughters, Peggy and Betsy, asleep upstairs in the mansion, he would lounge on a bench in the luxurious flower garden behind the house and reflect in glorious solitude on the events of the day while puffing on one of his long-stemmed clay pipes and glorying in the symphony of crickets.

This was one of two homes Schuyler owned. The other was a mansion of comparably palatial dimension at Saratoga, miles to the north, where Schuyler presided over a prosperous farm rich in grain, flax, hemp and, thanks to the mills Schuyler had erected along the Hudson's shore, lumber. Much of the land's income was derived from tenant farmers who paid the lord of the manor one-tenth of their earnings, as tenant farmers had paid Schuyler's Dutch ancestors after they'd arrived in the New Netherland colony in the sixteen-hundreds. Schuyler loved the farm. He delighted in the careful cultivation of crops and the tender nurturing of livestock. It caused him no small degree of sorrow to reflect on the farm's vulnerability as the English advanced southward.

The English would attempt to maintain a supply line of fully four hundred miles over water and rough country, all the way back to Quebec. As an experienced supply officer — that was, in fact, Schuyler's military specialty, acquired during the war against the French and the Indians — he knew than an army that size could consume up to ten tons of supplies daily. Its length alone would render the supply line of questionable reliability, so the enemy would be forced to live off the land as well — Schuyler's land, in all probability, once they probed that far south. Schuyler would have to burn his fields, of course, as would his tenants. That could be done quickly enough. The livestock would be another matter. The animals would have to be fed to Schuyler's troops to save the beasts from lending aid and comfort to English and German stomachs.

Schuyler thought of his prize cattle, drained of their rich milk and then slaughtered for their meat. A small price to be paid, he supposed, for freedom from the rule of royalty, if freedom actually could be obtained. If not, Schuyler imagined, the loss of his cattle would amount to little compared to the loss of his life. If the revolution failed, he surely would be hanged as a traitor to the Crown.

And to his class as well, he supposed. As a member of one of the oldest and richest families in the Hudson Valley — and as the husband of Catherine Van Rensselaer, a member of another such noble and monied family — Philip Schuyler was more prominent and influential than any of his peers among the Livingstons or the Van Schaicks. He had run for governor of the New York colony. Unlike many of his class, he was uniquely capable in useful matters — skilled at construction and boatbuilding, fluent in several Indian tongues, an experienced man of commerce whose prosperous estates supported what amounted to a self-sufficient personal empire. While many of his fellow gentleman farmers were fighting for nothing nobler than the right to keep their money, others remained resolutely loyal to the king. They blissfully ignored the reality that they and other people of substance, like Philip Schuyler, had evolved into the true royalty of North America. Schuyler's class was composed of the thriving sons and daughters of original settlers, heirs to a meritocracy long since abandoned in Europe, where the blood had thinned from generation to generation — and where rank, arrogant idiots like George III often ruled in the place of resourceful, long dead forebears who'd taken power through force of personality, wit, will and superior weaponry.

Schuyler puffed his pipe as he pondered both the peril and complexity of the circumstance confronting him. He was fighting for the rule of gentlemen over the continued rule of hereditary nobles an ocean away. He was fighting for the benefit of both gentlemen and the rabble — although he was acutely aware that the rabble distrusted him, perhaps even more than they distrusted most men of wealth, breeding and authority. As the leading member of New York's Patroon aristocracy — living in a city where most residents spoke Dutch, not English — Schuyler was despised by the stiff-necked New Englanders of English heritage, even though it had been the Dutch settlers, not the English, who had invented the term "American," thinking of themselves as independent citizens of a new land rather than as transplanted Europeans with loyalty to nobility at the other end of the ocean.

Both John and Samuel Adams, cousins and influential members of the Continental Congress representing the Massachusetts Bay

Colony, made no secret of their animosity toward Schuyler. Publicly, they criticized him for what they characterized as too delicate a personal constitution for military leadership. Schuyler was prone to illness, especially agonizing bouts of gout, and all too often was out of commission while fighting off this sickness or that one. Privately, the Adamses denounced Schuyler as haughty and overbearing. He supposed there was a measure of truth to that charge; Philip Schuyler did not suffer fools gladly. He understood, however, that the true source of the Adams' hatred for him was his wealth and ethnicity. Unfortunately, the Adams cousins represented large political constituencies. New Englanders trusted them, and they distrusted Schuyler.

That was one reason Schuyler had experienced such difficulty in attracting manpower from the militias. Conspicuously, New England militia members had failed to flock to his banner since the rowdy colonial politicians of the Continental Congress had, at George Washington's urging, reluctantly appointed Schuyler commander of the Army's Northern Department. His inability to build a following among people of English heritage, Schuyler knew, was the single most noteworthy vulnerability of his continued tenure as commander — even more pronounced than Schuyler's failure to establish what he had hoped would become a perfect rapport with General Washington.

As a matter of pride more than practicality, it was that second matter that concerned Schuyler more. The rabble were only rabble, and Schuyler was personally unconcerned with their views, although he did wish at this crucial juncture that he were more popular with them. Washington, however, enjoyed great sway with the petty politicians of the Continental Congress despite his own status as one of the wealthiest men in all the colonies — richer by far than Schuyler and his prosperous Patroon cousins. As a fellow gentleman farmer, Schuyler had expected to enjoy a strong relationship with the Virginian who served as commander-in-chief. Washington, unfortunately, was a tight-lipped and austere figure — not at all the warm, magnetic leader Schuyler had imagined he would be as commander of the Army of the United States. Schuyler's polished personal style, to his disappointment, had failed to establish for him the intense personal connection he'd hoped to enjoy with his commander. As a result of those two factors and his own lack of serious battlefield experience, Schuyler was well aware, his hold on this command was tenuous.

With a major battle looming, he had to find some way to attract recruits, to mount a force with some chance of withstanding the English assault when it came. If he failed to manage that, Schuyler's outnumbered regulars would be mowed down like wheat on the battlefield. Even if he'd commanded a force comparable in size to what St. Clair believed the English to have on Lake Champlain, Schuyler knew he would be at a distinct disadvantage. The Army of the United States was in dreadful shape. His ragged troops were up against His Majesty's Royal Army, after all. They were facing the finest fighting force in history. Schuyler knew he was matched against a new version of the Macedonian army — a hardened corps of modern-day Alexander's soldiers armed with sabers, bayonets, Brown Bess muskets and cannon.

In all, counting the four thousand men in St. Clair's command — now conducting a frantic, fighting retreat from Ticonderoga, according to Wilkinson — Schuyler had fewer than seven thousand regular soldiers and militia available to him. He'd written of his plight to John Hancock, president of the Continental Congress. Begging for more money, Schuyler had bemoaned the misfortune that "we should be necessitated to retain Indians and Negroes in our ranks." Now he was faced with a daunting swarm of enemy soldiers moving down from the lower end of Lake Champlain and an as-yet undetermined number moving in from the west along the Mohawk. Schuyler had appealed to Washington for more troops from the south. He'd received a responding message that some help, at least, was on its way north. Washington, however, was hard-pressed himself in the middle colonies. He'd been driven with almost casual ease from Long Island and New York City. The commander-in-chief had won a minor clash on Christmas Day in Trenton, but Washington had few troops to spare, and Schuyler knew it.

The problem was nothing less than immense. It would be eased only slightly if Arnold was successful along the Mohawk in halting the advance of the English expedition from the west under St. Leger. If anyone could do it, Schuyler knew, Arnold could.

A former apothecary raised by an often absent father and a mother whose life revolved around religious zealotry, Arnold was wildly impulsive, easily angered and had inherited his father's unfortunate fondness for spirits. He took extreme offense at every slight, real or imagined, and chafed under any hint of authority. At the same time, he was a dynamic leader of troops with an almost mystical capacity to motivate men under combat conditions. He was so personally courageous under fire as to qualify as foolhardy. He was gifted with an uncanny ability to inspire similar bravery on the part of terrified men who seemed ashamed to display less courage than their commander. Arnold was, Schuyler supposed, the finest pure warrior in the Army of the United States, all factors considered. He was a gifted strategist, and he could lead men in battle simply because he had a gift for making them care what he thought of them.

Yes, Schuyler had heard the complaints both from fellow generals and from nervous members of the Continental Congress. The politicians had retained for themselves the right to name and promote generals, although they tended to take Washington's recommendations seriously. They'd made Arnold a brigadier, but they'd steadfastly refused to advance him further in rank despite his marvelous record in battle. It was true, Schuyler admitted; Benedict Arnold was incorrigible and uncontrollable — probably more than a little insane, actually, if the matter were to be examined closely enough.

Without a moment's hesitation, though, Schuyler would have given up most of his fortune for an entire army composed of such lunatics.

Burgoyne. 1777

Hands on the rails, pulling him up the steps, Sir Francis Carr Clerke made his way from the ship's bowels to its deck. Planting his boots firmly on the planking, he gazed about, taking in the sweep of the scene — the hundreds of small boats at the shoreline, the bustle of activity on the beach, the military band forming up beneath fluttering pennants back at the edge of the forest. The towering stone bulk of Ticonderoga loomed up on the western shore, the Union Jack waving in the gentle breeze above its walls. What a striking day this was.

Clerke was a trim man of twenty-nine, the seventh baronet of Kitcham. His noble upbringing coupled with a sunny, confident temperament had left him with a knack for getting things done — for tasks performed adeptly, for orders delivered clearly. As a result, he served as General John Burgoyne's chief aide. Footsteps sounded in Clerke's ear. He turned toward them. Moving down the deck from the vessel's bow, the ship's royal navy captain approached the young officer.

"Is he yet prepared to disembark, Sir Francis?" Captain Thomas Pringle demanded.

"Shortly, Captain," Clerke said. "There's a certain ritual associated with these affairs, as you know. Please be patient, if you will."

As they spoke, a roar of cannon burst forth from the woods beyond the shore, rolling back from the trees and out over the lake. Clerke glanced toward the sound and spotted a rolling cloud of bluish-gray smoke rising like mist from the leafy treetops.

"Now, what's that about?" Pringle demanded.

"General Phillips remains annoyed that the rebels deprived him of the pleasure of reducing Ticonderoga to rubble with his guns," Clerke explained. "So, this morning, he's flinging grapeshot into the trees to clear them of snipers. The rebels have been sharpshooting at our patrols with gleeful abandon since we drove them from the fort. It wouldn't do at all to have them mar our formal landing this morning with a few more stray murders, now would it?"

Another booming burst of cannon fire produced an expression of distaste on Pringle's face. "A damned racket, is what that is."

"It's the thunder of captains," Clerke said.

"Say again, Sir Francis."

"From the Book of Job, Captain. 'And he smelleth the battle afar off, the thunder of the captains, and the shouting.' This army will make increasing racket as we move southward, I assure you."

"A soldier quoting scripture. That's a new one for me."

Clerke smiled slightly. "My uncle is a bishop. He drilled into me appropriate scriptural quotations for all occasions."

"All this talk of Bibles and cannon," Pringle grumbled. "I need to return to Quebec for more supplies for this hungry army of yours. I just want my ship back."

"You'll have it soon enough," Clerke assured him — and more than a little dismissively, too, the ship's captain noted. Scowling, Pringle strode away as Clerke moved to the ship's rail to survey the scene.

Except for a narrow spot at Crown Point, most of Lake Champlain was so vast that it could have been an ocean. For a man standing on one shore on most of the lake's length, the other shore was too distant to be visible. At the foot of the lake, though, Champlain narrowed until it was as slim as a ballerina's flanks. At the lake's southern tip, Champlain became a river, Wood Creek, that served as the lake's outlet. The river snaked back through the forest as the backbone of a little valley before it babbled to its death as a stream of yellow foam amid high rock mountains. It was along the edge of Wood Creek, deep in the forest, that General Phillips had dragged cannon and from which he now had his gunners hurling death through the tree branches.

Grapeshot was composed of nails, bits of chain link, broken metal tools, snapped knife blades, leftover musket slugs, shotgun pellets and small-bore cannon balls, all packed into the barrel of a cannon with a heavy powder charge and fired as a spray of shrapnel over a wide area. In the open field, grapeshot took down entire lines of opposing troops as they approached a fortified position, killing dozens with a single blast. At sea, grapeshot was used to clear the decks of opposing vessels. In the forest, where Phillips was now employing it, the ordinance whistled through trees, dusting them free of snipers in a hailstorm of blood spray and ragged bits of flesh.

As the stream left the lake proper, it divided into two distinct waterways. One flowed to the south and west, narrowing as it went, and into the northern end of Lake George, serving as that body's inlet. The second waterway was called South River. It ran to the south and east, ever narrowing, down to Fort Ann, where it subdivided into a diverse network of tiny tributaries that, ultimately, made their way to the Hudson River at Fort Edward.

Only the smallest English boats could go further. As the early morning sunlight sprinkled down on the lake like a shimmering torrent of golden coins the English flotilla of fully five hundred vessels was moving to the shoreline, disgorging its cargo. Hundreds of whaleboats, bark canoes and flat-bottomed, square-nosed, thirty-six-foot-long bateaux were already pulled up on the shore amid a frenzy of activity as they unloaded passengers and gear. The shoreline was alive with men, English and Germans in various uniforms and in civilian clothing, unloading themselves and the vital materiel of war — food, gunpowder, cannon, tents, cooking utensils.

The boats also were unloading women — nearly three hundred wives, sweethearts and salacious, adventurous whores from both Germany and the soldier-oriented fleshpots of St.-Jean-sur-Richelieu, Quebec. The women clambering out of the small boats were the property of the enlisted men and junior officers. The women of the senior officers had traveled aboard the large sloops flying regimental flags that had made the trip down Champlain under sail at the center of the flotilla. Those women, along with their children and personal servants, had traveled and slept in relative comfort and safety aboard those large vessels. Meanwhile, their lowlier sisters had paddled the open boats as vigorously as had their men all the way down from Quebec. Each night, they'd gone ashore with their husbands and lovers to share their rough blankets on the dirt in lakeside camps.

Riding at anchor that morning at the southern tip of Champlain, at a safe and discreet distance from the pandemonium at the shoreline, were four such sloops manned by crews supplied by His Majesty's Royal Navy. The smallest were the Carleton and the Lady Maria, on whose deck Clerke was standing. A larger vessel, the Royal George, lay anchored a hundred meters away and boasted two dozen cannon. Larger still was the Inflexible, bristling with twelve- and eighteen-pounders. It was, however, the relatively luxurious Lady Maria that served as the flotilla's flagship. The vessel flew the flag of the empire and, just below it, the banner of the Queen's 16th Light Dragoons, the home regiment of the expedition's commander. Clerke leaned back his head, gazed upward and surveyed the flags fluttering high aloft atop the Lady Maria's rigging. As he did, John Burgoyne stepped on deck.

He was a relatively tall, rangy man – square jawed, dark eyed, dark haired and youthful in appearance despite his fifty-four years. This morning Burgoyne was clad in the full regalia of a general in His Majesty's Royal Army. Wig powdered a glowing white, Burgoyne wore a full dress uniform — shocking scarlet coat with bright blue facing, gleaming brass gorget, gold braid, crisp white waistcoat and breeches, shiny black leather boots and an ornate saber hanging at his side over a burgundy sash. A navy blue cloak was thrown across his shoulders and hung down to his heels despite the balmy weather. Burgoyne appeared more properly dressed for a military parade through London than for the beginning of an arduous trek through swampy forests alive with enemy sharpshooters.

What a dashing chap, Clerke thought. The troops call him Gentleman Johnny for a reason. When I grow up, I suppose, I hope to look precisely as he does.

"All is ready, Sir," Clerke told the general. "The whaleboat is alongside. Your mount has been unloaded from the Royal George and waits at the forest's edge."

As he spoke, another burst of cannon fire boomed from the streambed in the woods. Burgoyne turned toward the sound.

Clerke said, "General Phillips is clearing the forest. It's the—"

"—Yes, yes, I know," Burgoyne said. "The thunder of captains and all that. I imagine, Sir Francis, should we ever meet, that I should find your clerical uncle most disagreeable."

"It's a view widely held in the family, Sir. Will Madame be accompanying the general this morning?"

"She'll follow in the carriage, with Lady Acland and the baroness. I can establish the headquarters on my own. Please stay behind and see that the carts are properly loaded and that all the ladies' needs are met, Sir Francis. Madame, as you may have noticed, can exhibit an exacting temperament."

Clerke merely nodded in assent. He didn't trust himself to utter even a word in response. Then the commanding general was hauling himself over the rail, moving deftly down the rope ladder, cloak flapping in the breeze, to the waiting whaleboat. Sailors straining at their oars at his knees, Burgoyne stood in the middle of the whaleboat all the way to the shoreline, erect and conspicuous, surveying the frenzy of the scene. As waves from the lake lapped on the beach, regimental banners were being unloaded and unfurled. He spotted the banner of the 47th Regiment of Foot, and that also of the 29th. In all — although some troops were already deep in the woods, clearing the path of rebel marksmen — Burgoyne had seven English regiments and five more regiments of German mercenaries hired with the empire's gold coin from the petty princes of Hesse-Hanau and Brunswick. Eight hundred of his troops were being left behind to garrison Ticonderoga.

His own men were clad in short coats of vivid red. Before the army had departed Canada, an ill wind had blown off course a vessel from

England carrying fresh uniforms, so Burgoyne's men had received permission to trim off the tails of their regulation uniform coats to serve as patches for their deteriorating jackets. The Germans wore coats of blue or forest green trimmed in a dull red or varying shades of blue with silver facing, depending on their provincial allegiance in the Fatherland and their military specialties. The German grenadiers wore high, metal helmets. Burgoyne's own grenadiers wore tall hats of bearskin. Burgoyne was short of horses for his German dragoons. As a cavalryman himself, he knew that those German troops were of only limited use afoot and would bitterly resent marching with the sixty-pound packs that were the lot of the foot soldier. He would have to forage for the horses, however, as he also would have to forage for food for his troops. Pressed for room on the ships for oxen to haul his guns and supplies, Burgoyne had brought only a few horses by ship from Quebec.

One was the general's showy white charger, transported all the way from London. As the whaleboat neared the shore, he spotted the animal awaiting him, its reins tightly held by a groom, surrounded by a few other mounts. Burgoyne took in also the military band forming up along the tree line to herald the commanding general's arrival with appropriately stirring martial music. On the beach, near the horses, he spotted Colonel Philip Skene and other officers of the royalist brigade — colonists fiercely loyal to the Crown and driven from their homes into Canada early in the rebellion. Now, in their uniform coats of Tory green, they were now returning in glory to reclaim their dwellings, shops and fields and all that was rightly theirs. Were the rebels to succeed in this rebellion, the loyalists knew, their property would be confiscated and distributed to soldiers of the winning side. For Skene, lord over thirty thousand acres just south of Champlain, loyalty to the Crown meant considerable financial risk.

The Indians were nowhere in sight. Burgoyne knew they were in the woods, scouting ahead of his troops, "purifying" the path, as Le Loup would put it. Burgoyne would have to meet personally with the Indians, he knew, and fairly soon. They would benefit from hearing their instructions directly from the man that some of them, apparently, believed was King George himself. The savages were worrisome but necessary, Burgoyne knew. They were matchless scouts and fierce woodland fighters. They terrified the troops of the militias. He knew also, however, that an uncontrolled mob of red men sweeping over the land ahead of his regular forces — raping, murdering and scalping promiscuously — would create more problems than they would solve. The common man of the colonies, Burgoyne understood, remained largely loyal to the Crown, but Indian bloodshed against ordinary citizens would harden the resolve of the militias against the English. In the end, he was acutely aware, it had been the irresponsible, uncontrolled use of the fathers of these very same savages that had cost the French so dearly in North America two decades earlier. That's why Burgoyne planned to lean hard on Le Loup to tightly control the Indian troops as the British army advanced toward Albany.

Standing tall in the boat, Burgoyne knew that he made an inviting target for any rebel sharpshooter who'd managed to escape detection and the havoc wrought by Phillips' grapeshot whistling through the tree branches. It was crucial, however, for the commanding general to show himself to the troops and to display, to the greatest extent possible, a serene disregard for his own safety on all public occasions. It was a burden of leadership, one of only many, and Burgoyne had borne it without complaint for a quarter century. He'd long ago made his peace with the harsh reality that sudden death was no more than an occupational hazard in his chosen profession.

As Burgoyne's whaleboat approached the shore, the troops began to cheer at his appearance among them. The commanding general grinned broadly, removed his tri-cornered black hat with its gold trim and white plume and waved it grandly over his head as the boat's bow nudged against the rocky beach. As Burgoyne stepped ashore, the snare drums began their beat, and the band burst into a lively march, brass blaring over the cannon fire from the woods beyond.

Colonel Skene was immediately at Burgoyne's side, saluting smartly and then shaking the general's hand in greeting.

"Welcome to the New York colony, General," Skene was saying.

"This is hardly my first visit to the colonies, Colonel," Burgoyne said. "My stay in Boston was made memorable by the graciousness of the Massachusetts ladies and the ill-mannered belligerence of their brothers, sons and husbands at Breed's Hill. I believe, however, that events here at Ticonderoga have offered us a most encouraging start to this current undertaking."

Skene smiled broadly. He was a big, red-faced man of perhaps fifty, born in Scotland, a retired English officer who'd married a wealthy woman and had founded a tiny community that bore his name, Skenesboro, on land he'd received as a royal grant. For some years, Skene had been a landowner of some gravity and the operator of a lucrative sawmill. As the revolution unfolded, he'd been briefly imprisoned by his neighbors for his royalist sympathies and had later fled to Canada to organize resistance to the revolt. He was only one of the commanders of Tory forces in service to the Crown, but the irregular regiment of one thousand loyalists Skene had put together in the king's service could be invaluable here, Burgoyne knew. That's why the commanding general had brought them with him from Quebec, untested though they were in battle. They knew the territory, and they knew who among the colonial population could be trusted as the Royal Army swept southward.

Skene was saying, "General, please meet Lieutenant David Jones, my aide."

Jones saluted smartly. He was a clean-cut man not yet twenty five. A boyish face — like so many of the faces in every such expedition, Burgoyne reflected, and they looked younger with each passing year. Burgoyne returned the salute with only a nod and a slight smile.

"Most of us fight for land and loyalty, General," Skene was saying, "but David here fights for even nobler stuff. My young aide fights for love."

"The loftiest of motivations," Burgoyne said.

"This campaign will reunite me with my sweetheart, Sir," said Jones, his face now as red as the general's coat. "We're to be married as soon as we can get back together. I asked General Fraser to send scouts to find her and bring here to me."

"I'm certain he'll strive to oblige," Burgoyne said. "General Fraser is an incurable romantic. I have a friend in Parliament, Charles James

Fox, who delights in saying that bigamy is having one spouse too many, and so is monogamy. I prefer General Fraser's more optimistic view as well as your own, Lieutenant."

Burgoyne then turned to Skene. "I'm told you own a house nearby, Colonel."

"I do, Sir. It's a number of miles down South River on the way to Fort Ann. The small boats can make it to my property. Then, from the fort, it's two dozen miles to the Hudson — half by water and then the rest overland, through swampy territory, before we'll reach Fort Edward on the river. My home, of course, is at your disposal."

"Very good. My chief aide, Sir Francis, will be ashore momentarily to spread the word among my senior officers. We'll dine at your house this evening, Colonel, and confer there as well. Would you be so kind as to grace us with your presence for a dinner meeting in your own abode?"

"I would be most honored, Sir."

Burgoyne motioned to the groom for his horse. As the animal was led forward, Skene, Jones and the other loyalists climbed atop their own mounts. Moving in behind the group, in tight formation, was a contingent of foot-bound English dragoons. In front, several troops of the 29th Foot were taking up marching position. With the ease of a born horseman, Burgoyne swung up easily on the magnificent white charger. Settling into his saddle, he turned his eye down the road along South River.

"Onward," ordered General John Burgoyne.

The journey to Skene's house along South River was uneventful. Along the route, a few stray shots from the woods sailed through the English column, but Skene's Tory scouts darted in and out of the forest, keeping the enemy at bay throughout the journey. Upon the party's arrival at Skenesboro, Burgoyne was taken somewhat aback at the grandeur of Skene's yellow stone mansion nestled behind gracious fields against the slope of a mountain near the fading creek. Burgoyne had expected a vastly more modest dwelling in this rough, uncivilized region. Instead, Skene's grand home would have looked perfectly appropriate on the rolling fields of Herfordshire.

The column had been followed by upwards of more than forty ox carts bearing Burgoyne's personal belongings — his luggage, fine china and silver, cases of expensive wine, gin, scotch whisky and delicacies of all descriptions, his headquarters equipment, maps and other paperwork. And, most important, the campaign war chest. Under guard at all times, the war chest was always within Burgoyne's personal reach. It contained gold coin for the purchase of food and other essentials that couldn't be transported down from Quebec. Before embarking on the campaign, Burgoyne had met with his officers and warned them to travel with only vital personal gear — if possible, keeping their personal luggage to no more than a single bag. It was a rule, of course, that bore no application to the commanding general himself, although General Will Phillips stiffly insisted on bringing only the personal gear he could carry himself. Moreover, Madame's luggage took up four of Burgoyne's ox carts all by itself. Charlotte had traveled with Burgoyne on many campaigns, until her health had begun to fail. Early on, Charlotte had learned to travel light. It was a lesson — one of many, Burgoyne was aware — not yet absorbed by Madame.

Tents for the troops were being pitched in the fields around the house. Burgoyne was establishing his headquarters in Skene's parlor, using two enlisted men to unfurl and post maps and to arrange paper files, when the carriage arrived out front. It was a calash, a two-wheeled affair constructed by troops in Canada and pulled by a team of prancing matched grays. The general glanced out the window at the three women, two small children and Sir Francis as they stepped down to be greeted by Colonel Skene. Burgoyne marched out to Skene's porch to welcome them as they came up the steps.

He said, "Greetings, ladies — and, of course, Sir Francis. Welcome to our new headquarters."

Lady Harriet Acland glanced around, studying the mansion with a discerning eye. She was a restrained and charming woman of twenty seven, the daughter of an earl, and just beginning to swell with pregnancy. Beside her in the calash, slobbering on everyone within five feet, was her dog, Jack, a massive, pleasant, panting black Newfoundland. Burgoyne very much liked both Lady Harriet and her husband, Lord John Dyke Acland of Devon. He was a major, the commander of Burgoyne's grenadiers, and was one of Burgoyne's most capable younger officers. Lord Acland was now in the forest ahead, hunting down rebel gunmen with his troops.

"Rather lovely, actually," Lady Acland said.

"Ya," said the baroness, her English thick with heavy teutonic pronunciations. "We vill be ferry comfortable in zis houze."

Burgoyne bowed low before Baroness Frederika von Riedesel, her two young daughters, Frederika and Gustava, crowded around her ample skirts. She was a tiny, ruddy, blonde woman in her early thirties, petite but wiry, with a ready smile and never a complaint. The daughter of one general and the wife of another — and a noblewoman to the very marrow of her bones — the baroness was nonetheless as hardy a military campaigner as any man in Burgoyne's command. The general took her hand and kissed it. He then turned his attention to the third woman emerging from the calash.

"I trust that Madame's journey was pleasant," Burgoyne said, taking her hand in his own.

"The conclusion is most pleasant," Madame replied with a dazzling smile and only the slightest hint of musical French accent in her speech. "I have now arrived for the matchless pleasure of the commanding general's company."

Burgoyne's lips touched the back of her hand and lingered there for just a moment. He then squeezed the soft hand gently, kept it wrapped in his own and gazed into her azure eyes. Her hair a shimmering cascade of inky blackness, her flesh a glowing ivory, Madame was easily the most beautiful woman he'd ever laid eyes on, Burgoyne reflected once again.

"Your rooms are on the second floor, ladies," he told the other two women. "Sir Francis will have the servants show you the way and see to the unloading of your bags." He then turned back to Madame. "You would perhaps grant me the honor of joining me for a tour of the grounds?"

The smile faded slightly from Madame's lush lips. "It was a wearying journey, but the general's companionship shall no doubt be reviving."

"For only a few moments, Madame," Burgoyne said jovially,

taking her arm in his. He turned to Clerke. "See to the ladies' comforts, Sir Francis. When I return, please join me, if you will, in the map room, and bring my other aides as well – especially Tommy."

"Indeed, Sir," Clerke said. He well knew that pleasant, smiling Sir Thomas Stanley, one of Burgoyne's junior aides, was probably nosing about the women who'd traveled down from Canada with the army. Clerke knew, too, that Stanley felt the freedom to absent himself from his duties all too often because the young officer had the ability to refer to the commanding general as "Uncle Jack."

Burgoyne and his lady moved back down the steps and out onto the grounds of Skene's mansion. Burgoyne guided the woman toward the bubbling waters of the stream. All around them was a flurry of activity, with soldiers unloading supplies from small boats and pitching neat rows of tents that stretched from the house across the fields to the edge of the woods. Off at the forest's fringe, they could see latrines being dug and cooking tents being erected. An entire, surging city of canvas was being erected on Skene's farm.

"The ladies treated you well?" Burgoyne asked.

"Lady Acland is quite gracious at all times. We're becoming fast friends."

"That's excellent," Burgoyne said. "You should study her, my love – study the way Lady Harriet speaks and conducts herself."

"I am doing that," Madame said. "As for the baroness, well ..."

"A bit stuffy, I surmise," Burgoyne asked.

Madame nodded silently. She was acutely ill at ease in the company of women of noble breeding, and Burgoyne was well aware of it. Noblemen were a different matter. From childhood, Madame had never met a man immune to her charms, whatever his station in life.

"She is a baroness, after all," Burgoyne said, "and acutely aware of her status at all times. She's of a type you'll have to grow accustomed to in London, my love."

"Then London is a place I dread," Madame said.

"Oh, no. London is not at all a place to dread — not for you. Not for the lady of Gentleman Johnny Burgoyne."

Madame smiled slightly and tightened her grip on the general's arm as they made their way through the sweating, swearing mob of men. "The house is quite impressive."

"Indeed. I think we might stay here a while. I'm awaiting word from New York City concerning reinforcements, and you were surely cramped on the journey aboard ship. Accommodations further south should be distinctly Spartan until we reach Albany. I shall, of course, be comfortable enough in a tent when the situation calls for that, but you deserve some time in a real bed amid gentle surroundings before we plunge ourselves into such an uninviting environment."

"That's thoughtful of you, Jack. Thank you."

"We're throwing a dinner this evening, you and I. Converse only in English, if you please. Your French accent is most attractive in English, but your French itself is marred by decidedly colonial pronunciations. You must become accustomed, Madame, to serving as a hostess in such settings. London is one long, unending swirl of such gatherings, you know."

"So you've told me."

Burgoyne stopped, faced her and took both her hands in his.

"This is the beginning, my love. There is much for you to learn, but you can learn from these ladies if you watch them and study their conduct. Quebec is now firmly in your past. London is in your future — on my arm, of course."

She smiled — a glitter of white teeth and soft, gentle, fetching curves in her face. "As you wish, my Lord."

Burgoyne laughed. "Not your lord just yet. But soon enough, I would imagine."

Back at the mansion, Skene and Clerke snapped orders to soldiers to unload the ox-carts and to Skene's Negro servants to escort the ladies to their rooms. Few of the troops had ever seen people with skin so dark, and they openly marveled at their appearance. Skene took the occasion to introduce himself to the young officer as the women ascended the curving staircase to the mansion's sleeping quarters.

"Extraordinary house," Sir Francis observed.

"Took me ten years to build it," Skene said. "The damned rebels threw me in jail for a while and then chased me out of here last year and up to Canada, fleeing for my hide because I wouldn't abandon king and country. The same thing happened to most of the men with me. Now we're back, though, aren't we?"

"You are indeed, Colonel. King and country aside, I can now appreciate what you fight for."

"I was unaware, Sir Francis, that Madame Burgoyne was French. I must observe that she's a positive vision."

Clerke frowned slightly.

"Madame Burgoyne is dead, actually. She died last year in

London, as the general was working in Quebec to prepare for this campaign. She'd been in frail health for some time. Now, there was the very image of a lady, Colonel Skene. Madame Burgoyne was the daughter of the Earl of Derby, you know."

Skene's face took on a confused expression. He said, "Then who ..."

Clerke's upper lip curled slightly as he spoke. "This woman is the wife of a junior officer in Canada — still quite married, unfortunately. It seems that the general was needful of comfort and companionship upon learning of the passing of his wife of nearly three decades. Madame was more than eager to provide the necessary consolation."

What Clerke longed to say — but would never say aloud to anyone, out of loyalty to his commanding general — was that Madame was, in Clerke's view and in that of virtually every other senior officer associated with the campaign, a conniving, low-born strumpet unworthy of Burgoyne's serious attentions.

Skene's eyebrows rose.

"I see. It's a complex matter, then. Has the general any children?"

"Long ago, there was a daughter. She died quite young."

"Well, then ..." Skene began cautiously.

"Yes," Sir Francis Clerke said, abruptly cutting off further conversation on the topic. "Well, then. That's what we all say about it, you know."

∞

After dining on roast chicken and beef with his key officers and their ladies in Skene's cavernous dining room, Burgoyne ordered maps brought in. They were unfurled and locked into their wooden frames at the head of the table, where the general had sat throughout the meal, his glorious mistress at his right hand. Burgoyne had been making small talk about party life in London and the countless personal quirks and foibles of his fellow members of the House of Commons. Around the table, among others, were Clerke; General Phillips, the artillery officer; Lord Acland and his lady; Colonel Skene; the invading force's chief chaplain, a handsome young clergyman named Edward Brudenell, and the baroness Frederika and her husband, the Baron Friedrich von Riedesel, who commanded Burgoyne 's five German regiments.

General Riedesel was that rarest of creatures, Burgoyne had observed to Clerke — a fat cavalryman. Short, chubby and solemn with pinched lips and a glassy stare, Riedesel nonetheless sat a horse with the skill of a jockey. He understood both cavalry and infantry tactics and maintained iron discipline over his troops. Unfortunately, he spoke little English. Burgoyne spoke some German but preferred to deal with Riedesel in French. When that was impractical, as it would be this evening as Burgoyne addressed the entire group, Burgoyne knew that the baroness would translate his words. Burgoyne spoke enough German to suspect that the baroness offered her husband her own observations as she translated the commanding general's words. After all, the translation couldn't take that much longer than the original remarks. Sitting on the baron's other side was Colonel Nicholas von Breymann, a stern, hard-eyed man in his mid-forties who served as the baron's chief infantry officer.

Technically, Phillips was Burgoyne's second in command, since he was the senior English officer in the expedition, while Riedesel was third in command. That pecking order had no meaning, however, as long as Burgoyne lived. Were Burgoyne to be killed, then Phillips would take over. While he breathed, however, Burgoyne ceded authority to no man in any matter, large or small. Clerke and the chief aide's deputies handled details for the commanding general and transmitted his orders, but Burgoyne's only true counselor was General Simon Fraser, who commanded the expedition's hard-edged advance troops.

Fraser was not at dinner. He was in the forest ahead, killing as many rebels as he could manage in advance of the campaign's next thrust southward. Burgoyne had sent a messenger ordering Fraser to report to headquarters to confer with the commanding general at the earliest possible opportunity. In actuality, Burgoyne wanted only to spend a few hours with Fraser over a fine vintage. The two had been fast friends since early in the Seven Years War.

"Now," the commanding general said to the assemblage, rising at the head of the dining table, "on to matters of serious moment. Specifically, that's my fifty guineas."

The group sat silent. Burgoyne paused for effect, searching each of their faces with sharp eyes. More than a little wine had been consumed here this evening, and he wanted to be certain that he had everyone's full attention.

"Last year," the commanding general said, "before leaving London, I made a wager with a fellow member of Parliament, Charles James Fox. If I return to London, victorious in this campaign, by Christmas of this year, he owes me fifty guineas. If I do not return with victory by that date, then I must pay him a similar sum. Ladies and gentlemen, I implore you: employ all of your efforts during this campaign to save me from so cruel a fate as ridicule by Fox. It's bad enough that the fellow is such a poor loser. When he actually wins a wager, he's truly monstrous."

The group around the table laughed. Burgoyne paused to permit the laughter to subside. Then he added, "I do believe, given my recent history with cards and horses, that the time is ripe for me to win at least one wager."

Now the laughter was even more spirited. Burgoyne's reputation as a gambler was legendary, exceeding even his standing as a London bon vivant with a healthy appreciation for the companionship of stage actresses.

"It is time," the general said, "sitting in this fine house after this most pleasurable meal, to acquaint you all with the theory of this expedition. You are aware that we are moving south to crush the rebellion once and for all. For reasons of security, however, I have kept the campaign details closely held. I now deem the moment propitious for you to become familiar with the Grand Strategy."

He certainly had their attention now, Burgoyne noted. Grabbing a carving knife from the table to employ as a pointer, he stepped to a large map of the New York and New England colonies and lower Canada as well.

"We began here," he said, "in Quebec. We are now here, in Skenesboro, to the south of Lake Champlain. During the next phase of the operation, we'll portage boats to Lake George and move a portion of our forces down that body of water to take the rebel fort at the end of the lake. At the same time, we'll be moving the bulk of our troops down a wet and soggy dirt road, here, taking Fort Ann and Fort Edward as we go. Along this second road, we'll bear with us, overland, boats to carry supplies down the river with us and the components of a bridge over which we shall transport our supplies and cannon to the far side of the Hudson. I expect Fort George, here at the far tip of Lake George, to fall without a fight, as did the forts at Crown Point and Ticonderoga — and as will both Fort Ann and Fort Edward as well, I surmise. The rebels are well aware that these tumble down, wooden fortifications at Fort George, Fort Ann and Fort Edward provide no protection against General Phillips' cannon. They'll abandon them and retreat — ultimately, I'm confident, all the way to Albany. When they do that, we'll have them cornered."

As he spoke, he noticed the baroness translating his words into German and Riedesel muttering into his wife's ear in response.

"Baroness," Burgoyne said, "does the general have a question? In fact, all of you, this is the moment at which questions might and should be asked about the Grand Strategy."

"Ze baron," said Frederika von Riedesel, "vants to know if Albany is our ultimate goal. And, if zis is so, how vill ze capture of zis single town end ze rebellion?"

Burgoyne smiled. "Last year, I had the pleasure of a meeting with both His Majesty and Lord Germain, the colonial minister. It was after that meeting that the king authorized funding for this campaign. The plan, my dear baroness, is more complex than I've yet explained."

Burgoyne moved back to the map. "As we move down the Hudson toward Albany, Lord Howe in New York City shall shortly receive orders from Lord Germain in London to begin moving his army up the Hudson to join us. At the same time, from the west, Colonel Barry St. Leger commands a substantial force from Canada moving east along the Mohawk River, here, that will join with ours just north of Albany, here. In short, we are converging on the town from three distinct directions with a powerful force constituting each prong of the assault. Albany will fall, and quickly. When it does, the real campaign will begin."

"The real campaign, Sir?" Clerke asked.

"Indeed, Sir Francis, the real campaign. Of itself, Albany is insignificant in the overall scheme of the rebellion. However, once the town is conquered to form the center of an iron line controlled by the Royal Army all the way from New York City to Canada along the Hudson River, we shall then sweep eastward, through New England, all the way to the sea. Along the way, we shall hang every rebel we find. I served in Boston during the early days of this treasonous revolt. It is my belief — and that of the king and Lord Germain as well — that New England is the intellectual center of this rebellion. It began there, and we can kill it there by decapitating it. We can end this entire sordid business in a matter of months by hanging the original imaginers of this revolt — as we should have hanged them long before the first shot was fired at Concord. That, ladies and gentlemen, is the Grand Strategy. That is the mission of our campaign."

For a long moment, there was silence as the assemblage took

in Burgoyne's words and studied the map beside him, imagining his words translated into action. Yes, it all made sense. The entire strategy held together — assuming, that was, that a three-pronged Royal Army force really could defeat the rebel army's northern forces.

Breymann, the baron's deputy, cautiously raised a hand. In more or less accent-free English, he asked, "General Burgoyne, how much difficulty do you expect if the enemy does not retreat into Albany but instead chooses to meet us on ground of its own choosing somewhere north of the town?"

Burgoyne smiled slightly. "Reassure yourself, Colonel, that we are up against only an undisciplined mob, not soldiers. They will do all within their power to avoid confronting His Majesty's troops in the open field. They'll huddle in the forest and strive to fire upon us from ambush, as they've been doing ever since they abandoned Ticonderoga. That's why your foot soldiers were subjected in Canada to special training to function more effectively in the woods. That's why I had join us here that contingent of savages who so disturb the digestion of our good General Phillips here."

Phillips, not a man prone to smiles, smiled slightly at the remark. His friendship with Burgoyne stretched back decades. Solemn and taciturn in his own style, Phillips nonetheless enjoyed his commander's wit and style.

"Our doctrine of battle is quite simple, really," Burgoyne explained. "We outnumber them. Our troops, man for man, are vastly superior to theirs. Colonel Skene's loyalist regiment — and, especially, our band of bloody red savages — will drive the rebel forces from the woods and, ultimately, into the open. There, upon the field of battle, we shall then make short work of them with our cannon, with our concerted volleys of musket fire and, finally, with our bayonets. Essentially, they have no bayonets, you know. Imagine, an army without bayonets."

Burgoyne glanced around the room, searching face after face for any hint of doubt or confusion. He saw none. Questions would come to him later, he knew, as various details of the campaign became complicated, as they invariably would. War was never a tidy business. For tonight, however, Burgoyne had his key officers both united and optimistic. He wanted them going to bed in precisely that frame of mind.

"Ladies and gentlemen," said the commanding general, "a busy day awaits us tomorrow. Good night to you all, and God save the king."

§⃝

In Philip Skene's spacious master bedroom suite, Burgoyne removed his boots and sword and tossed his heavy formal uniform coat across a chair. He removed his powered wig and placed it in its stiff, round leather case. Tomorrow morning, the showy formalities of arrival behind him, he would don a regular field uniform, and the wig would be stowed by his valet with the rest of the general's gear. Burgoyne probably wouldn't need it again until Albany — until the victory celebration.

Under other circumstances, the valet would be in this room with the commanding general, tending to Burgoyne's clothing as he prepared to retire. Tonight, however, the valet slept on the floorboards of the hall outside the room as Burgoyne, settling into a throne-like wing chair, watched Madame undress. These Frenchwomen, he noted, suffered from no false sense of modesty, as did so many of their more cold-blooded English sisters. Madame's gown and undergarments went from her flesh directly to the floor. Then, smiling, she strode from her side of the bed across the room in all her naked, unabashed and unadorned splendor to curl atop Burgoyne's knees. He wrapped his arms around her, drawing her close, holding her protectively. She was a tiny woman who fit neatly into the tall man's lap.

"Bab, isn't it delightful to be off the ship and on solid ground once again?" he asked her.

She snuggled her head beneath his chin. "It is delightful to be able to sleep with you again. That little cabin on the boat, and the three of us so crowded in there. The baroness, she snores. Did I tell you that?"

Burgoyne chuckled. "No, although it doesn't surprise me. I don't snore, do I, my love?"

"Oh, no," said Madame. "Tell me again, Jack, how it will be in England."

Burgoyne leaned back in the chair, clutching the warm bundle of alluring feminine flesh to his chest. "England has winter, but it's never as bitterly, brutally cold as Canada. The sun hides a good deal, but air is always moist and gentle. London is a scintillating city, Bab. You'll especially enjoy the stage shows. You've seen nothing in Quebec to rival the sheer, sparkling magic of the London stage. I have myself written a few plays, actually. One was performed on the Boston stage before we were forced to retreat out of that city by rebel misbehavior."

"And it is true that I shall be the wife of the prime minister?" she asked.

Burgoyne smiled as he gazed at the ceiling. "Eventually, perhaps. And, after that, perhaps the wife of a baronet or even an earl. His Majesty is famous for his generosity to those who serve him well. Lady Bab, you shall be, my love. There is, however, much for you to learn before you can move in sufficient comfort in such circles. Watch the baronness. Study Lady Harriet in particular, as I've advised. She's a woman of excellent breeding and style."

Madame huddled close to the general. When she spoke, her voice was a low, serious whisper. "Will they truly accept me in London, Jack? I will not be shunned as some hopeless rustic — as no more than the whore of a celebrated general? You can promise me that?"

"Indeed. Of course — especially if you acquit yourself properly."

"How can you be so certain?"

Burgoyne squeezed her gently. "I will be the general who put down the colonial revolt. If I insist that they accept you as my beloved Lady Bab, then they must and they shall."

Slowly and lovingly, Burgoyne kissed Madame full on the lips, lingering there a long moment. It was one of those rare kisses between the two that did not involve passion. She was so young, Burgoyne understood. Lust had its proper place, and he prized it all the more as he aged – and this woman stirred that lust as no other woman ever had — but Babette would be on his arm long after his passion had faded.

"And that, my love," he told her, "I most assuredly shall do."

Franklin. 1777

Late on a hot July morning, with the previous night's rain rising as steam off the sun-splashed, cobble-stoned streets of Paris, Charles Gravier, the Comte de Vergennes, leaned over to his teenaged mistress at a sidewalk cafe near the Church of St. Germain. In her ear, through her golden curls, the count whispered an endearment. He then whispered a bawdy suggestion as to how they might pass the coming evening.

The girl giggled. Vergennes leaned back in his chair with a smile. He enjoyed making her giggle almost as much as he enjoyed evoking laughter from his granddaughters, who were a few years younger than this lovely girl. He was about to expand on his remark when he spotted, approaching their table, a thickset man with straight, graying chestnut hair falling down from a balding pate to brush against the detachable fur collar of his brown coat. Walking slowly and haltingly, leaning on the thin tree branch that he used as a walking stick, the American commissioner to the court of Louis XVI smiled broadly and raised a hand in greeting.

Vergennes rolled his eyes. Just what he needed, a morning of theater. Behind his eyes, his head ached slightly. He was in no mood for this. He also could see no way to avoid it.

"My dear count," said Benjamin Franklin in his heavily accented French. "It's such a pleasure to happen upon you like this."

"It is always a distinct pleasure to share your company, Dr.

Franklin," said the French foreign minister, rising and taking Franklin's hand. "Please join us. This is ... well, you may simply call her Angelique. She is the daughter of old friends."

"Mademoiselle," Franklin said with a smile, taking a seat at the outdoor table and then proceeding to ignore the sixteen-year-old girl in favor of her sixty-year-old lover. "A lovely day. I was taking my constitutional, as I do daily. Exercise, my dear count. As with the companionship of young women, it keeps old men vibrant."

Vergennes nodded. "I trust you remain comfortable at the Hotel d'Hambourg."

"Very much so, although I'm giving some thought to larger quarters just outside the city. I've looked at a splendid house in Passy, only a half hour out of the heart of Paris. It has lovely gardens and congenial neighbors. As you know, I lived simply and happily in just a few small rooms during all those years in London, but I have my grandsons with me during this assignment. For boys of fifteen and seven, the atmosphere of a hotel can be stifling. They need some open ground on which to frolic."

"Indeed," the count replied. "And to what purpose might I ascribe the pleasure of your company this morning?"

Franklin smiled sheepishly. His hotel was a good distance from this spot. Vergennes knew this meeting was more than mere happenstance.

"I have news," Franklin said. "A dispatch reached me yesterday from Philadelphia. You may, very soon, have information for the king that he's sure to find heartening. In mid-June, a sizable English invasion force embarked from Quebec to invade the New York colony. The invasion is commanded—

"—by General Burgoyne," the count broke in. "Surely you realize that we have our own sources of information, both in Quebec and London."

Franklin smiled slightly. "And in Philadelphia as well, no doubt."

"No doubt," the foreign minister said quietly. "We already know of Burgoyne's invasion, but it intrigues me to learn that you view this as information that would cheer His Majesty. Why do you so interpret it? I should imagine that just the opposite would be the case."

Franklin nodded. "That's because you believe that our soldiers cannot stand against the English army. If you did believe that we could successfully defend ourselves, then I would have no purpose here in Paris. There would be no need for me to come to you — hat in hand, day after day — begging for the military aid from France that could permit us to defeat the English quickly and decisively and firmly establish our independence once and for all."

"And ..." the French foreign minister said.

"And," Benjamin Franklin said, "this invasion represents good news simply because it will be repulsed in a clear and convincing fashion. When that occurs, my dear count, all arguments against French aid to our cause will evaporate like morning mist."

Vergennes leaned back in his chair. "More than ten thousand English and German troops. That's what our information tells us. And that's only what embarked from Quebec. You're aware that there's another English force moving in from the northwest? You're aware that still another force of undetermined size may be moving up from New York City under Lord Howe?"

"We're aware of all of that and more — although the disposition of Howe's forces remains an open question, according to our sources in London. General Burgoyne is not without enemies in high places."

"Even without Howe," the foreign minister said, "what your army faces is formidable."

Franklin smiled. "Formidable but not insurmountable. Certainly not invulnerable."

Vergennes raised his eyebrows. Then, his voice tinged with amusement, he said, "Your self-confidence is most inspiring, Dr. Franklin."

"By definition," Franklin told him, "revolutionaries are confident people. We will manage this military crisis, my dear count; have no doubt. Think, however, of how much easier it would be for us if we had available from France the military materiel that could bring this clash to a quick and decisive end. France is engaged in a massive modernization of its military forces. Your army is awash in out-of-date cannon and muskets — materiel no longer of practical use to you. Why not give it to us immediately? In return, we'll provide you with shiploads of tobacco. We're willing to pay you for what you'll otherwise be disposing of without payment. To you, this aged weaponry is useless; to us, it represents vital tools for achieving victory."

Vergennes sighed slightly. This was an old argument. Franklin had been making it at least once a week since his arrival in Paris six months earlier. The count said, "You ignore the fact, Dr. Franklin, that His Majesty has already been helpful, despite his reservations about the viability of your revolution. Virtually all the powder your army uses comes from France. All your uniforms, several hundred cannon, thousands of muskets — all this came to you through the generosity of Louis XVI. And yet your forces continue to suffer defeat after defeat at the hands of the English on every battlefield. You could not hold New York City or its environs, after all."

"General Washington did take back Trenton on Christmas day," Franklin pointed out.

"A small victory, six months old, against hired German troops and not the cream of the English army, which is what you face in this invasion by Burgoyne. Tell me now, and please be candid, what is the advantage to France in further provoking the English by lending additional support to what any thoughtful observer must now view as a likely lost cause?"

"The cause is not lost," Franklin said firmly. Now the American commissioner was sitting straight up in his chair, shaking a finger at the French foreign minister. "There is great advantage for France in supporting us further, my dear count. If you have any hope of reclaiming Canada—"

"—We harbor no such fantasy," Vergennes said, shrugging. "Canada is lost to France for all eternity. We are reconciled to this."

"France possesses vast territories west of the colonies in the North American continent," Franklin argued. "Permit the English to defeat us, and those territories will soon become the part of the English Empire. We both know that, my dear count. We know also that an English victory in North America would threaten French sugar colonies in the West Indies, the revenue from which is crucial to your nation's welfare after all those years of warfare with the English. You know, and I know, that anything that weakens the English Empire in the Western hemisphere strengthens France. Anything that aids my nation's revolution works to the advantage of France in securing its holdings in the New World."

"If you win, Dr. Franklin," Vergennes said softly, "and only if you win. Moreover, if you lose and we have aided you, then we will have succeeded only in provoking King George and further endangering our New World holdings."

"We'll win," Franklin said calmly. "But, in the interim, let us not pretend that the help France has provided us thus far has been a simple act of charity. France's self-interest is inextricably intertwined with the self-interest of my own country."

"Your own country only if you can hold it," Vergennes said.

Franklin smiled slightly. For the past six months, since his arrival in Paris, although Benjamin Franklin was perhaps the most famous man in the civilized world as a result of his achievements as a scientific thinker, he'd played the jovial, grandfatherly bumpkin — mangling his French purposely, affecting his fur collar and fur hat as the garb of an American frontiersman, even though he was actually a fabulously wealthy printing magnate back in Philadelphia. Franklin's amusing act brought him invitations to the finest homes in France, where he entertained in salons as he made his arguments to influential people close to the king. He'd never fooled Vergennes, though — not for a moment — and Franklin knew it.

"We'll hold it," he told the French foreign minister. "We really have no choice now, do we? And we'll hold it most immediately against Burgoyne. You have my promise on that, my good count. Burgoyne will go down to defeat before the snow flies."

Vergennes turned to the girl and patted her hand gently. Franklin recognized the gesture of affection as a sign of dismissal. He stood and bowed.

"Keep that promise, Dr. Franklin," the French foreign minister said, "and I will then speak to His Majesty on your behalf. You are completely correct, you know. We do have more cannon and muskets than we know what to do with."

"We would certainly know what to do with such an embarrassment of riches."

"Yes," the Comte de Vergennes said. "It's also true, however, that, like General Burgoyne, France has many more enemies in London than she needs."

Burgoyne. 1777

In the pre-dawn July darkness, as the sun began to wash away the darkness over the eastern horizon, Burgoyne sat at a table on Skene's front porch and sipped tea he'd brought with him from London. He'd risen early, a soldier's habit. In the sea of canvas tents around the house, in bedrolls in Skene's barns and other outbuildings, his men were awakening, tending to their weapons and preparing for a day of killing in the woods and swamps to the south and west. To the south, across Skene's fields, Burgoyne spotted a horseman emerge from the shadowy forest beyond the tents. As the rider drew near the porch, the commanding general recognized him. Burgoyne rose in greeting.

"Simon," Burgoyne said, "you're the sorriest of sights."

Brigadier General Simon Fraser swung down from his foam-flecked gray gelding. He was a square-jawed man of forty-eight whose broad, expressive face radiated good humor. Beginning against the French and the Indians, Fraser had spent the bulk of his military career campaigning in North America, although he'd first met Burgoyne when each had been serving in Ireland. As a young officer, serving with Burgoyne under Howe at Quebec, he'd saved Burgoyne's life, forming a lifelong bond with the man who was now his commander. This morning, Fraser's field uniform was stained and torn, and his boots were coated in thick, dried mud. As they touched the ground, he snapped to attention and saluted Burgoyne, who returned the gesture only casually.

"The formalities have been properly observed," the commanding general said. "Now, sit down and breakfast with me. And tell me about the ground to the south."

Fraser came up on the porch and took a seat as Burgoyne ordered a Negro servant to find the general some tea and eggs. Fraser stank of sweat. The night had been none too cool to begin with. Now the sun, just nudging up beyond the tree line, was already transmitting the message that this day would be as sweltering as the previous day had been.

"It's evil country," Fraser said, the burr of Scotland marking his speech. "The road is but a wilderness trail through marshes and wide ravines and raging creeks. The rebels destroyed all the bridges over those creeks, and each needs to be rebuilt for the cannon and the ox-carts to cross successfully. The damnable rain has left the earth soaked and spongy, and the rebels have even dug trenches from the swamps to ensure that the water makes its way to what otherwise would be dry, hard ground. The horses' hooves sink into the dirt all along the trail. So do men's boots. So will the wheels of the cannon and carts, Jack. It'll be slow going with an army this size."

"We missed you at dinner," Burgoyne told him.

"It was late last night when I received your order to report," Fraser said. "There was work to be done, and I figured you'd be abed by the time I arrived, anyway. So, here I am for breakfast, Jack. A bit early for gin, unfortunately."

"Who'd you leave in command?" Burgoyne asked.

"Balcarres for our troops, Baum for the Germans. You know, for an earl, the Balcarres boy fights rather nicely. Both our young noblemen — Balcarres and Lord Acland, too — have been more or less pleasant surprises out there in the wilderness. Acland even sustained a flesh wound from a sniper that he's shrugging off rather manfully. Perhaps there's something to this blue blood business after all."

Burgoyne smiled. "Very little, from my observation. I'm the son of a nobleman, you know — a bastard son, at any rate. Whatever worthwhile traits I possess, I assure you, came to me through my mother's common lineage and not through the watery blood of Lord Bingley. And you, Simon, ideal specimen of Scottish peasant that you are, are more soldier than perfumed dandies like Balcarres or Acland will ever be."

Fraser smiled. He was not of noble stock, to be sure, but he was no more a peasant than was Burgoyne. Clan Fraser was an old Scottish family with some money. Simon had been born the tenth child with no hope of inheriting enough for a life of leisure. Military life had not made him wealthy, but it had given him stature. He was a colonel in the regular English army and a brigadier in the colonies only, but he enjoyed the rank that had given him sufficient authority to issue orders to lords and earls.

"Well, they seem good men so far, Jack," he said. "I'm glad we have them. As noblemen go, each is a vast improvement over that fat, pompous, Brunswicker baron. Riedesel should be half the soldier his wife is."

"I know you don't care for him personally, Simon, but you fought beside him against the French, and we both know that he's rather good — certainly good enough for our purposes on this campaign. He is, by the way, nagging me to find him two hundred mounts for his dragoons. The poor chaps are already sore of foot."

"They're huge fellows for cavalrymen. Each German dragoon must weigh nearly as much as his horse."

"Did you stumble across any acceptable mounts for them on your foray south?"

"None worth stealing," Fraser said. "The rebels are grabbing everything themselves as they pull back — mostly to deny it to us, I presume. Every cow, duck, goose, sheep and chicken has been gathered up, much less the horses. They're fighting hard, Jack — better and smarter than I'd expected."

"Go on," Burgoyne said, listening and assessing.

"We took custody of all the cannon and supplies they'd left at Ticonderoga. Then I took half my brigade, left the big guns behind and chased the bulk of their forces east and south. At a place called Hubbarton, we came across a stubborn rear guard of New England militia firing at us from the greenery while the main force moved away at a dead run. We killed about forty and wounded another hundred or so. We took several hundred prisoners. But they killed sixty of our people and wounded another one hundred seventy. Arthur St. Clair commanded the fort, you know."

"I remember him from the war with the French. He married some colonial politician's daughter, did he not?"

"Granddaughter — and heiress, by the way — of Governor Bowdoin of Massachusetts. St. Clair has much to protect here, and he's doing it efficiently enough. When he abandoned Ticonderoga under cover of darkness, the baron and his men were bogged down in the swamps on the lakes eastern shore, but my regiment was only an hour behind St. Clair's fleeing garrison. I'd hoped to move to his left and push him here to you and to the main body of our army. Unfortunately, we were in rough, wooded country, and St. Clair refused to fall obligingly into the trap I'd tried to set for him. Our savages were ranging ahead. They captured a rebel sentry. That's how I learned it was St. Clair."

"Unfortunate."

"Yes, well, the heat was intense, and they truly are better in the woods than we are, Jack."

"We won't be in the woods forever."

"We'll be here for longer than we like," Fraser said. "St. Clair got far enough ahead of us to set his men to work with axes and saws all along the path to Fort Ann — and, I presume, the road beyond that to Fort Edward and the river. The road has been effectively blocked. The rebels took down every other tree along the route, dropping them into the road from either side and leaving them there, branches intertwined, to hinder the passage of our cannon and our supply carts. When I left the scene to report here to you, gracious young Alexander Lindsay, the sixth Earl of Balcarres, was nobly engaged in swinging an ax along with eight hundred and fifty other men. Trees fall more easily than they can be chopped into pieces and dragged away. The rebels took down those trees much more quickly than we'll be able to clear them."

"That's because so many of them are farmers, accustomed to felling trees to create farmland. How long to open the road, Simon?"

"Two solid weeks with them firing at us from the forest as we work — possibly longer. Luckily, they miss most of the time, and we always get their marksmen eventually, but it takes time and no work goes on while the hunt is in progress. It's a bloody nuisance, really."

Burgoyne's lips pursed. Fraser and his hardy advance corps could sweep the path of rebel soldiers with relative ease, he knew, but the expedition could not advance without its supplies and big guns. The damned supplies, Burgoyne grumbled to himself. They were the soft underbelly of any large expeditionary force. Every invading commander was forced to spend vastly more time fretting over how to feed his army than how to fight with it. You could kill the enemy and move your men forward, but you could sustain none of it unless you could feed your troops when their bellies rumbled — unless you could provide oats and hay for your animals, unless you could keep your men well stocked with powder, ball and flints. An army of ten thousand, Burgoyne knew, couldn't live entirely off land this sparsely settled. The road must be cleared for supplies before the army could move in full force.

"Distressing," the commanding general said softly.

"Well," said Fraser, "it's no more than a delay. I've sent scouts to survey Fort Ann and Fort Edward, but it's my guess that St. Clair will have cleared them of all but a few rear guard troops and will soon swing west to be cross the Hudson to march south and join Schuyler. Once the road is open, however, we should be able to march straight to the Hudson and proceed to Albany unimpeded. We can carry the small boats overland and then move our supplies by water down river. Oh, and by the way, I ordered the savages back to their camp as you commanded in your message to me. What's that about, might I inquire?"

"I'm going to their camp later today to speak to them personally. General Phillips fears that they're getting out of hand."

"They're always out of hand. Isn't that why we brought them along in the first place?"

"To a point, yes," Burgoyne conceded. "The savages are certainly useful, but I cannot countenance widespread violence against the civilian population. The colonists are the king's subjects, after all, Simon, and most of them remain loyal."

"You're quite right, of course," Fraser said. "If you'll permit me a few hours sleep, I would be delighted to accompany you to their camp. I've been there already. You'll find it quite a spectacle, I assure you."

Burgoyne chuckled. "A scene to be recounted at length when I'm back home at Christmas. The London ladies grow delightfully aflutter at tales of naked red savages."

ॐ

Sir Francis Clerke hadn't expected it, but he found himself distinctly ill at ease as they rode into the Indian camp. There were four of them — himself, Burgoyne and Fraser, neither of whom betrayed the slightest hint of discomfort, and the obviously terrified civilian driver of an ox cart laden with barrels following behind. The only other white who would be on hand, Sir Francis knew, would be Le Corne St. Luc – or, as he was known to both whites and Indians alike, Le Loup, the wolf.

Le Loup was a towering, menacing-looking French-Canadian scout, thought to be part Mohawk. With a black patch over an empty eye socket, a scalp lock of bristly white hair thrusting up from his otherwise bald skull and a still rock-hard frame draped in black and buckskin, he'd been a fabled fighter in his younger days on behalf of the French against the English – so effective that he'd been knighted by the French king. Now sixty-six years old, the Chevalier Le Corne St. Luc sold his services as a commander of Indian forces to the English. Attached to the command of the overseer of His Majesty's forces in Canada, Sir Guy Carleton, Le Loup – in exchange for a high rate of pay – served as Carleton's liaison to the Indian nations. At Burgoyne's urging, Le Loup had been ordered by Carlton to make this journey against Le Loup's wishes. His response to this ill treatment at his advanced age had been to render himself insensible with rum during the journey southward over Lake Champlain. He'd steadfastly maintained that condition upon landing in his bark canoe at Skenesboro, where he'd vomited loudly on the creek shore and demanded to know the whereabouts of more rum. He'd since sobered up, more or less, to exert whatever control he could muster over the four hundred Indians in his charge — which was precious little, if General Phillips were to be believed.

Refreshed by a nap in his tent, Fraser was in a clean field uniform, but Burgoyne — always the calculating showman and polished performer — had once again donned his finest parade dress. Astride his white horse — all scarlet, gleaming white and gold braid and lacing — the commanding general was an impressive sight, and the Indians reacted to it as he'd imagined they would. Knotted around cooking fires as darkness approached, the Indians stood slowly and followed in a growing group as the three horsemen rode in stately fashion into the camp and through their ranks. At the camp's center, next to a large fire surrounded by a dozen squatting Indian men of middle age, the now half-sober Le Loup stepped out from an army issue tent as he heard the hoofbeats. Le Loup was in his trademark black blouse and greasy buckskin pants. He saluted as Burgoyne's horse pulled to a halt before him.

"We are much honored to receive you in our humble camp, mon general," Le Loup said in heavily accented English as he bowed and belched simultaneously.

At least the old man seemed less drunk than usual, Sir Francis noted.

"I've come to address your people," Burgoyne said. "Would you be so kind as to translate for me?"

"I can translate into three native tongues," Le Loup said, "Ottowa, Mohawk and Algonquin. I can also communicate your words in sign language. Some of these chiefs understand French. The substance of his excellency's message will be understood by most and explained to the others by their brothers."

"I'll speak in French, then," Burgoyne said. "I want to be understood by all here, Le Loup. Now, gather them together, and find me a place from which to address them."

Le Loup extended an arm toward the nearby fire, where all the middle-aged men who had been squatting a moment before were now standing. "This is the council fire, mon General. These men are the chiefs of the nations. They await your words."

"Very well," Burgoyne said, and strode to the fire in his gleaming black boots. Fraser moved easily behind him. Nervously, Sir Francis moved with his superiors into the center of the tightening circle of glowering red men. All were in war paint — striped or smeared in blacks, blues, reds and yellows. Some, he noted, wore their hair long, midway down their backs. Others wore scalp locks or hair adorned with shells and beads. Still others wore cloth coverings over their heads decorated with feathers and carved ornaments of bone. In the summer heat before the council fire, virtually all were shirtless. Some of the hundreds of red men crowding in on the scene wore only moccasins and bits of cloth or buckskin over their private parts.

"A curious wardrobe," Sir Francis muttered to Fraser.

"They're dressed for war in the woods," Fraser responded, wiping the sweat from his brow with the back of his hand. "Has it occurred to you, Sir Francis, that in this beastly wet heat these chaps might have precisely the right idea?"

Le Loup found and placed in front of Burgoyne an empty wooden ammunition crate. Burgoyne stepped atop it and gazed around, hands on hips. Now, more than a head taller than any of the hundreds of Indians crowding in on him, the general motioned for Le Loup to stand next to him on the crate.

In flawless French, Burgoyne called out, "Greetings from his great and royal majesty, King George, our common father across the sea."

Immediately, Le Loup began gesturing to the assemblage with his hands while he barked out a quick sentence in an incomprehensible language and then two other sentences in tongues that were both different but, at the same time, surprisingly similar. Burgoyne waited until the chevalier had finished. Then, his voice loud and strong, Burgoyne continued.

"His Majesty feels immense gratitude for the loyalty of his children. My soldiers and I esteem you as brothers in this war — as our comrades in friendship and glory. Your loyalty shall be richly rewarded. The rebels against whom we wage war are disturbers of the public order, peace and happiness. Our common father has authorized me to reward with treasure warriors who bring me their scalps."

Le Loup called out in his babble of tongues as his fingers flew. Immediately, a clamor of assent went up from the Indians. It was a shout of approval in several languages. Sir Francis watched the

Indians as they nodded and called out. He was taken aback by Burgoyne's offer to pay for scalps. The general had mentioned this macabre incentive to no one. That was, as Burgoyne later confided to his chief aide, because the idea had not been Burgoyne's. Paying the Indians for scalps had been the personal brainchild of King George III.

"However," Burgoyne called out, "His Majesty will pay more treasure not for the scalp of a rebel but for that same man taken prisoner and brought to my tent."

Immediately, as Burgoyne's words were translated, the noise died down. Now the Indians were silent and attentive.

"Our common father knows," Burgoyne went on, "that his red children are matchless in their enterprise, their perseverance and in their ability to resist hunger, weariness and pain. He urges us, his white children, to emulate your spirit and your hardiness. Our common father knows, too, of the magnanimity of character of his red children. He therefore urges you to refrain from bloodshed when you are not opposed in arms. Aged men, women and children must be held sacred from the knife or hatchet, even in time of actual conflict. These are the wishes of our common father, King George, and he has given them to me to give to you."

Hundreds of pairs of hard, dark eyes focused on Burgoyne as he stood on the crate, gazing out over the now-silent crowd in the growing darkness as Le Loup moved his hands frantically and shouted out the general's words in his three languages. When Le Loup grew silent, Burgoyne examined faces in the assemblage, his sharp eyes moving from face to face. Then, after a long moment, the commanding general spoke again.

"Nor will our common father permit the wounded to be scalped or for the wounded to be killed for the purpose of scalping. He urges his red children to curb their passions and to remember always that it is nobler to spare than to slay."

In the moments that followed the translation, Sir Francis spotted Simon Fraser's right hand creep across his middle and slowly move to the hilt of his saber, lingering there.

"Warriors," Burgoyne shouted out, "on the next dawning you are free to go forth in your valor and might to strike at the common enemies of King George, myself and of you as well. You are free to take treasure as you may find it. You are free to defend yourselves as is necessary in the course of warfare. I urge you only to take note that our common father has many loyal subjects dispersed along our line of march and that these are your brothers and sisters deserving of your mercy."

For a long moment after the translation, an ominous silence hung over the scene. Then, unexpectedly, one of the older men who'd been squatting around the council fire when the party had arrived stepped forward. At the top of his lungs, for perhaps a minute, the man shouted in Burgoyne's direction as the general stood on the ammunition crate, utterly expressionless.

"Prepare yourself, Sir Francis," Simon Fraser whispered ominously.

As the Indian finished, a broad, toothless grin spread across Le Loup's face. The chevalier turned to Burgoyne and looked up.

"This man is a chief of the Mohawks," Le Loup said. "He says that he loves his father across the sea and that all their hatchets have been sharpened with affection. He says that there will be obedience to all that King George has ordered and prays that the Father of Days gives you many, mon general — and much success as well."

From the crate, Burgoyne glanced at the semi-drunken old Frenchman with the black eye patch.

"Then we'll survive this gathering, I take it?" the commanding general asked softly, a smile playing about his lips.

"Yes," said Le Loup, grinning broadly. "Isn't that wonderful, your excellency? For a moment, I was almost certain that we would not."

"In that case," Burgoyne told Le Loup as he stepped down from the ammunition crate, "inform your children that the ox cart that followed me into camp is laden with barrels of rum — a gift to his red children from our common father across the sea."

As Le Loup shouted out the news in various languages, the warriors shifted their attention from the three red-clad officers to the ox cart. They swarmed over it like a tidal wave, rolling barrels to the ground and smashing them open with hatchets amid laughter and war whoops. The civilian driver was on the run the moment the Indians turned toward the ox cart. The ox, he knew, would end up in cooking pots tonight, but he'd been paid for it and wasn't prepared to fight four hundred savages to rescue the creature.

Fraser moved to Burgoyne's side and said, "I do think, Jack, that this might be an opportune moment for us three to be on our way."

"General Fraser has a point, Sir," Clerke said. "We've just encouraged them to murder whites, and now we're serving them rum."

"Very well," Burgoyne said. "Mount up, gentlemen."

As Fraser swung up on his horse, he said to Burgoyne, "They'll do as they please, you know. They came here not to defend the king's honor but to loot and plunder."

"Ah," said Burgoyne, gazing down on Le Loup from the saddle of his white horse, "but the chevalier will see that they follow orders. Won't you, now?"

Le Loup shrugged, a uniquely French gesture. "I will do my best, mon general."

Burgoyne smiled in amusement. Then, in a low voice, he said, "I'll hang the man who violates the order — along with he who permits its violation, either directly or through drunkenness or neglect. And bear in mind, Le Loup, that we're in country rich in tree limbs."

Babette: Before it all began

It was late April before the rains came.

As they poured down in a relentless, drenching torrent, day after day, the hard-packed Canadian snow began to melt beneath the usual dark shroud of thick, forbidding clouds. The winter had been brutal even by the exacting standards of St.-Jean. Now, as the snow receded, raindrops dug into the frozen Earth like warm, probing fingers pulling the chill from the dirt. The Richelieu River began to swell between its muddy banks with this new downpour and with the melting snows. By mid-May, the river was running high and fast. The first, fragile blossoms of spring were popping out on the trees. It was just after dawn one gray morning in late May, with the fragrance of new life permeating the air outside the two-room officer's quarters occupied by Captain Peter Loescher and his wife, that Babette felt the first pain. It took her breath away.

"Peter," she called out from the bedroom.

He appeared in the doorway, gazing in, his expression tense with alarm.

"It's coming," she told him.

"Get dressed," he ordered. "I'll take you to the surgeon's."

In the bed, Babette grimaced as a wave of pain passed through her. She rolled up in a ball and said, "I can't travel like this. Bring the surgeon here to me, please."

"It'll take twice as long," he warned.

Babette's only response was a dull, muffled scream of agony that she choked off by jamming a portion of blanket between her teeth. A moment later, she opened her eyes, gasped with temporary relief and heard the thud of hoofbeats in the soft mud outside the cabin. Something was wrong here, Babette suspected. No, she didn't suspect; she knew. This wasn't right — not right at all. As the pain knifed through her once again, she felt her heart flutter with fear. She'd spoken with the wives of the other officers, absorbing their knowledge, experience and advice. She thought she'd known what to expect, and this wasn't it. This was the wrong sort of pain. It was wider and sharper than she'd been warned of — not at all the steady, rolling spasm and gradually building pressure that she'd been told she could expect. Her mother had died in childbirth. Ettiene LeDoux had never forgiven his daughter for killing his beloved wife — not really. When surly with drink, a common circumstance, he would tell her so.

Later, Babette could not recall how long it had taken Peter to return with the regimental surgeon — forever, it had seemed. The surgeon was slim and youngish and, oddly, more than a little feminine in manner. At first, a candle in one hand to combat the dim light of the bedroom and a small, leather bag containing his instruments in the other, he was pleasant and confident.

"Do you have rum, Captain?" he asked as he sat on the bed next to Babette.

"I do," Peter said. "Do you need it?"

"No," the surgeon said. "You do. Go into the other room and get royally drunk. Celebrate the impending birth of your child. Leave me alone with Madame, if you will."

Babette glanced at her husband. Peter's broad face was flushed with excitement.

"And shut the door, please," the surgeon said as he set down his bag and threw back the blankets.

As the pain returned, the surgeon rolled up Babette's nightgown. He examined her carefully — taking what seemed an eternity as he poked and probed at her in the light of the candle. As this activity continued, Babette watched his expression undergo a transformation. Without a word, the surgeon suddenly covered her, stood and left the room. Through the half-opened door, Babette could hear him confer with Peter.

"Get me a woman," the surgeon snapped, "another officer's wife, perhaps. I'll need another set of hands. And please don't bring me some flighty girl, Captain. Bring me a sensible, mature woman who has given birth more than once."

"What's wrong?" she heard Peter say.

"She's a small woman," the surgeon said, "and this is a large child. It's also in the wrong position, I fear."

"What can you do?" Peter demanded.

"Turn it — perhaps. If not, then I may be forced to take it. You understand my meaning, I trust."

Babette heard only silence. Peter was not responding.

The surgeon said, "Your wife is slim in the hips — not at all built for childbearing. Moreover, if I must take the child, there'll likely be an infection that follows. If she survives, she'll probably be left unable to conceive again."

For a long moment, through the half-open door, Babette heard nothing. Then Peter rasped, "Do you realize what you're saying?"

"This is divine will, Captain — God's work. Take hold of yourself."

"No children?" Peter choked out.

"Not with this wife," the surgeon said. "Now, find me that woman. And see that she washes her hands, please. That seems to help with infection. No one knows why."

As Babette heard the hoofbeats once again, the surgeon moved back into the tiny bedroom. He stood above the bed in the dim, flickering light, gazing down on her as she fought back another wave of pain.

"I heard you," Babette whispered to him.

"Yes, you were meant to," the surgeon told her. "You're entitled to know."

"I shall not die," Babette said through gritted teeth. "Do what you will, but I shall not die."

The surgeon gazed down upon her thoughtfully. Then he moved to the foot of the bed and threw back the covers once again. His eyes fixed on hers, he took off his scarlet coat and tossed it into a corner of the room.

"Do you understand what I must do to assure your survival?"

Her mouth a thin, determined line, Babette nodded.

"As you will, then, Madame," the surgeon said softly as he reached into his leather bag and brought out a knife-like implement. "It's entirely possible that you shall not die after all."

Schuyler. 1777

After dispatching Arnold and a force of nearly one thousand men to Fort Stanwix to meet the English invasion from the west, Schuyler moved the bulk of his army, totaling nearly three thousand regulars and militia, out of Albany to form a defensive line north of town. His forces settled in at Cohoes, just south of the Hudson's juncture with the Mohawk.

Then, with a relatively small contingent of troops, Schuyler crossed the Hudson and rode up the river's eastern shore for Fort Edward hoping to meet St. Clair — not knowing that the commander of Ticonderoga had been forced fifty miles to the east and was setting up shop in a region known as the Hampshire Grants, although some natives of the area still called it Vermont, a perversion of the French

Vert Mont, or green mountain. It was there that St. Clair hoped
to reform his widely scattered army and prevent what he feared
would be a wave of desertions. At each stop on the journey, Schuyler
composed letters at his folding field desk and sent them off by courier
in every direction, pleading with the local militias to join him.

Like St. Clair, Schuyler was worried that the intense bloodiness of
the clash with the pursuing English south of Lake Champlain would
spark desertion from his army. In his heart, Schuyler feared that when
he did hook up with St. Clair the former garrison of Ticonderoga
might be down to no more than a thousand men. Schuyler had
received word that a brigade was being sent north from Peekskill,
under the command of Brigadier John Nixon, but he knew that even
a full brigade would never make up for the desertions from St. Clair's
army.

At Fort Edward, Schuyler ordered a force of Massachusetts
militia to join St. Clair's men in felling trees and obstructing the road
between the river and Fort Ann. He also fired off a steady stream of
dispatches by express rider begging all commanders in the New York
and New England colonies for cartridge paper, powder and musket
balls. Schuyler also urged the transfer of bullet molds, raw lead and
carpenter's tools to replace all that had been lost to the English at
Ticonderoga. He needed wagons. He needed shovels to dig defensive
positions. He needed cannon and more supplies, supplies, supplies.
If, by some miracle, he actually succeeded in rallying the militia,
Schuyler knew, they might well starve as they awaited the arrival of
English bayonets.

Then, his work at Fort Edward finished, Schuyler crossed back over the Hudson and continued down the western shore to Saratoga, near his country home and farm, scouting for favorable ground on which to make his stand against the English army moving down from the north. Schuyler knew the country in that area, and he had a spot in mind. On the crest of a high, sloping bluff overlooking the western shore of the Hudson River, near a tavern on the river road operated by a farmer named Jotham Bemis, Schuyler stood one July day at noon surveying the site. With an outstretched arm, he gestured for Wilkinson's benefit as the summer sun blasted down on the hillside.

"They can't cross the river further south of this location," the commanding general said. "Below here, the Hudson grows too wide for the erection of a pontoon bridge steady enough to bear the weight of their supplies and cannon. That means that they'll have to cross north of this spot, probably up near Fort Edward. They'll have to march along this road to reach Albany. From here, Colonel, we can train what cannon we have down on them from above. This bluff constitutes a fortification cunningly constructed by the Almighty."

Wilkinson gazed down on the scene, imagining a huge English army moving southward on that road and a fortified Army of the United States force dug in on the hillside, atop the bluff and along its northern edge.

"Can we stop them, Sir, with so few cannon?" he asked.

"We must," Schuyler said simply.

"And if they come up the hill after us?" he asked.

"They will," Schuyler said grimly. "Then it'll all boil down to whether we can hold this high ground. If we can do that, then we will have halted the invasion from the north. They'll have no choice but to flee back to Canada."

"Couldn't they retreat to Ticonderoga and winter there?" Wilkinson asked.

Schuyler shook his head. "Once ice formed on Champlain, they would face huge problems in moving supplies south on the lake from Canada. I deem it unlikely that they would sit at Ticonderoga all winter and risk starving amid the snow, Colonel. Whatever else Gentleman Johnny Burgoyne might do, it won't be that."

Jane. 1777

Her eyes opened as the first, filmy rays of the sun glinted off the river and formed a regiment of glimmering, glittering pinpoints of light dancing atop the water. Jane awakened to the light and to the distant, muffled sound of musket fire off in the woods.

She sat bolt upright on her straw pallet on the dirt floor of Mrs. McNeil's cabin. The older woman lay in her bed on the other side of the room, wrapped in homespun covers, snoring loudly and blissfully unaware of the turmoil outside the cabin. Through the open window, Jane heard the frenzied voices of men, the dull thud of running boots on dirt. She threw aside her cover and leaped to her feet. Silently, bent over and staying low, she crept across the earthen floor of the one-room cabin to the door, opened it just a crack and spotted the running men outside. The rebels were in full flight, scampering down to the river, paddling across in bark canoes and rowboats toward the Hudson's western shore in total retreat. They were abandoning Fort Edward to the advancing English army.

David is near, she thought. He's coming for me. She felt her heart turn over in her chest. Despite her awareness of imminent peril, Jane felt a surge of delighted excitement. She'd waited for David for so long now. Finally, today, they would be together again. Slowly, and with appropriate caution, Jane opened the door. A line of perhaps two dozen rebel soldiers was at river's edge, kneeling and taking up firing positions to cover the retreat of their comrades as they clambered into the boats pulled up on the shoreline. She watched the members of the rear guard picket reload their aged French muskets. They ripped open paper powder packets with their teeth, pouring the powder down rusting gun barrels, driving home one-ounce lead balls and wadding with ramrods, using the leftover powder to prime their firing pans.

The English had to be very near, Jane knew. The muskets had smooth-bore barrels three feet long. Their effective range was no more than a hundred yards. She spotted several rebel soldiers loading and firing at targets off to the right. Yes, there was no doubt now. The English were no longer near; they were here.

As she watched, Jane saw several of the rebels in the rear guard fall, one with an arrow through his middle and protruding from his back. Then, as the last of the boats set off from the shore, the rear guard was overwhelmed. From the right, a swarm of Indians swept into her line of vision. There were perhaps three dozen of them, no more than forty yards from where she watched through the half-opened cabin door. They poured out of the woods with bloodcurdling war whoops. Wielding tomahawks and firing muskets and loosing bows as they came on, the Indians roared into the tiny rear guard, cutting them down ruthlessly in hand-to-hand combat. A knife blade flashed in the morning sunlight. Blood gushed like a scarlet fountain from the throat of one rebel soldier. Jane heard the dull thud of steel hatchet blades against skulls. For a moment, she turned her eyes away. Then, fascinated with the horror of it all despite herself, she turned back to gaze once again upon the bloody scene.

The rebels were throwing down their empty muskets and standing, their hands raised in the air. The Indians were at work on the surrendering prisoners with knives and hatchets when a gigantic old man in buckskin pants and black shirt and with a black patch over one eye came running in from the right and leaped among them, shouting at the savages in a strange language, pulling them away from their prey. Jane pulled back into the cabin and closed the door as Mrs. McNeil came awake.

"What's the fuss outside?" the older woman demanded, throwing off her covers.

"They're here," Jane said. "The rebels are fleeing."

"Well, God save the king," Sarah McNeil shouted triumphantly as she bounded from her bed. "Gather your things, girl. You have ground to cover this fine day."

Jane was about to respond when the cabin door burst open. Jane turned and caught just a glimpse of flying black hair and copper skin and red and yellow paint smeared across a foreign face. She felt an elbow smash into her forehead. Instantly, Jane went down, dazed, her back thudding against the cabin's dirt floor. She felt strong hands grasp her elbow. She heard Mrs. McNeil's harsh, outraged shriek as

Jane felt herself dragged across the floor, her mouth filling with dirt, and outside into the sunlight, into the dying screams of the doomed rebel rear guard, into the war whoops and the stink of gray clouds of gunpowder billowing in the air. A hand dug into her waterfall of hair, pulling her head up. She opened her eyes then, and she saw the knife near her face.

And she screamed. Jane McCrea screamed mightily.

Then the huge old man with the black eye patch was grabbing at the dark hand with the knife, pulling it away from her face. Still dazed, she heard angry voices ring out over and all around her as she lay in the grass, just barely conscious, outside the cabin door. She felt blood trickle from her nose. She coughed as the blood poured down her throat, and she turned her head, the blood flowing down her cheek into the grass. From the corner of one eye, she could make out two Indians dragging Mrs. McNeil from the cabin. The older woman was totally naked now, an egg-shaped mound of quivering white flesh, and screaming insanely, her voice a mixture of rage and terror, mostly terror.

Jane couldn't move, didn't dare move. The angry voices roared above her. Then a strong hand clutched at her elbow, and she felt herself dragged to unsteady feet, her hair tumbling across her face. Jane felt lightheaded from the blow she'd suffered, fearful that she would faint, fighting it, terrified at the prospect of losing consciousness. In front of her, a big, muscular savage was locked in a shouting match with the even bigger old man with the eye patch, who held Jane firmly by the elbow. The one-eyed man turned to her, shoving his face toward hers, only inches away.

"Who are you?" he demanded in heavily accented English. "Your name?"

"J-Jane McCrea," she managed to choke out.

"You are the woman of David Jones?" he demanded.

Groggily, Jane nodded.

The towering one-eyed man turned his face away from her and shouted some more at the huge savage who'd dragged her from the cabin. The Indian glared at him and at her, too. In a lower voice now, the old man snapped at him in that strange tongue. Somehow, Jane knew it was an order. She watched as the Indian, his dark eyes smoldering, turned away and moved toward the pasture where Sarah McNeil's old, decrepit horses grazed near the fence gate, unaware and unperturbed.

"He is taking you to the English camp," the one-eyed man told her. "General Fraser sent me to find you."

Slowly, Jane was returning to full consciousness, although her head ached horribly from the blow she'd sustained. The scene around her was madness, a hell of blood and violence. The powder stink was choking her. Along the river's edge, Indians were lifting up the corpses of fallen rebel soldiers by their hair and sawing off their scalps. Off to the side, she saw two Indians struggling to load the naked, shrieking Sarah McNeil aboard one of the woman's ancient horses and failing at the task. Mrs. McNeil slid off the animal's back and hit the ground hard. Finally, one of the savages pulled her to her feet by her gray hair and wrapped her wrists in rope. Then the Indians headed off to the woods, leading Mrs. McNeil like a cow. The older woman was no longer screaming. Now she was praying in a loud, quavering voice.

"Don't leave me to them," Jane begged the one-eyed man.

"I must stay here," he told her emphatically. "If I leave them to take you back to camp, they'll butcher everyone in the village for their hair. Panther knows who you are. You will be safe."

The big Indian was back now with the other of Mrs. McNeil's horses. Wordlessly, he grabbed Jane by the waist and swept her effortlessly up to the animal's bony back. She clutched desperately at the horse's thin mane to avoid falling. Then the horse was moving, and Jane was leaning forward over its neck, digging frantic fingers into the animal's sparse mane to keep her seat. The savage led the animal at a brisk trot toward the forest while Jane bounced on its back and her head swirled. Through a haze that seemed to have settled over her eyes, she gazed down upon the savage's broad, muscular back. As they entered the woods, he glanced over his thick shoulder at her, his dark eyes boring through the war paint up into her face. The breeze quickened, gathering strength in the warming air.

With a brand new surge of terror, Jane McCrea felt her cascade of bright copper hair flowing out behind her like a banner in the brisk morning wind.

Burgoyne. 1777

In Philip Skene's spacious dining room, with candlelight flickering off the pale beige walls, Madame struggled to open a tin of caviar.

"I so miss Simon's company," she was saying. "He's so charming and always so gay. And he's so skilled at opening these horrible tins."

"Simon and my Freddie," the baroness said, "Zey stay in ze field day and night."

"These men and their warfare," Lady Acland replied, smiling and stroking the huge head of the panting, drooling Newfoundland sitting beside her. "Leave them to their own devices, and they would play at it all the time. That's why I insist that mine come in from the forest now and again, as he has done this evening."

"Ya," said the baroness. "I told mine to come in also, but here he is not. Madame, a kindness I vill do you und open zis."

Concerned that she was being patronized, but fearful of challenging the baroness if she were, Madame smiled and handed over the tin and the metal can opener. Frederika von Riedesel took the items in her small, strong hands and grinned widely at the pleasure of the task. She had been opening tins of food in camps near battlefields since early childhood. It was a skill learned young by the children of soldiers. Her own young daughters were highly adept at such tasks.

"Zere," the baroness said with satisfaction as the opener's steel teeth bit into the tin.

The women were clustered around one end of the long, gleaming cherry wood table. Meanwhile, a body of men chatted over Madeira at the other end. In all, not quite two dozen people occupied the large room — the three women on their private turf at their end of the table, Burgoyne and his inner circle of top officers and Philip Skene and his young aide, Lieutenant David Jones, at the other.

Burgoyne and his staff had taken over the house completely.

Senior officers, their ladies and servants occupied the second floor sleeping quarters while more junior officers slept in servants' quarters on the third floor or on bedrolls on the hardwood floors of downstairs rooms. Skene and his senior officers slept in one of the estate's large barns. These nightly gatherings over fine food and wine, followed by gin, scotch whisky and brandy, were now routine. Sometimes Lady Acland would entertain by playing the pianoforte in Skene's sitting room, while Madame sang French folk songs in a sweet, soaring soprano. More often, the group would simply talk and drink and listen to Burgoyne hold forth on one or more of the many and varied topics on which he was undeniably expert. The commanding general was a captivating master of ceremonies, and he seemed starved for both fine food and idle conversation in the evening when he emerged from his headquarters in Skene's parlor at sundown.

As usual, dinner had been sumptuous. One of Skene's young, fat sheep had been butchered that morning and prepared in the late afternoon in fine style in the cooking shed behind the mansion. The roast had been served with new potatoes and fresh vegetables and with fluffy, crusty bread baked in stone ovens behind the house. It was a topic of complaint by the German troops that the English commissary officers issued only flour and not the baked bread to which the Germans were accustomed in their home quarters.

Now, the meal behind them, and the dishes cleared by Skene's black-skinned servants from the far away sugar islands of the Caribbean, the senior officers and their wives were drinking and chatting while Madame had ordered the serving of some of the fine, imported delicacies Burgoyne had brought from Canada. She especially loved the beluga caviar. Burgoyne had brought along perhaps half a hundred pounds of the stuff, along with tins of smoked oysters, delicate European cheeses dipped in wax to keep them fresh and tin after tin of dried, candied fruit to appease his mistress's relentless sweet tooth. Ox cart after ox cart groaned under the weight of Burgoyne's smoked salmon and sausages and cases of fine wines, cognacs and prime whiskies.

At his end of the table, Burgoyne was leading a discussion on Shakespeare. He was of the firm opinion that such marvelous plays could never have been crafted by some crude, unschooled Avon merchant — that they were, in fact, the work of some nobleman who'd refused, for his own reasons, to sign his own name to the works.

"The details of life in the upper classes," Burgoyne was saying, "are far too precise for this Shakespeare chap to have known from his own experience — the life of the court in particular. If a cow could talk, gentlemen, she would truly be a remarkable creature, but she could never hope to describe with faithfulness the experience of flight. That's because she would never have flown. Yet whoever really wrote these plays could, and with minute accuracy, characterize the lives, language, foibles and manners of the noble classes. And these plays are the work of a member of the merchant class? Highly unlikely, I would conclude."

Lord Acland was intrigued. He lacked Burgoyne's intimate knowledge of the theater arts, but he knew Shakespeare's work, which was becoming quite popular on the London stage.

"Then how, Sir, would this Shakespeare fellow's name have

become attached to the plays?" the young officer asked.

"A misunderstanding, perhaps," Burgoyne said. "The goddess Athena was the patron of the theater in ancient Greece. She was often portrayed in statuary holding a spear. She was sometimes referred to, in Shakespeare's time, as the spear shaker. Some educated nobleman with a sense of humor could have signed a play with a pseudonym in her honor. Much later, as the plays endured and interest in their long-dead author grew, that work could have been erroneously attributed to someone on the fringes of the London theater with a similar name — like this hard-drinking merchant, Will Shakespeare. It was all a few centuries ago, my Lord. The truth, I fear, is lost forever in the shroud of time."

Skene said, "You must miss London terribly, General — the stage in particular."

Burgoyne shrugged and sipped his Portuguese Madeira. "I don't miss the intrigues of Parliament. I miss not at all the shoddiness of London politics. Here, Colonel, we are all engaged in the legitimate business of empire — holding the Crown's possessions by force of arms against those who would purloin them. Yes, I do miss London and its lights and its stages. Yet, I would rather be here, in true service to my king, than back in London dodging political daggers hurled continually at my spine."

Lord Acland said, "It's that bad in Commons, is it, Sir?"

Burgoyne shook his head wearily. "Oh, yes. His Majesty, unfortunately, is served by ministers whose primary interest is not the empire's welfare but their own. Lord Germain is the worst of them."

"He's the colonial secretary?" Skene asked.

"Indeed," said Burgoyne. "As George Sackville, long before becoming Lord Germain, he commanded cavalry and was cashiered out of the army for malfeasance and cowardice at Minden in the Seven Years War. A man with less impressive family connections would have been shot. He then attached himself to the rising political star of Lord North. As prime minister, Lord North gave his protégé the colonies to administer — and you can judge for yourself what a stellar job he has done. Thanks largely to Lord Germain's ineptitude, we now have a revolt to put down. As you might imagine, Colonel, the colonial secretary and I do not hold one another in the highest regard. Behind the scenes, he opposed this campaign, of course. Luckily, I had direct access to His Majesty, and the king was vastly more reasonable."

Sir Francis Clerke smiled. "That's because, Colonel Skene, when this campaign succeeds and the rebellion is put down, Lord Germain fears being replaced as colonial secretary by the man who quelled the revolt."

Skene nodded slowly. "Now I understand."

Burgoyne smiled slightly. "You further understand, I trust, why I miss the London stage but not the London politics."

As Burgoyne spoke, a large, pear-shaped form filled the doorway. Baron Friedrich von Riedesel's blue uniform coat was splattered with mud. He bowed low to the group.

"Forgive my tardiness," the baron said in French. "I have been abroad with General Fraser tending to rebels."

Riedesel's arrival signaled the end of conversation in English, leaving Skene and Jones as the only people present unable to decipher the ensuing conversation in French. They leaned back in their chairs to observe and to listen to what was largely gibberish to their ears. A year of exile in Quebec had been too brief to permit either Skene or Jones to function effectively in this strange tongue.

"Freddie," the baroness said disapprovingly from her seat at the end of the table, "you should wash and change your uniform before you join us."

"Not at all," Burgoyne said expansively from his chair at the other end of the table. "The baron's presence this evening only serves to remind us in our decadent comfort in this fine house that war remains a dirty business. Please let him know that, Baroness." Then, in his own smooth but limited German, Burgoyne said, "Come in, my good Baron, and aid us in reducing our oversupply of Madeira. We're all delighted to see you."

Riedesel crossed the room in muddied boots and took the goblet of wine Burgoyne poured for him. He downed it in one gulp and held out his glass for a refill.

"It is good to return to this place," the baron said. "When at last no one returns from war it will be because war finally has been properly organized. We are, it seems, General Burgoyne, some distance from that point this evening."

"Trouble on the road?" asked Sir Francis.

Slumping into a chair, the baron said, "There is only one narrow, rutted path cut through the woods to the river. So much dense woodland I have not seen since the Black Forest. In a dozen days we have made less than a half dozen miles. We chop up the trees the rebels felled on the road and pull the pieces off to the side. And all the while the rebels fire on us from the forest and then fade away when we drop our axes to charge them."

"Yes," said Lord Acland. "The damned cowards refuse to stand and fight."

"At some point they must," Burgoyne said quietly. "That's when we'll have them, my Lord."

Riedesel said, "There are many small bridges along the way that they have destroyed. These must be rebuilt before we can move supplies and cannon over them. When I saw it on the map in Brunswick, this route from the lake to the river seemed so quick. But the map does not show you the roughness of the land. It is fearfully swampy with many biting bugs. And poisonous snakes with rattles on their tails."

"Yes," said Burgoyne. "It looked easier on the maps in London as well. Reality all too often tends to temper optimism."

"This is good wine," the baron said. "Thank you, General."

"Is General Fraser coming in this evening?" Clerke asked.

"No," the baron said. "He has Le Loup and his savages prowling the forest at night. He says he must stay and watch them. General Fraser displays little faith in Le Loup's ability to control his savages."

Burgoyne smiled slightly. "That's only because Simon knows Le Loup, and he knows the savages as well. How much longer on the road, my dear Baron?"

Riedesel shrugged. "A week. Perhaps two."

The commanding general frowned. "It's taking longer than we'd planned."

The fat cavalryman laughed out loud over his wine glass. "We both understand, General, that the best battle plans are invariably subject to revision after the first shot is fired."

"Indeed," said Burgoyne. "Still, I'd hoped by the end of this week to be on the western bank of the Hudson advancing toward Albany."

The chubby German general shook his head vigorously. "Perhaps by the end of next week. We still have many miles to clear for the ox carts and the horses. Speaking of horses, General, I—"

"I'm well aware of your concerns, my good Baron," Burgoyne said. "It pains you to see your dragoons afoot."

"It does," Riedesel said. "They cannot give you their best without mounts."

Burgoyne leaned back. "Very well. We've had little luck foraging, I take it?"

"None to speak of, Sir," said Lord Acland. "What horses the rebels haven't taken for themselves they've killed and eaten. While we dine here on fine mutton and caviar, they dine on horseflesh to keep us from mounting our dragoons."

"Hardly sporting for the horses," Sir Francis commented in English, mostly to himself. He was somewhat drunk.

"What's not sporting?" asked Skene, finally catching a few words he could comprehend.

"The rebels," Sir Francis said, slurring his words slightly. "They're eating every horse in sight. We can't find mounts for the baron's cavalry."

"Well," Skene said, "There are horses aplenty to the east, in the Hampshire Grants. Bennington is home to an entire rebel supply depot with plenty of food and horses, too. It's off our route, but we seem delayed here anyway."

"You're right, Colonel," said David Jones. "A foray into the Bennington area would take no more than a few days."

Interested, Burgoyne sat up in his chair. "An expedition to the east for horses? Yes, I suppose that could be done." The general turned to Riedesel and said in French, "Would your troops welcome a few days from the labor of clearing the road to make a jaunt to the east for horses, my dear Baron?"

"Most assuredly," the baron said. "We would need some scouts to show us the way, but we would need no help in whatever fighting might be necessary. My men need a fight, General. The long journey in the boats and now this swinging of axes in the heat is taking the edge off them."

"Very well," Burgoyne said. "Colonel Skene will supply a guide for your forces, Baron. Have one of your officers take what troops might be required tomorrow morning and move east to scour the land for horses and supplies."

"It won't be an easy venture, General," Skene said. "The journey to Bennington runs through dense forests alive with rebel militia. That's where most of the garrison from Ticonderoga fled, after all. The baron would require as many as three thousand men to absolutely ensure success. It would be wise, too, to take cannon to spray grapeshot."

Burgoyne translated Skene's remarks into French for Riedesel's benefit. The baron frowned at the mention of three thousand men. He wanted his horses, but he also wanted a clear road to the Hudson.

"I can do with less," Riedesel said. "I will send Colonel Baum with regimental strength composed of my dismounted dragoons, light infantry and some gunners. I will ask General Fraser for some of his sharpshooters as well. For my own part, I will stay here. I want to see this pathway opened to Albany as quickly as possible."

Burgoyne nodded in agreement. He viewed Skene as a good man in a fight, but he was hardly an experienced, senior-level military strategist. Burgoyne was not about to send nearly a third of his army into the wilderness to the east simply to obtain horses for a few hundred German dragoons and perhaps some food supplies. The commanding general stood.

"It grows late, gentlemen," he said. "We have days of trial and tribulation ahead of us. I bid you all a good evening."

Then, nodding for Madame to join him, Burgoyne and his mistress left the dining room and climbed the stairs to the mansion's second floor. Around the table, the officers, one by one, took their leave with bows to Lady Acland and the baroness. As Lord and Lady Acland climbed the stairs, leaving only the baron and baroness in the room, Frederika von Riedesel rose and approached her husband, who sat sipping wine from his glass. She placed a hand on one fleshy shoulder. She could feel his weariness through her palm.

"You must rest, Freddie," said the baroness.

"In a moment," the baron snapped out.

She sat down beside him and patted his hand. "Do not be cranky with me."

"Is this what goes on here while we clear the road and exchange fire with the enemy?"

The baroness nodded. "Night after night. The commanding general enjoys his social life. It is her, I think, more than he. He seeks to keep her entertained. He seeks also, I think, to train her — to teach her the ways of her betters."

"Men are dying out on the road," Riedesel said in a low voice. "We would lose more if the rebels shot better. As it is, they fire high most of the time. Still, we lose too many during each day of labor. We left eight hundred to garrison Ticonderoga and to protect the supply line. It all adds up."

She took his chubby hand in her own. "Come to bed with me, my Freddie, so you can rest and be alert tomorrow and you do not become one of them."

The baron frowned. "A party every evening, as though he was back in the swirl of London. We're losing crucial time. The woman clouds his judgment."

"He commands," the baroness said simply, pulling gently on her husband's arm to get him to his feet and off to bed.

"Yes," said Baron Friedrich Adolf von Riedesel, rising in his muddy boots and tilting slightly to one side in sheer exhaustion. "As do you, my beloved one."

Fraser. 1777

All along a four-mile stretch of the soft, slim, rutted dirt road that snaked through the dense forest, General Simon Fraser had nearly a thousand men swinging axes, wielding saws, sweating, groaning, hauling and lifting. In the hot, still, afternoon air, the stink of human sweat hung over the scene like a sour, reeking cloud. It combined with the earthy stench of ox manure. The large, lowing animals were invaluable in hauling away chunks of tree trunk weighing hundreds of pounds.

On his prancing gray horse, Fraser rode at a slow, measured pace along the road, watching his men strain. It was soul-killing work for soldiers, although Fraser took a certain perverse delight in watching the fuzzy-cheeked Earl of Balcarres stripped to the waist in the summer swelter, laboring side by side in the mud with privates and non-commissioned officers. This was the boy's initiation to the mundane rigors of army life, and he cheerfully performed his labors beside the enlisted men he commanded, setting precisely the example a good commander should set, in Fraser's view. Soon — very soon, Fraser hoped — the boy would learn what soldiering was really all about.

Fraser longed for the opportunity to face the enemy in the open, man to man, across a field. A burst or two of grapeshot from the cannon to thin the enemy ranks, then a volley of musket fire, then another and perhaps a third. Then, with each side advancing with no more time to reload, the two lines would close with musket butts, bayonets and sheer nerve as the dragoons swept in at an angle on their horses, sabers flashing. At close quarters with cold steel — that was where battles were won or lost. Face to face, heart to heart. That was how empires were built and held, an inch at a time.

The Romans had known. They'd waged war with short spears and shorter swords — weapons built for tight, elbow-to-elbow combat. Look them in the eye, suck the stink of their terror into your nostrils and then chop them down, step over their bleeding corpses and move on, marching relentlessly forward. Fraser was curious about how the boyish earl and Lord Acland might react to that. Reasonably well, he supposed. Despite their gentle upbringings, the youthful lordlings seemed made of sterner stuff than Fraser had imagined.

That was what was happening further along the road, Fraser knew. He had Le Loup's savages paving the way, followed by Fraser's own hardened advance troops moving through the woods toward Fort Edward and the river. By the time this road was cleared for cannon and supplies, the path to the water would be littered with corpses. Any rebel between Fraser and the Hudson would be dead or a prisoner of the Royal Army.

Still there were these nettlesome sharpshooters in the trees along the road, firing on his troops as they worked at moving the tree trunks. A single man with a musket in the woods could kill at a hundred yards through an opening in the leaves, fade back into the underbrush and cost Fraser up to an hour of labor at that spot as his troops dropped their axes, picked up their muskets and pursued the sniper through the woods. That's why this chore was taking so long. The men working on the road were fired upon three dozen times a day, usually unsuccessfully but with accuracy often enough to be disturbing. Fraser had lost four men that morning. Armed sentries along the forest's edge were no deterrent to the snipers; they simply shot the sentries first.

Atop his gray gelding, high above the laboring troops in his scarlet coat, Fraser knew he was a tempting target for any rebel sniper. He knew also that his men wouldn't work if they were frightened, and if they perceived that their general was fearful they would lose their nerve. So, hour after hour, Fraser rode among them on the soft, muddy road, offering words of encouragement and offering himself to the rebel sharpshooters, bolstering the courage of his troops. Further down the road, he knew, Baron Riedesel was doing the same, and fat Freddie was an even larger and more inviting target than Fraser.

Glancing down the road, he saw another officer approaching on horseback. In a few moments, he recognized the newcomer as Sir Francis Clerke, Burgoyne's personal aide. As they met, they exchanged salutes.

"The general's compliments," Sir Francis said. "He has sent me to observe and report back to him on the progress along the road."

"It's going well enough," Fraser said. "The snipers are fewer and further between since we sent Le Loup and his savages ahead to the river. We're only a day or two from completion now, I would say. It might be time for General Burgoyne to consider moving his headquarters to Fort Edward."

Sir Francis smiled slightly. "Only if he can get an ox cart of fine food and drink to the fort, I'm afraid. Madame requires diversion."

Fraser shook his head wearily. "All this attention to Madame's needs, Sir Francis, constitutes a distraction that Jack could do without."

"I'll not be the one to say that to him, General."

"Nor will I," Fraser admitted. "Any word from New York City?"

Sir Francis shook his head. "We've sent four couriers to Lord

Howe with no word in response on when he'll begin to move his forces northward along the Hudson."

"Do we know if those couriers got through?"

"We presume they did. We've had word from St. Leger, and his couriers have come through territory thicker with rebels than the Hudson's eastern shore, which is the route we assigned our couriers to New York City. St. Leger reports that he's meeting resistance."

"Yes," said Fraser, "well, so are we, but it's only a temporary circumstance here. Is St. Leger in trouble?"

Sir Francis shook his head. "No—" he began ...

... just as his three-cornered uniform hat sailed off his head into the mud, the victim of a sniper's musket ball. Instantly, both officers were down from their horses, hunched over and ankle-deep in the mud, and the men around them were dropping their axes and saws, grabbing their muskets and pouring into the woods. Drawing a pistol from his sash, Fraser followed them. Bareheaded, Sir Francis Clerke did the same.

"The blighter nearly got my head instead of my hat," Clerke muttered to the general.

"They tend to shoot high," Fraser whispered. "This is not well-trained opposition we face, Sir Francis, but it does seem to be enthusiastic opposition."

The two officers moved shoulder to shoulder, bent at the waist and the knees, into the forest, slapping away the mosquitoes and the ferocious black flies as they went. They'd advanced into the thick woods perhaps fifty yards when, off to their right, several muskets barked. They moved toward the noise, joining a knot of shirtless, sweating English soldiers gathered in a circle around a still form in the bushes.

The sharpshooter had been no more than a boy, perhaps fourteen. He gazed skyward sightlessly, a swatch of red soaking the front of his brown homespun shirt.

"A near thing that was," said Sir Francis. "By Jove, General, they're sending their children to fight against us."

"War against irregulars can be an untidy business, Sir Francis," Fraser said in a low voice, gazing down on the boy's dead face, replacing his pistol in his sash and turning to move back to his horse on the muddy road through the forest.

Babette: Before it all began

The commander's quarters in St.-Jean was a sturdy, three-story stone house easily five times the size of any private structure in town, most of which were constructed of logs. It occupied a high hill overlooking the military port along the river. As the hired, covered calash carrying Peter and Babette Loescher pulled up before it on a bitterly cold night in snow-bound December, the building was ablaze with light. The music poured from the open door, where fully one hundred other guests — the garrison's senior officers with their wives or mistresses — were arriving for the ball to celebrate the arrival from London of General John Burgoyne.

"Remember, be on your best behavior," Peter ordered. "Speak only when you're spoken to, and smile politely at all times."

Babette said nothing in response. Any word she might utter would surely infuriate her husband. Peter's fury was often near the surface these days, and Babette was frightened of it. He'd never done her violence, but she would never forget his willingness — perhaps even his eagerness — to inflict violence on her guardian on the day they had met. Moreover, she would never forget Peter's unfettered rage when, after their marriage, she'd confided to him that the old Indian he'd chased away from her father's cabin had, in fact, been her dead mother's father. Peter had been so incensed to learn that his wife was half Ottawa that, for a moment, Babette had literally been in fear for her life. It had been a memorable experience — one that forever would be imprinted on her brain cells. Peter, she suspected, would never take her home to Portsmouth when he retired from military service. Babette had concluded that her fate was to be his colonial wife, scheduled for abandonment at the appropriate moment. It was a common happening with these English officers in the wilds of some foreign outpost. There would, Babette was now certain, ultimately be a proper English wife to warm Peter's bed as he grew old across the sea — and to bear him children, too, as the current Madame Loescher was both unwilling and unable to do.

At the broad, double door — flanked by red-coated guards, stiffly at attention with bayonets pointed toward the glittering winter stars — they left the calash. Peter stepped down first, offering his wife his hand in a perfect — and, Babette understood, completely ceremonial — display of chivalry as her feet touched the frozen ground. Inside the building's entryway, they surrendered their cloaks, hats and gloves to liveried servants. Peter was resplendent in white wig, ceremonial saber and full dress uniform. Babette was glorious in

a slightly worn formal burgundy gown she'd managed to borrow from the wife of another officer after she'd solemnly pledged to wash it before returning it to its owner. She knew she was lucky to have the dress for this event. The color was appealing on her, and her relationships with the wives of other officers had cooled drastically since Peter, in his cups one night with his comrades, had confided that the woman he'd married had Indian blood.

As they entered the ballroom that the center of the building, Peter nodded and shook hands with fellow officers. As instructed, Babette smiled and nodded politely, casting a cautious glance at the enormous crystal chandelier that hung over the dance floor, clearly an import from the Continent. In niches around the building, she noted, stood marble statues of assorted Greek gods and goddesses in various states of undress. Peter had told her once that she had the breasts of a statue. That had been in the beginning. Now, when they made love, he grunted and groaned atop or behind her, but he never uttered endearments. His love had died; his lust lingered on and required regular satisfaction.

The garrison orchestra was at the far end of the room, playing a waltz. A quick survey of the room told Babette that no one below major, Peter's new rank, was in attendance here. He'd been both surprised and pleased to receive an invitation, but he'd also understood that this was only one many gatherings to welcome Burgoyne, whose mission remained unclear to the garrison's rank and file. Other, more intimate dinners and receptions had featured no officer below field grade rank. In His Majesty's army, generals seldom rubbed elbows with majors unless the major was well born,

which Peter was not. Neither Peter nor Babette had ever before been inside the commander's quarters.

"There's Sir Guy," Peter whispered to her as they made their way into the cavernous ballroom. "That must be Burgoyne beside him."

Babette glanced at a knot of officers and ladies near the large marble fireplace that dominated one wall of the ballroom. She'd seen Sir Guy Carleton on several other occasions, during his visits to St.-Jean from the fort at Quebec, although she'd never had occasion to directly address the military governor of Canada. He was a solemn man in his early fifties with a stiff, humorless manner. Beside him was a slim, smiling, broad-shouldered man with an elegant bearing who towered half a head above Sir Guy. So, that was Gentleman Johnny Burgoyne, Babette thought. Undeniably, a handsome fellow — and one of both gravity and presence as well.

She nudged at Peter's arm. "Let's go meet the general."

"No," Peter said. "I'm certain there'll be some sort of receiving line later on."

Babette paused only a moment. There was a decision to be made, and it must be made now. She took a step away from her husband.

"You need to be noticed," she said, pulling gently at his arm. "You'll be lost in the crowd in any receiving line."

"Babette ..." Peter began, but by then she winding her way purposefully through the dancing couples, and he faced the choice of staying behind or joining her. In just a heartbeat, Peter had caught up and was at her side.

"We'll just say hello and then fade away," he muttered. By then, however, Babette was already edging through the knot of men and

women surrounding the two generals and extending her hand.

"Sir Guy," she said, "I'm Madame Loescher, the wife of Major Peter Loescher."

Carleton smiled slightly and took her hand. Burgoyne turned to her, his smile broadening as his eyes took her in. Immediately, he reached out with both hands to free Babette's hand from Carleton's rather limpid grasp. The general bent over and gently brushed the back of Babette's fingers with his lips.

"Madame Loescher," he said, raising his head, "it is a pleasure of enormous magnitude to make your acquaintance."

"And this is my husband, Major Loescher," Babette said, reaching out for Peter's arm and drawing him close.

"How do you do, Sir?" Peter said softly, clearly discomfited.

Burgoyne bowed slightly and silently to the junior officer and then turned his gaze once more to Babette.

"I detect a touch of French in your speech, Madame," the general said. "My wife and I lived in France for a number of years. What province are you from."

"I am from Quebec, Sir. I regret that I've never been to France."

"A pity for you, Madame," Burgoyne said, "but a far greater pity for the French. Your presence there would do much to beautify their country, as does your presence here on behalf of the pristine wilds of Canada. Well, now, this is a lovely tune the orchestra is playing. It's quite popular in London these days. Do you dance, Madame?"

Babette cast a quick, sidelong glance at Peter, who stood as stiff and as unmoving as a stone monument.

"I simply adore dancing," Madame told Gentleman Johnny Burgoyne.

Which was how it all began.

Clinton. 1777

With screaming seagulls gliding over the forest of tall, wooden masts in the vast harbor, New York City was coming awake. The bustling port town that huddled at the southern tip of what the English called York Island was a metropolis of twenty-three thousand souls housed in two- and three-story brick and wooden structures. Below the ruins of the wall across the island that the Dutch had erected more than a century earlier to keep out English invaders from New England, the gabled two- and three-story buildings lined narrow streets littered with horse manure and the soggier dung of pigs and sheep. As the day began, those narrow mud lanes and cobblestone streets began to buzz with wagons bearing crops from Long Island and the lower Hudson Valley, with lowing cattle ferried over from New Jersey for slaughter. Wagons laden with furs taken by trappers in the upriver wilderness around Albany moved ponderously amid the milling livestock.

Bellows wheezed and metal clanged in blacksmith shops. Brewery workers filled barrels of beer and loaded them on carts. As druggists, candlemakers and bakers opened their shops, weary whores slunk home from taverns, fleeing the bright, oppressive light of day. Sailors staggered, drunk and all their other hearty human appetites temporarily slaked, back to their berths aboard ships from around the globe. At night, New York City was a wide open seafarer's town, alive with raucous Germans, Swedes, Frenchmen, Spaniards and Dutchmen. In daylight, it was home to the black workers, both free and slave, tradesmen, money counters, clerks, laborers and street hucksters who had been the lifeblood of this uniquely vibrant town from the moment the Dutch had founded their New Netherland colony here, only to have it grabbed at gunpoint by the English six decades later. And soldiers, of course — many, many English soldiers filled the streets of New York City with the accents of East London and Yorkshire mixing with the dozen or more tongues routinely spoken there.

Sir Henry Clinton had been awake for hours. It was his custom to rise well before dawn. Always, he was alert before the sun came up, active and in full uniform before the men in camp around him were roused from slumber by the bugle's blare. He clung to that encampment routine both in London and here, in this colonial outpost, which he considered an encampment despite having grown up in New York City, the nephew of an earl and the son of the colonial governor. Raised in the colonies, Sir Henry Clinton nonetheless viewed himself as an Englishman. Any assignment outside England was, in his mind, essentially duty on foreign soil.

In the brownstone mansion he occupied on Broad Street near the battery of big guns that overlooked New York Harbor, Clinton had been sipping tea, dining on fried shad and scones and reading daily reports from the various segments of his command. With immense interest, he'd also read an eyes-only dispatch that had been delivered as Clinton slept. The dispatch had been borne by a weary courier from the colony's northern wilderness. It had been carried in the hollow heel of the courier's shoe hundreds of miles through dense forest and villages infested by rebel sympathizers. The dispatch had been hand-written by Burgoyne, Clinton's friend and comrade in arms for nearly two decades despite the fifteen-year gap in their ages. It was a friendship that had been cemented several years earlier when the two had sailed together from Britain to the colonies, each anticipating a major command. While Clinton had remained in the colonies to await his chance for more responsibility, Burgoyne had instead sailed back home after the rebellion had begun in the Massachusetts colony to argue for a chance to implement his Grand Strategy.

Outwardly, the message scrawled on the page appeared no more than a cordial letter to a friend. Clinton knew better, as would have a savvy Army of the United States officer if the message had been intercepted. It was only when Clinton placed over the letter a special decoding device that the true message revealed itself. The decoding device was a scrap of cloth with a pear-shaped hole cut out of its center. Laid over Burgoyne's seemingly innocuous letter, the template blotted out irrelevant words on either side of the true message. In his actual communication, Burgoyne was expressing alarm over having received no word from Lord William Howe, Clinton's commander, concerning troops that were supposed to have been sent from New York City north, up the Hudson, to reinforce Burgoyne as he neared Albany.

Clinton read the message repeatedly. In language only lightly veiled, Burgoyne was asking his friend to spy for him. Burgoyne was urging Sir Henry to learn what he could about Lord Howe's orders and intentions and to relay that information to Burgoyne by courier at the earliest possible opportunity. The request placed Clinton in a difficult position. As Burgoyne's friend, Clinton felt an obligation to aid him. As Lord Howe's deputy, although Clinton felt considerable antipathy toward the man, he felt an obligation to place his loyalty to his commander above all other considerations. And, obviously, if Lord Howe possessed information on troop movements that he wished to impart to Sir Henry he would have done so already.

It was that realization that most disturbed Clinton. As a lieutenant general at the relatively tender age of thirty-nine, he was bright, capable, somewhat full of himself and privately critical of many of the more senior English commanders, especially Howe, whom Clinton regarded as no more than a buffoon. If, in fact, Billy Howe had the orders from London that Burgoyne's dispatch assured Clinton were in Howe's possession, then Clinton's commander was not confiding in him. And what, precisely, might Lord Howe have in mind?

As the sun crept up over the eastern edge of what the English referred to as York Island, Sir Henry's valet was placing the white, powdered wig atop the general's head. For a long moment, Clinton studied himself in the mirror. He was appropriately elegant in scarlet and glowing white with vivid blue facings. He reached for his gold-trimmed, plumed hat and strode out the door onto Broad Street as the first rays of daylight splashed across the cobblestones.

Clinton's daily trek to the English headquarters at the battery on the southernmost tip of York Island was brief. New York City was a small, surging, busy port built on the finest natural harbor on the east coast of the North American continent. Many of the newer buildings were constructed of timber and walled with wattle and daub, much like most of the buildings in London, a city largely built of wood. The bulk of York Island to the north of the port and the farms that lay beyond it consisted of meadows, streams, waterfalls and forest. York Island offered the English not only a fine port, a passageway up the Hudson River to the north and access to the Mohawk River, which could take vessels as far west as the Great Lakes, it also provided an abundance of food. Mussels, oysters and clams came from the salt marshes that bordered the island. Fish populated the harbor and rivers, and an abundance of game roamed the woods. Those woods also provided a wealth of lumber for construction – basswood, oak, sweetgum and soft, pliable pine. But the older buildings, those erected by the Dutch who'd settled this long, slender island more than a century and a half earlier, were constructed chiefly of masonry, and many of those early structures were built of brick created by the Dutch knickerbockers, or brick makers.

The English army's headquarters was a collection of older masonry buildings near the battery. Like Clinton, Lord Howe lived elsewhere and commuted to his offices to conduct his daily duties. Except in the vilest of weather, Clinton made a point of marching briskly to the battery every morning. Peevish and nervous by nature, he found that discharging energy was crucial for him in controlling his temper. Nearing middle age, he also valued the exercise. Clinton was a short man, about which he could do nothing, but he fought a gallant, losing battle daily against his unfortunate family tendency toward corpulence. Howe habitually arrived by carriage, which he was doing as Sir Henry rounded the corner at the battery and spotted his commander disembarking.

"Good morning, my Lord," Clinton said.

"Good morning to you, Sir Henry," Billy Howe said expansively.

At age fifty one, he was a large, dark-eyed, olive-skinned man with bad teeth and a fleshy middle. The softness of his waistline was the product of routine social overindulgence in the company of his gorgeous mistress, Elizabeth Loring, who was regularly on his arm when she wasn't in his bed. The open affair with the wife of one of his commissary subordinates was the stuff of scandal for Lord Howe even in London, where lame jokes routinely circulated about Howe lying snoring after whoring with Mrs. Loring.

"This damnable heat," Howe said. "It's barely daylight, and it's already warm enough to bathe a man in sweat. I do so miss the gentle English mornings, Sir Henry, especially this time of year."

As they climbed the stone stairs together, Howe said, "Has it occurred to you, Sir Henry, that both of us have probably spent more of our adult lives away from England, missing it, than at home in the first place? It's a soldier's burden, I suppose — just one of many. Please drop by my headquarters after you've settled in. I'll have tea, and I have much to discuss with you."

"As you wish, my Lord."

Howe paused at the top of the steps, gazing out over the harbor and the screeching seagulls soaring lazily above the waves. A vast, floating thicket of ships' masts poked skyward in the gently rolling water — hundreds of commercial vessels and, directly in front of the battery, a large portion of the incomparable English navy riding at anchor on the greenish, rolling swells. When Washington had been driven from New York, much of the firepower used against him had been generated by more than one thousand big, booming guns on thirty formidable English warships.

"An inspiring sight," Howe said. "There's the real key to the empire's strength, this fleet. It's English oak that commands the seas, Sir Henry — stout oak beneath our feet and even stouter oak in the spines of His Majesty's sailors."

"Indeed, Sir," Clinton said, frowning slightly. He knew that Lord Howe was merely quoting his older brother, Admiral Richard Howe, the commander of what was, without question, the finest navy on Earth. Richard was his younger, slower brother's patron. Without him and without the Howe family's distant blood link to King George, Lord William Howe would command only his personal servants — and, in all probability, perform that chore ineptly.

Later, in Howe's spacious office, Clinton informed his commander of the dispatch from Burgoyne.

"A secret dispatch, you say?" Howe asked.

"Well, a private one, anyway."

"Yet you share the contents of this private communication with me?"

Clinton nodded. "Jack Burgoyne is my friend, my Lord, but you are my commander. My first loyalty, therefore, must lie with you."

Howe digested the remark. He was acutely aware that Sir Henry Clinton viewed him with more than a little disdain — more disdain, in fact, than Clinton harbored for most of humanity, which he tended to view with a cynical, withering contempt. Nonetheless, Clinton was placing duty to Howe above friendship. Howe did not ask, however, to see the dispatch. That would be too much. He could either trust Clinton's recitation of its contents or he couldn't. Howe doubted that Clinton would have brought up the matter had he planned to lie about it, so actually reading the thing made no particular difference.

"I deeply appreciate your sharing this information with me," Howe said. "I know that you and Burgoyne are close. The timing of this is curiously coincidental. I had planned this morning to share with you the substance of communications I've received from London. Since rousting Washington out of New York and then wintering here, our army has been sitting long enough. It's past time to begin another offensive."

"So," Clinton said, "We're moving up the Hudson after all."

"Not immediately," said Lord William Howe. "It is my assessment that Burgoyne should be able to take Albany without undue difficulty."

"I must express my doubts on that, Sir," Clinton said.

"Oh?" said Howe. "And on what do you base those doubts, Sir Henry? Do you question General Burgoyne's competence?"

"I do not, my Lord," Clinton replied. "Jack is as fine a general as I've ever seen. My concern, however, is that his heavily laden expedition down from Canada plays to the rebels' strength and to our own weakness in this colonial terrain."

"What strength?" Howe demanded. "They've demonstrated no strength thus far."

"Actually, my Lord, their strength is deceptive. True, they are sloppy, dirty and ill inclined to follow orders, but their lack of discipline is more than compensated for by their familiarity with the wilderness, by their ease with weaponry and by their resistance to native diseases that plague our forces so often. Our relatively easy victories here in and around New York, in country that resembles

Europe, might be difficult to repeat in the forests that line the Hudson."

"I see," Howe said slowly. "And your plan to accomplish Burgoyne's goal of crushing New England, Sir Henry, would have been what, precisely?"

"Had the decision been mine," Clinton said, "We would first have moved north to capture West Point and then sailed frigates filled with troops up the Hudson to Albany. Such an action would have prevented the movement of rebel troops or supplies between this region and Albany. As you noted, ours is the finest navy in existence, my Lord. Surely, we should use it to our advantage. Only then would I have moved a force down from Canada – a leaner, more mobile force than Jack now leads with all his cannon and ox carts filled with supplies. As things now stand, West Point and its surrounding highlands region are well defended and will have to be overcome by a force of some magnitude if we're to move to Albany successfully. If we fail to do that, then I fear that Burgoyne might well find himself cut off and isolated."

. Howe shook his head. "We disagree, Sir Henry. I have complete confidence in Burgoyne's ability. Therefore, my plan is to move the fleet to Philadelphia, take that city from the rebels, engage Washington in New Jersey and then march northward to meet Burgoyne once the rebels are crushed here in the middle colonies."

For a moment, Clinton remained silent. Then he said, "That's what Lord Germain ordered?"

Howe said, "The colonial secretary stated a preference, Sir Henry, that I move up the Hudson to join Burgoyne, which I most assuredly shall do in the fullness of time. Lord Germain did not instruct that such an expedition to the north need be undertaken immediately. First, therefore, I deem it more vital to focus on the Continental Congress in Philadelphia and to put this rump rebel government on the run. And that, Sir Henry, I shall do with utmost pleasure."

"My Lord," Clinton said cautiously, "would not such an action constitute violation of a direct order from the colonial secretary?"

"Not at all," Howe said, lifting up a sheaf of papers from his desk and digging through them. "Yes, here it is. Lord Germain closed his dispatch with the following: 'Every man of common understanding must see that orders given at such a distance presuppose a discretionary power.' So, Sir Henry, it is quite clear that the colonial secretary expects me to exercise my own best judgment as to when to march on Albany. Frankly, I see no absolute necessity of doing so before next spring. An offensive against the New England colonies, which is the entire point of Burgoyne's campaign, will take some months and could not occur until the snows first fall and then melt in the north."

Clinton leaned back in his chair. His face was impassive, but he understood precisely what was going on here. Germain had issued an order that was not really an order. If Howe marched north before this year's winter and bolstered Burgoyne's efforts in taking Albany, then the Grand Strategy would succeed and Germain could always contend that he'd issued the order that had made the plan a success. If Howe marched north now and the campaign failed nonetheless, Germain could argue that his New York City commander had acted recklessly and displayed poor judgment. Essentially, Germain had issued an order so vague as to cover Germain in any eventuality. He could claim credit for anything successful that might occur from this operation in the north and, at the same time, deflect blame from himself to his generals for any failure.

Now Howe was going the colonial secretary one better, which led Clinton to suspect that Germain might have sent Howe a separate, private letter urging him to leave Burgoyne to his own devices in taking Albany. That was the only explanation Clinton could imagine for Howe's plan to relegate Burgoyne's campaign to secondary status in favor of one Howe himself would initiate against Philadelphia — and for which he would receive full and more or less exclusive credit if successful. After that, anything Burgoyne might accomplish to the north would be viewed in London as a matter of lesser importance.

Clearly, this was all London politics, Clinton concluded. Inwardly, he cursed all politicians and the politician-generals who ran the Royal Army. This was why France still held lucrative colonies in the New World twenty years after the English capture of Canada. London was a foul, fetid sea of venality, and so was the military. It overflowed with generals whose bank balances and bloodlines had bought their rank and whose focus was struggling to outshine one another while serving as impediments to rivals' various maneuvers for advancement.

Clinton himself was not immune to this atmosphere. He was acutely aware that he was senior to Burgoyne and, by rights, should have been given permission to carry out the plan he'd just outlined to Howe. Someone in London, however – and Clinton presumed that to have been Lord Germain – had decided that any plan authored by

Clinton would be too difficult to appropriate and, therefore, should be ignored. Moreover, Clinton was on less intimate terms with the king than Burgoyne, who'd been the monarch's morning riding partner for some years now. So, at the moment, Clinton's primary interest was to save his friend from disaster – a disaster he was certain that Howe was conspiring to expedite.

"My Lord," Clinton said, "it occurs to me that the conquest of Philadelphia would most assuredly leave you with too little time to make your way north to Albany before ice and snow close in on the region this coming winter. Albany is three hundred miles from Philadelphia, after all. Unless Washington chooses to meet you in the open field you'll be forced to chase his army all over New Jersey."

"I'll be taking thirteen thousand troops, Sir Henry — more than half the population of the entire city of Philadelphia. Moreover, Philadelphia is a hotbed of loyalist sympathy. Once the royal fleet moves up the Delaware River and begins its bombardment, loyal subjects of His Majesty will pour from their homes to join us in our liberation efforts. I'm confident that I can take Philadelphia in relatively short order, leave half my force to chase Washington's army of three thousand or so all around New Jersey and still, if it becomes necessary, move to Albany before the leaves fall this year. In addition, I would be heading north with a force fully two-thirds of what Burgoyne brought down with him from Quebec."

Clinton said, "The leaves fall earlier in the north, my Lord. I must stress to you my concern that General Burgoyne might be unable to reach Albany unaided."

Howe made a dismissive gesture. "He won't be unaided. He has a separate force under St. Leger moving east along the Mohawk. He simply won't receive his aid from me until after I take Philadelphia. We're talking about the rebel capital, Sir Henry. It might even be that, with Philadelphia about to fall, Washington will be forced to abandon his elusive tactics and meet us, at long last, in the open field. If that happens, then it's utterly incidental whether or not Burgoyne reaches Albany and then sweeps eastward through New England to the sea. With their capital captured and the main body of their army destroyed, the rebels will have lost the war."

Clinton did his best to leave his face an impassive mask. "Am I to accompany you to Philadelphia, my Lord?"

"That's not at all necessary. You're to stay here in New York to command the remainder of the garrison. That'll leave you with what — six thousand troops or so?"

"Rather less than that, my Lord — the effectives, that is. At the moment, I have more than a thousand men down with smallpox and other assorted ailments."

Lord Howe shrugged. As both he and Clinton were aware, disease had proven a far more daunting opponent for the English than the rebel military forces. Jamming thousands of troops into close quarters with shoddy sanitation and limited hygienic procedures was a perfect prescription for epidemics. While the English held full control over the New York City region, they exercised vastly less control over the ravages of typhoid, dysentery, malaria and other ailments common to crowded conditions. On average, disease killed three times as many eighteenth-century soldiers as battle itself.

Howe said, "That's more than enough to hold New York against anything Washington might send against you — assuming that he sends anything at all, and he will not. His focus will be defending Philadelphia, not trying to re-take New York City against a superior force."

Clinton said, "Unless he moves north to engage Burgoyne. Washington will understand, my Lord, that he cannot prevent you from having your way with Philadelphia. Faced with the choice of losing both Philadelphia now and New England in the spring — and unable to defend Philadelphia effectively — Washington would be a blockhead not to march north to protect the New England colonies. If he does that, and Burgoyne receives no aid from here in New York City, then Burgoyne is quite possibly lost, and the revolt will remain in full bloom. The Continental Congress would simply reconvene in Albany or Hartford or Boston. The taking of Philadelphia would have won us nothing of substance."

Howe's brow furrowed. Clearly, it annoyed him that his deputy was presenting him with a tactical argument that Howe couldn't refute.

"I've made up my mind, Sir Henry," Howe said abruptly. "This is no longer a subject fit for debate."

"I'm not debating you, my Lord. I'm offering my best advice."

"Which has been heard, considered and rejected as unsound. If you're so concerned about Burgoyne, then lead a force of your own up the Hudson. I must insist, however, that you leave enough here in the way of troops to protect New York City and Long Island should Washington, against all logic, move to re-take this territory. You may, of course, employ your own best judgment in the matter."

Nicely done, Clinton thought. Howe had given him permission to reinforce Burgoyne, but he'd left in Clinton's hands both the decision itself and a judgment as to how many men would be necessary both for that task and for the simultaneous defense of New York City. Now, if Burgoyne went down, it would be Clinton's responsibility, not Howe's. Moreover, if Clinton took enough men now to ensure his arrival in Albany, past the rebel-held forts along the Hudson highlands, he would have left New York City essentially undefended against a potential attack by Washington. Clinton knew immediately that he could not move north until more of his ailing men were out of their beds and on their feet to protect this city or until reinforcements arrived from Europe, and he had no idea when that might take place.

Inwardly, Clinton cursed bitterly. Howe had just outmaneuvered him, and he hadn't expected that. It served to confirm his suspicion that Germain had sent Howe private instructions to accompany Germain's official orders. Howe would never have come up with so deft a scheme on his own, Clinton was certain. Furious, and containing that fury behind an expressionless mask of restraint, he rose from his chair and bowed low.

He said, "My deepest thanks, my Lord, for your faith in my judgment."

Clinton then went to his own office, placed a decoding template over a piece of paper and scribbled a brief dispatch to Burgoyne on the portion of the paper exposed in the opening. He then removed the template, added more, misleading words to the blank space that surrounded the true message and waved the paper in the air to dry the ink from his quill pen. Then, leaning back in his chair, Sir Henry Clinton read the letter he'd just composed.

> My dear Jack,
> I have been cheered to learn of you setting off for Albany with such a strong force. I vowed to offer you my congratulations at my earliest opportunity, and I am doing so in this brief missive. As is ever the case, I shall strive to be of sufficient aid in buoying your spirits and in faithfully bolstering both your courage and good fortune. Yours always in service to His Majesty, H.C.

Clinton then replaced the template over the faux letter and carefully examined the actual message he'd written to Burgoyne — the one Burgoyne would discern when he placed his own cloth template over this document. It read:

> setting off for Albany
> at my earliest opportunity
> shall strive to be of sufficient aid
> courage and good fortune.

Was this clear enough? Would Burgoyne grasp from these words that Clinton was unable to move north right away? Would he discern the depth of Clinton's fear that he wouldn't be able to fight his way past the Hudson highlands at West Point?

Yes, Clinton thought, the words "earliest opportunity" as opposed to "now" or "presently" should alert Burgoyne to a delay. Moreover, the word "strive" should adequately convey both

Clinton's commitment and his doubts. The dispatch would be copied four times and sent out hidden in the hollow boot heels of multiple couriers under the assumption that at least one of them would get through rebel-held territory without ending up dangling from a tree limb. With hard knuckles, Sir Henry rapped the ship's bell on his desk. At the sound, the general's aide, Colonel Nichols, immediately stuck his head through the door.

"Sir?" he said.

"Give this to the couriers," Clinton said, holding out the letter. "Have this missive copied and then dispatched to General Burgoyne at their most expeditious pace."

Schuyler. 1777

Atop their horses on a high bluff on the west bank of the Hudson, Schuyler and Wilkinson were discussing the problem – the ever present problem for all military forces, they both knew — of supplies. As the two men spoke, Wilkinson glanced to his right and spotted in the distance a line of men moving northward along the slim, dusty river road toward the Army of the United States camp. There were hundreds of them, he noted. With muskets on their shoulders, the distant line of men resembled a snake with a high, ridged back crawling toward them. He raised an arm and pointed toward the advancing troops.

"Look there, Sir," Wilkinson said. "Is that a portion of our forces moving northward from Cohoes?"

Schuyler squinted his eyes and studied the formation. "I gave no such order. What we might be looking at, Colonel, are reinforcements from General Washington in New Jersey. Let's hope so. We should ride to meet them."

The two men moved back off the bluff and guided their mounts into the camp. All along the top of the plateau, on farm fields where Schuyler had ordered his troops to make camp, white canvas tents poked up in neat rows stretching back to the beginning of the forest. Thin tendrils of smoke rose from campfires into the sunlight. Schuyler's army was eating its midday meal. Mess groups were established around groups of six. Each group had been issued a cast iron kettle, a hatchet with which to chop wood and daily rations of a pound of flour and beef. The meat from Schuyler's freshly butchered prize cattle was being roasted over open fires on woodsmen's long knife blades, on the tines of pitchforks and on the curving blades of wheat and corn sickles.

The men needed the food. They'd spent months on salt pork and beans and, sometimes, only flour mixed with water into a doughy soup. Most of those who weren't down with smallpox suffered intermittently from fever or the bloody flux. Virtually every member of the army below colonel was ill with some ailment, large or small. Schuyler ached inwardly at their torment. In recent weeks, he himself had eaten so little that the nagging gout in his feet had disappeared.

As he moved among them, the commanding general spotted soldiers placing flour on flat rocks, mixing the powder with water from the streams leading down to the river, pounding the mixture into a coarse paste, then setting the flat stones near the fire to cook the concoction. Fire cakes, the troops called them. Generally, they were made when the army was short of beef, fish and salt pork to fry. As Schuyler rode among the cooking fires toward the horse pen, he spotted soldiers supplementing their rations with greens looted from the farm fields and with the occasional fish someone had managed to scoop from a stream or from the Hudson itself. Food remained short, however, despite Schuyler's sacrifice of his cattle and sheep, and every mess group had fire cakes baking near the flame. They tended to fuel dysentery, but they provided starch for energy, and the cakes supplemented the army's meager rations of meat.

On this day, energy was called for. Along the edge of the woods, hundreds of men were busy with axes. Under the direction of Schuyler's youthful Polish engineering officer, Thaddeus Kosciuszko, they were taking down trees for the eventual creation of fortifications along the front of the bluff and along the northern face of the plateau. Behind such log fortifications, men could fire down from shelter on the open hillside near the shoreline and across the fields if the English attempted to flank them from the north. Such fortifications would be effective enough against musket fire, Schuyler knew, but they would be useless against cannon. To protect his men against that, Schuyler would need to construct shields of earth many feet thick. If the shovels arrived, Kosciuszko would do that well, Schuyler knew. The man spoke almost no English, but he was a master builder. If the shovels never appeared, the men would dig with knives or their hands. One way or the other, Schuyler knew, Kosciuszko would get it done.

There was much work to do here — weeks of it. Perhaps months — if Schuyler had months, which he doubted. He could manage the construction of proper fortifications only if St. Clair could reform his army and further delay the English as they tried to move southward from Skenesboro. From spies and captives taken to the north, Schuyler knew that the enemy force was commanded by Burgoyne, a cavalryman, and that the cavalryman was short of horses for his dragoons. He hoped fervently that Burgoyne would delay his trek southward until he'd managed to forage enough horses from the countryside to properly equip his cavalry. One of St. Clair's orders was to steal every horse he could find to keep the animals from the English.

Once clear of the camp, the commanding general and his aide spurred their own horses and galloped off to meet the line of advancing men. Schuyler guided his mount down the face of the bluff at breakneck pace. Following behind more cautiously, Wilkinson noted that the older man rode easily and effortlessly — a gentleman born to the saddle, his skill on horseback honed on fox hunts and on long, leisurely rides across his formerly bountiful fields, now reduced to charred wasteland to thwart the English.

The two of them reached the narrow road at the foot of the bluff just as the line of marching men arrived at the same location. They were led by two riders. One, a huge man clad in buckskin beneath a broad-brimmed hat, was a stranger to Wilkinson. The other was General Horatio Gates, whom Schuyler had replaced as commander of the Army of the United States' Northern Department that winter. For months now, Gates had spent most of his time bearing messages back and forth from Washington and from the Continental Congress in Philadelphia — and, Schuyler had no doubt, maneuvering with the Adams cousins to get his old command back — while serving as Schuyler's primary deputy when he was in attendance in Albany.

"General," Schuyler said from his saddle, "seeing you and this party is a profound pleasure. How many men have you brought me?"

"We have roughly five hundred," Gates said. "General Schuyler, I'm sure you recall Colonel Daniel Morgan, the commander of Morgan's Rangers."

Morgan was a hulking, hard-eyed man in his early forties. He saluted smartly.

"Good to see you again, Colonel," Schuyler said. "Upon his return from the west, General Arnold will be pleased to see you once more. I recall with great pride the assault on Quebec you made with him."

Morgan nodded, reddening slightly. "We nearly made that work, Sir, that Quebec business."

"So, you did," Schuyler said.

No other words needed to be spoken on the topic. When Arnold had been wounded in the assault on Quebec the previous summer, Morgan had taken command, even though he'd been outranked by several other officers. Once his heavily outnumbered force had been surrounded by the Royal Army, he'd stood with his back to a wall, shouting challenges to any English soldier to try take him prisoner. When none would go near the raging, bellowing, tomahawk-waving Morgan, he'd finally surrendered to a passing priest, cursing every English soldier in sight as a coward. Upon his release in a prisoner exchange, he'd been promoted — and justifiably so. Schuyler was delighted to have him.

Slowly, Schuyler gazed down the road upon Morgan's force lined up along the river behind the two riders. Garbed largely in buckskin, they were a rustic-looking lot — largely bearded, some in fur hats despite the intense heat. They stood in the blazing summer sun, tomahawks bristling from their belts. They were a force designed to counter Burgoyne's Indians, and Schuyler had no doubt that Morgan's men could handle that chore. Each man, Schuyler noted, bore not a regulation brown Bess or ancient French surplus musket, as the general's own troops carried, but a Pennsylvania rifle — long-range weapons good for three to four times the reach of ordinary military firearms. Morgan's Rangers were skilled forest fighters — the deadliest single force in the Army of the United States. Still, only five hundred men?

"I take it that General Washington will be sending more troops as the battle draws near," Schuyler said softly to Gates.

Gates shook his head. "He hopes to dispatch a force under General Lincoln at some point soon, but for now this is all the commander can spare. He's still dodging Howe's army in the New Jersey colony, and he has Philadelphia to defend, after all. He must at all costs defend the city where the Continental Congress sits, General Schuyler."

His face expressionless, Philip Schuyler nodded, although he suspected that Washington would not waste his army to defend the armchair generals of Congress. Washington would keep his troops safe and let the politicians run for their lives. Scrambling for their own hides, they would be less likely to interfere with him.

"So, he must, indeed," Schuyler said. "Colonel Wilkinson, please escort Colonel Morgan and his men to our encampment. I'm certain we can find some appropriate nourishment for them after their long and difficult journey. General Gates, things have changed markedly since your last tenure here. Permit me to familiarize you with our current circumstance. As always, I value your good judgment."

Wilkinson moved forward on his mount to lead Morgan and his rangers up the face of the bluff to the camp. As he did, Schuyler wheeled his horse northward and motioned for Gates to join him. Gates nudged his mount with his spurs. He was a stooping, jowly man of fifty, graying and tending toward softness in the middle. Spectacles perched on the end of his long nose. In manner, he tended toward the fussy and officious. The troops referred to him as "Granny Gates," and Schuyler had always felt the appellation appropriate. A transplanted Englishman who'd served as an officer in the Royal Army before becoming a planter in Virginia, Gates understood the logistical mechanics of soldiering—the supply aspects of military work especially — but Schuyler felt the man was too cautious by nature and tended toward pettiness. Schuyler had never really warmed up to Gates, and he knew the feeling was mutual. There was, Schuyler suspected, a certain degree of class envy in their relationship. Gates despised nobility and gentlemen alike, although he was nakedly ambitious. Schuyler, with inherited social position and more money than he could ever spend, harbored no ambitions beyond dealing as best he could with whatever immediate challenges life might throw his way.

The two generals rode side by side along the bottom of the bluff, the river at their right, as Schuyler gestured with this left hand, laying out to Gates his thinking on the military virtues of this location.

"If we're to stop them," Schuyler said, "this is the best place from which to try. If they get past us here, Albany is theirs. We can't engage them directly anywhere north of here. There are simply too many of them and too few of us."

"I know Burgoyne," Gates said. "I served with him against the French, and Fraser, too. They're capable men with capable subordinates."

"We're also capable, General, and we have capable subordinates as well. I'm delighted to have Morgan and his men. I'll send them north tomorrow to aid St. Clair. They'll be good in the woods. That's where we have the edge. It's in the open field against European tactics that we're vulnerable. That's why I chose this ground."

"It's fine ground," Gates conceded. "An excellent selection, General Schuyler. But they outnumber us even before the English force under St. Leger arrives here from the west."

"I've sent General Arnold to stop St. Leger at Fort Stanwix. If anyone can do that, it's him."

"Arnold is demented," Gates said coldly.

"Assuredly so," Schuyler replied. "Immensely useful, however."

"I don't share your faith in him. The man is unacceptably rash. I learned that last year when I commanded him and his force at Valcour Island."

"I appreciate your reservations. I feel, however, that Arnold's virtues outweigh his shortcomings. Moreover, General Gates, we are beggars here, and not choosers."

Gates frowned. "I struggle to remain objective on the subject of

Arnold, but I have reservations about his stability. Ever since his wife died ..."

"I know," Schuyler said quietly. "It was a frightful loss for him. But the same fever would have taken her even if he'd remained an apothecary in Connecticut. He understands that; I've spoken to him on the subject. Arnold doesn't blame himself for her death."

"No, but his loss seems to have left him unconcerned about whether he himself lives or dies. General Arnold's personal bravery is entirely commendable, General Schuyler, but he leads troops. It's one thing for Arnold to display too much courage for his own good. It's another matter entirely when that foolhardiness endangers the survival of the forces entrusted to him. As you said, we're already outnumbered."

"Yes," Schuyler said. "I'd hoped for more support from Washington."

"He has no more support to offer."

Schuyler frowned. "I need men, General. Our intelligence tells us that Burgoyne's forces are half again what I can muster. Between what I have here and to the south, and with General St. Clair's forces included, I can muster no more than seven thousand effectives. Even with this good ground in our favor, and even if Arnold halts the English expedition at Fort Stanwix, those are not encouraging numbers."

Gates said, "New England had one hundred thousand men eager to defend their homes. The New England militias should be rallying to the cause of the commander of the Northern Department."

Schuyler reddened. Gates was right, and Schuyler knew it. "In addition," Schuyler went on, "Burgoyne's force is well-equipped. You know what we have here — men with no footwear, clad in rags, some of them carrying matchlocks a century old. The condition of St. Clair's men was no better before they were routed from Ticonderoga. It's bound to be worse when they finally fall back here to join us for the big fight."

Gates was silent for a long moment. Then he said, "If we had more support from the militias ..."

"I know," Schuyler said, shaking his head. "I've had little success in rallying them."

For a long moment, silence fell over the two generals as they sat astride their horses on the river bank. Then, without a word, Gates reached into his coat and produced an envelope. Wordlessly, he handed it over to Schuyler. The commanding general took it and eyed the thing. It bore the wax seal of the Continental Congress. Schuyler broke the seal and opened the envelope. He unfolded the document and read it, quite carefully, twice, noting at the bottom the large, flowery signature of John Hancock. Then he glanced up at Gates, whose face was impassive.

"So," Schuyler said, his voice completely even, "you're replacing me as commander of the northern department."

Gates said, "It's the will of Congress, General. I played no direct role—"

"Oh, please," Schuyler said. "It's only the two of us here, General Gates. Let us be direct and honest with one another. Congress rules the colonies, unchecked by any other power, executive or judicial. You've cultivated allies in Congress — like John and Sam Adams.

General Washington is your friend—"

"—He is, Sir. I say that with pride."

"Understandably so," Schuyler said. "And what is the official rationale for my replacement?"

"Ticonderoga," Gates said. "It was surrendered without resistance. John Adams maintains that Congress will not hold a fort until it shoots a general."

"And in this case, I'm the general being shot — figuratively, at any rate. Ticonderoga was given up to preserve the army, General Gates. I'd repeatedly communicated to General Washington and to the Congress General Arnold's assessment that the fort was vulnerable. We couldn't garrison the mountains around it. We could barely garrison the fort itself. Anyone who has ever seen entire walled villages atop the mountains of Calabria would understand that mounting big guns on the mountaintops surrounding Ticonderoga was never an impossibility."

Gates reddened slightly. It had been Gates who'd stoutly maintained that the British could never drag cannon up to the summit of Sugar Loaf.

"General Washington has never been to Italy," Gates said simply. "Neither have Mr. Adams or most of the members of the Continental Congress."

"Then, now that you know what happened, you agree with me?" Schuyler demanded.

"It's not for me to agree or disagree," Gates said. "There's also was the matter of your personal weakness with the militia, General. It was felt by certain members of Congress—"

"—The Adamses."

Gates only nodded as he continued. "... that the only chance of repelling this invasion was the appointment of a new commander whose ability to attract recruits was likely to be superior to your own. You have my sympathies, Sir, but this decision was not mine to make. Like you, I can only abide by the orders I'm given."

Schuyler's expression never changed. "Young Wilkinson is efficient. He'll be as loyal to you as he has been to me, since his true loyalty lies with his own advancement. I suggest that you keep him on as senior aide to the commanding general. As for me, General Gates, I am at your disposal for whatever duty you feel appropriate. It would be my preference to join St. Clair in combat to the north against the English advance."

Gates glanced away from Schuyler and out over the slowly flowing water of the river sliding by in the bright sunlight. "It's the belief of Congress that recruitment from the militias would be enhanced by your complete departure from the field, General Schuyler."

Schuyler blinked twice, in rapid succession, as the meaning of those words sank in. Then, his voice nearly a whisper, he said, "I'm to leave the army, then?"

"Congress has not revoked your commission, General, but I have no need of you here. Might I suggest that a much-deserved period of rest and relaxation would be an appropriate course of action on your part."

Schuyler nodded slowly. "I see. Very well, I shall, of course, remove myself from the field entirely. Deftly done, General Gates. My compliments."

Gates said nothing in response.

"I do insist," Schuyler told him, "on a court martial in the matter of Ticonderoga. I remain confident that a dispassionate examination of my decision would result in my exoneration."

"You are probably correct," Gates said. "I'll notify General Washington of your request."

For a long moment, the two generals sat astride their mounts, eyeing one another in silence. Schuyler, wounded and furious, betrayed no emotion. Gates was visibly flushed in the face with the glow of his victory.

"You've left me with good ground, General," Gates said finally. "I'll note that in my report."

It was a dismissal. Schuyler recognized it as such. Without another word, he wheeled his horse around and galloped northward toward the charred, blackened fields of his beloved farm.

Baum. 1777

Musket fire from the rebel militia, sporadic and ragged, began in the soggy swelter of early afternoon – from the bushes, as usual, as was the habit of the rebels, who dearly loved firing from ambush. The fire was tentative and, fortuitously, inaccurate, but it slowed what already had been a difficult march, and a scowling Lt. Col. Friedrich Baum was annoyed by both the din and the disruption.

His force had taken twelve hours to cover no more than twenty miles through dense forest toward the rebel supply depot in Bennington, in the Hampshire Grants, that contained stores Burgoyne coveted. The trek had taken Baum and his men up and down hills, through bursts of torrential rain and ferocious winds, over and around fallen and purposely downed trees. One of Baum's officers had complained to the commander that the English colonies seemed to be no more than "one prodigious forest bottomed in swamps and morasses." Baum agreed. This was ugly country, especially for horsemen without horses, which was much of his force. He hoped there were horses to be had in Bennington, a key rebel stronghold in this harsh region. Baum, more annoyed than disturbed by the periodic sniper fire, finally turned to his interpreter, a Tory regiment captain named O'Connell, and snarled in German, "Instruct your savages to some prisoners take for me."

O'Connell saluted smartly and shouted out a commend that was incomprehensible to Baum, who spoke only German and found the language of the savages both incomprehensible and repulsive. Immediately, a dozen red men slipped off the road and vanished into the forest. Baum, from the back of the few horses in the company, turned at the waist and gazed back at his ragged, ponderous command as it stretched along the sodden dirt road. He had nearly eight hundred muddy men behind him – mostly dismounted German dragoons, grenadiers and infantrymen, skilled marksmen from Fraser's command, a mob of undisciplined, buckskin and homespun-clad Tories and Canadians gathered from Skene's forces. Baum also had with him a few musicians to blare out marching music as the dispirited German troops slogged along in the stifling August heat. Behind the men came the women – perhaps fifty German wives and whores who'd been pressed into service across the sea to amuse the mercenaries as they plied their warlike trade in this primitive land. It was too bulky a force, Baum knew – too slow and heavily armed and burdened by cannon Baum had been too cautious to leave behind. But it was the force that Burgoyne had ordered him to take – one potent enough, whatever its shortcomings in terms of speed and flexibility, to overcome whatever obstacles Baum might overcome in his raid for horses and supplies from the rebels of the Hampshire Grants.

"The rebels have the advantage of knowing the ground," Burgoyne had haltingly explained to the German officer in his own language. "For our part, we must retain the advantage both of knowing how to fight and maintaining muscle sufficient to win that fight."

So, now that the maddeningly slow march with a command that had no hope of stealth had been slowed even further, Baum still had no idea what sort of opposition he might encounter as he swept down on Bennington, forty miles into enemy country and far enough from Burgoyne's main army to make a timely rescue from disaster not much more than a faint hope. Baum, however, moved ahead without fear. Tall, slim and intensely disciplined at age forty, he was not, by nature, a fearful man, especially on the field of battle. A professional soldier since his teens, Baum viewed death or dire injury as no more than acceptable vocational hazards. He was an expertly trained, combat-tested professional who felt fear only at sea on his way to bloody battlefields in lands far distant from his native Brunswick.

On each of the other military campaigns he had waged on behalf of the prince of Brunswick, who regularly sold the services of his troops to other European potentates, Baum's sea voyages had been limited to relatively brief sojourns along the European coast, with land always reassuringly in sight of the ship's deck. This jaunt had involved crossing an open ocean – a vast universe of instability and threat. The rolling swells of the daunting North Atlantic in a season of squalls and dimness the year before had unnerved Baum, a new experience for him. The shriek of ship timbers under stress had set Baum's teeth on edge. The sharp flap of canvas shrouds in the vigorous wind had turned his stomach. Water accumulating and actually forming waves in the bilge had sent thrills of alarm along his sturdy spine. Salt water streaming through a hatch had once washed a sleeping Baum from his bunk, leaving him tense and testy and sleepless for days. He had lived uneasily in the belly of the wooden whale for months until the vessel finally reached dry land in North America. After enduring all that, Baum had no fear of musket balls, cannon fire or hand to hand combat, at which he excelled, especially with his expertly wielded saber. As unpleasant as this campaign might be, he'd told his closest friend, Colonel Nicholas Von Breymann, it couldn't be more arduous than the sea journey back and forth to this vile wilderness.

The friendship between the two men dated back fifteen years. They were a study in opposites. Where Baum was low-key and taciturn, the somewhat older Breymann possessed a fiery temper. Where Baum's expression of amusement was no more than a tight smile, Breymann laughed easily and often. Where Baum bore hardship with placid acceptance, Breymann often complained bitterly that the world was not shaped to his desires. Most conspicuously, where

Baum, a non-swimmer, dreaded sea travel, Breymann was entranced with the wild beauty of open water. Oddly, the contrast in their traits and temperaments had drawn them together rather than kept them apart. Baum and Breymann were like brothers – although brothers with different fathers, von Breymann often joked.

In only a few moments, the red men were returning, dragging rebels with them and the horses the rebels had been riding. The prisoners were forced to their knees in the middle of the road before Baum's horse. The colonel, tall and slim and his face marked with the obligatory saber scar that his swordsmanship training had left on him, gazed down on them dispassionately. When the count reached five, O'Connell informed the commander that the other rebels apparently had escaped. Baum studied his quarry. Three were essentially children, no more than fifteen years of age. One man appeared to be about seventy. The other was about thirty five, bearded and glaring. All were caked in mud, and some were bleeding from various wounds. The red men were not gentle captors, Baum had noted, although he regarded their casual brutality as nothing less than appropriate to the circumstances.

"Ask them what before me lies," the colonel instructed O'Connell.

The Tory officer snapped out questions to the prisoners, none of whom responded. O'Connell kicked one of the boys and slapped the face of another. When the younger man protested, O'Connell drove a black boot into the man's middle.

"Kill that one," Baum ordered. "Let's see if that renders the others more talkative."

O'Connell did not hesitate. In a flash of movement, he pulled a pistol from beneath his green coat, pressed the barrel against the man's forehead and pulled the trigger. Blood and brains burst from the rear of the prisoner's head as he fell backward, eyes open and jaw agape as the other prisoners gasped audibly. The Tory officer rattled off a few more quick sentences. Immediately, the old man responded. The prisoner and the Tory officer conversed for several moments. Then O'Connell turned to his commander.

"There are at least fifteen hundred rebels at Bennington, Sir," he said, "perhaps as many as eighteen hundred. Some are stragglers from Ticonderoga but most are raw militiamen. A rebel militia general named Stark has been recruiting them for months now."

"Have they cannon?" Baum demanded.

"Nothing of note," O'Connell replied. "This man here predicted that they'll run at our approach. Most are poorly armed, he said – or armed not at all, and the militia has no muskets with which to supply them."

Baum pondered the circumstance. "Fifteen hundred rebels with no cannon and eight hundred of us with big guns. I would say that we effectively outnumber them, Captain. Hang these remaining and catch up with me."

O'Connell's face paled. "The boys, too, Sir?"

Baum's expression never changed. "All who oppose us, Captain. A boy with a musket is a man's game playing, and a man's penalty should to be his as well."

"Sir ..." O'Connell began.

"Very well," Baum snapped out. "Take their horses and set them free. You English are too gentle with these people. It's a lenient mindset you'll come to regret."

Within a few hours, Baum's force had reached a large mill at the confluence of a stream and what his maps informed him was the Hoosick River. Baum was in an ill humor. He'd lost two men to musket fire from the bushes, although the red men had routed the snipers with dispatch and returned to the column bearing bloody scalps, which Baum deemed offensive conduct. At the mill, however, which the rebels seemed to prize, resistance intensified dramatically. Musket fire from the forest and bushes grew deadlier, and Baum halted to deploy his troops. Three rebels were finishing the job of dismantling a small bridge over the narrow river – work they wrapped up with surprising hardiness under heavy fire from Baum's forces. The air grew thick with gunpowder, which shrouded all and blocked out the sun.

It was obvious now that the journey to Bennington would involve heavier fighting than Burgoyne, lulled by the lack of resistance at Ticonderoga, had imagined. Baum took the occasion to dictate a message to Burgoyne and send it off on via courier on horseback. In his note, Baum reported what the prisoner had told him about the size of the rebel force at Bennington and complained about the behavior of the savages, whom, he wrote, "cannot be controlled." By late afternoon, after many hours of bitter exchanges of fire, the rebels had largely been driven off and the bridge repaired. As Baum prepared to move his ungainly command across the river, a courier came galloping up on a foam-flecked horse with a message from Burgoyne.

"The accounts you have sent me are very satisfactory," the commanding general's note read, "and I have no doubt of every part of your proceeding continuing to be the same." Move on, Burgoyne instructed Baum, and hold ground as you do. If confronted by forces too heavy to engage, Burgoyne wrote, send me word, and I'll dispatch more troops to bolster you. Baum, sobered by the resolve and effectiveness of the troops he'd just encountered, immediately sent back a reply requesting immediate reinforcements. Then he sent ahead a party of red men to scout his way after he'd moved his force across the newly reconstructed bridge to its camp for the night on the river's eastern shore. He was now no more than a dozen miles from the Bennington Depot, and the mill he'd captured had happily contained food for his men as well as those still with Burgoyne – nearly eighty barrels of flour, about a thousand bushels of wheat and twenty more barrels of salt. Bennington, he knew, would contain even more riches for an army living off the land. And, he hoped, Bennington also would contain horses for his dismounted dragoons. In his tent that evening, Baum dozed uneasily with images of dark, green ocean swells rolling through his brain. The following morning, over tea and with a courier standing by as the sun rose over the forest to the east, Baum again wrote Burgoyne, with O'Connell scribbling down the colonel's German dictation in English, as he'd done the day before.

"I will proceed so far today as to fall on the enemy early tomorrow." Baum wrote. "I expect that fifteen hundred to eighteen hundred men are at Bennington but are supposed to leave it on our approach."

His men refreshed by a night's sleep and by a cool morning

drizzle, Baum left a detachment to defend the mill and then set as brisk a pace as he could manage that morning. By mid day, only a few miles from the mill and the river on which he'd camped, musket fire from the woods and bushes picked up markedly. Impressed by the volume of fire and seeking a better view of the conflict, Baum and a few of his officers galloped up a high hill as musket balls whizzed around them. From the hill's relatively clear summit, he could see more than a mile in every direction. It was a commanding view that permitted Baum to assess the strength of the rebel forces in the cleared fields to the south and east. What he saw made him glad that he'd asked Burgoyne for additional troops. The rebel force he spotted in the fields outnumbered Baum's by two to one, and the rebels weren't running. Instead, they were moving in no particular formation in his direction. There were too many men against him for Baum to risk a frontal attack, and none was necessary in any event with reinforcements from Burgoyne on their way.

Baum's hill was heavily wooded on three sides. Only the western slope was thinly forested, and he deemed it the only way the rebels could reach his forces in any numbers if Baum chose to dig in on this high ground and await reinforcements. He immediately ordered the wholesale felling of trees and the construction of wood and earthen barricades behind which he, his men and his cannon could hold off the rebels until the additional forces he'd requested of Burgoyne arrived. After several hours of labor under increasingly heavy fire from the forest below, Baum surveyed his new defenses with approval. A total of five barricades had been constructed – one nearly four hundred feet in length – across the hill and along the route back to the river.

The morning's drizzle had turned into a deluge, making any rebel charge up the mud-slick western hillside into Baum's muskets and cannon a decidedly dicey proposition. He wouldn't have tried it, Baum knew, and he doubted that they would either.

As the sun sank in the west and the officers' tents were erected, Baum chewed on hardtack and pondered the coming day. When his reinforcements arrived and attacked the rebels from the rear, Baum and his eight hundred troops would sweep down the hill and crush the rebels between the two forces. He held good ground here, Baum knew, and good ground was a foot soldier's best friend.

At eleven at night, a horseback courier plunged from the blackness into Baum's camp as rebel musket balls whistled across the hill's darkened western slope. The message was from Baum's friend, Breymann. He was leading the relief column, but he was now in camp to the west with cannon and six hundred and forty two foot soldiers, each with forty cartridges. The cannon, combined with the rain and rugged terrain, had slowed the progress of the reinforcements. Ammunition carts had overturned and had to be righted. Breymann's guide had lost his way. The march had been a disaster. Breymann estimated that his force had made no better than half a mile an hour in the drenching rain, and his troops were now exhausted. He would be underway at first light, however, rain or sun. Baum scribbled off a message of his own and dispatched the courier back down the hill into the darkness and musket fire.

Hurry, Baum had urged his friend.

As the sun rose and the rain intensified, the musket fire from below the hill began. Baum's men returned fire, but it soon became clear to the commander that his force was under attack not just from the front of his barricades but also, to his surprise, from the heavily wooded sides of the hill and all along the line back to the river. These farmers and squirrel hunters were better in the woods than he had anticipated – certainly better than his own highly trained infantrymen, he noted ruefully. Baum's response was to order the felling of more trees and the construction of additional barricades. All day, the forest rang with gunfire, with the ring of axes and the rasp of saws and with the grunts of men exerting themselves as the sky belched forth water at a blinding rate. As night again fell, Baum spotted rebels marching around the base of the hill and fired cannon in their direction, but he could see no damage inflicted on the enemy before the rebels fell back. He felt relief that no direct assault had forced him to concentrate his troops' fire in any single direction. He also felt concern that Breymann had not yet arrived. The rain, Baum suspected, had once again kept the heavily laden relief column's pace to only a crawl.

The rebel charge came the following afternoon, in bright summer sunlight. Over a period of about ninety minutes, roughly three hundred men, Baum estimated, came up the wooded north side of his hill and roared shouting, screaming and shooting over the barricades and into his compound. Several hundred more came charging up the thinly forested western slope. Baum's grenadiers were falling at an alarming rate. Some were dropping their weapons and raising their hands in surrender. He watched as two of his officers, in rapid succession, fell. The rebel forces were closing from all directions, Baum noted, although their fire had slowed as they strove not to shoot one another by accident. But tomahawks and knives had taken the place of musket fire, and Baum himself was now drawing his saber as he and his remaining troops drew together, back to back, in the center of the hill's summit. With almost casual skill, he used his saber to dispatch several of the rebels who approached him.

Still calm, although his blood ran high with the thrill of combat amid the continuous clap of thunderous musket fire, Baum assessed the situation dispassionately through the clouds of power smoke and reluctantly concluded that this engagement had been lost. Breymann would appear too late to save Baum's command. Snapping orders to his remaining officers and sergeants, Baum ordered a retreat back toward the river – a disciplined retreat, Baum hoped, to a location where he could link up with Breymann's forces later in the day and launch his own, vengeful counterattack. Everywhere, though, his troops were bunched and scattered, and the retreat by his wounded, exhausted men was both ragged and disorganized. His troops also were low on ammunition, Baum realized as he backed down the hill, slashing with his saber at a knot of rebels who were trying to surround him. He could hear the groans of the wounded and dying all around him. This was a cataclysm, he decided grimly, and he was already pondering the wording of his written report to Burgoyne when a musket ball tore into his middle with the force of a horses's kick.

Baum felt his knees buckle on the slope of the hill. He felt no pain as he went down, although he recognized this midsection wound as probably fatal, like virtually all battlefield wounds to the torso. He lay still for a long moment, awaiting the pain and surprised that it seemed not to be coming. He placed a hand over the wound and felt blood gushing from the hole. Then he was surrounded by a ring of his own men, all cursing and sweat and blood. As he felt strong hands grab his shoulders and begin to drag him down the still muddy hillside and back to the English stronghold on the river, the commander prayed silently that Breymann, who had to be near, could still save the day. Baum also consoled himself with one lingering thought.

At least he would be spared the incomparable agony of that return journey across the North Atlantic to Germany.

Burgoyne. 1777

The message from Breymann was brief and to the point. As he sat at his desk in his headquarters in Skene's mansion, Burgoyne studied the scrap of paper carefully.

" ... Two hundred and seven dead from both my command and from Baum's, including Baum, who expired in my arms after characterizing the rebel forces as men who "fought more like hell-hounds than soldiers.' An estimated seven hundred of our forces were captured along with all cannon and draught horses and supplies, including those captured earlier from the enemy by Baum's command. My best estimate, from surveying the field, is that the rebel forces suffered less than a hundred dead and wounded."

Breymann continued with a terse account of his own ill-fated clash with the rebel forces, which had outnumbered his own by approximately three to one. Skene, Breymann reported, had narrowly cheated death when he'd mistaken a group of rebels for Tories and had rushed on horseback to greet them. He'd had his horse shot out from under him and had managed barely to fight his way back to already abandoned English cannon before narrowly escaping on an artillery horse.

Clearly, Breymann speculated, news of the English advance on Bennington with Indians at their side had roused the local population and prompted them to turn out against the royal forces in numbers far greater than anticipated. The red men had fought bravely and effectively, the German officer reported, but he theorized that their very presence with the English forces had hardened resistance on the part of the colonists.

"Perhaps we should send them back to Canada," Breymann wrote in what Burgoyne recognized as a stunning display of emotional distress and unseemly impudence to a superior officer.

Burgoyne read the missive again as the mud-flecked courier who'd brought it stood by to transmit the commanding general's reply to Breymann, who was at that moment fighting a bloody retreat action on his way back to Fort Edward.

Not bloody likely that I'll send the savages back, Burgoyne thought to himself, reflecting on the regiment he'd left behind to garrison Ticonderoga. Not with me now down nearly two thousand men from the ten thousand troops who landed with me at the foot of Champlain.

He should have sent English troops to Bennington, Burgoyne thought, rather than Riedesel's forces. These Germans moved far too slowly, too methodically, always stopping to dress their ranks and following European marching formality slavishly at the expense of speed. If Breymann had made better time with his relief column, this disaster need never have occurred. Still, it made no sense now to fault the man who'd done what he'd been trained to do and was obviously grieving for the loss of his friend. The error, Burgoyne supposed, had been as much his as Riedesel's or Breymann's.

Burgoyne hurriedly scribbled a reply to Breymann to return with all possible haste and commended the German officer for managing to save a few hundred men from both his and Baum's command. As he wrote, Burgoyne saw the heavy wooden door open and Babette enter, resplendent in a summer dress of bright yellow. He scrawled his signature on the message, handed it to the courier and watched the man salute quickly and vanish through the door Babette had just passed through. Babette, ever sensitive to the general's moods, noted the troubled expression on his face.

"Jack," she said tentatively, "is anything wrong?"

Burgoyne rose from his chair, wrapped his red-clad arms around the woman, embraced her firmly and then kissed her, long and passionately.

"We're about the business of war, my darling," he said with a confident smile as he pulled his face away from hers. "That's seldom an affair conspicuous by its tidiness."

Arnold. 1777

Roughly one hundred and forty miles west of the Army of the United States' position on the Hudson's west bank at Saratoga,

Nicholas Herkimer lay dying in a large, brick mansion in the Mohawk Valley. The house was fairly new — about fifteen or so years old, Arnold estimated as he rode up to it. The building had been designed to look like a typical English country manor house, although its owner was the leader of a proud Germanic community that had emigrated many decades before from the Rhine River region. The one hundred and sixty acres surrounding the stately structure were lush and well manicured, as were all the farms of these industrious Germanic farmers in this region they found so reminiscent of the Fatherland.

A servant took the reins of Arnold's horse and that of his chief aide, Major Richard Varick, when the soldiers dismounted. Varick, a dozen years Arnold's junior, had been a law student when the rebellion had erupted. Like virtually every other enlisted man or junior officer in the Army of the United States, he looked upon Arnold with great regard – although, like most, he also understood that Arnold was a uniquely volatile personality.

"I'll see him alone, Dirk," Arnold told Varick. "He'll be weak, and he'll want to speak freely. The presence of a stranger should not be permitted to inhibit him on his death bed."

"Very well, Sir," Varick said. "I'll wait here with the horses."

Herkimer's tearful young wife, nearly thirty years her wealthy husband's junior, greeted Arnold at the door. Upstairs, in a large bed in a large room, Herkimer lay in a pool of slimy sweat, his long, white clay pipe clenched firmly between his teeth, his face pale as a potent infection ran wild through his burly, feverish body without interference. The room stank of gangrene. He struggled to sit up to greet Arnold, general to general. Gently, Arnold placed a hand on his chest and pushed Herkimer back in his bed.

"A man who gave a leg for his country need rise for no one," Arnold said.

Herkimer smiled weakly through what both he and Arnold knew would be his final agony, ending probably in no more than a few days. Infections after amputations were common, and no one could stop them once they began their ravages. Herkimer was no more than fifty. On his deathbed, the microbes assailing his every cell, he easily looked seventy.

"Rise I would were I able," he grunted out in English with the distinct German taint so common to the area, "for the hero of Quebec and Ticonderoga. When did you arrive?"

"Yesterday afternoon," Arnold said, "with a thousand men double-timing through the forest behind me – and only to find that the English bastards had already been repulsed by the Tryon County Militia and its gallant general. Congratulations on your victory."

"I'm glad we could keep St. Leger from closing on Schuyler's rear."

"Schuyler no longer," Arnold told him as he took a chair next to the bed. "We have imbeciles for leaders, General. The Congress replaced Schuyler with Gates, God help us."

Herkimer's lips pursed. "Not a man of perfection, Schuyler, but a better man than Gates. The Adamses are wrong about him. I recall when he came here in the winter more than a year ago to help me contain John Johnson and his Tories. Three thousand of us marched on Johnson Hall with knives and sabers flashing and put the fear of almighty God into the great man's son, who ran off to Canada after that. Schuyler was a good man to have at my side in that clash. Ya, a good man, that Schuyler."

It was the response Arnold had hoped for. Herkimer had reason to be grateful to Schuyler for help in controlling John Johnson, the son and legal heir of Sir William Johnson. Sir William's name alone might have rallied support for the Crown during the revolt's perilous infancy not just among the colonists but, more seriously, among the greatest Indian power on the continent, the Iroquois. As it was, the nations of the Iroquois confederacy were split, with the Mohawks and Senecas fighting for the English but the Oneidas siding with the rebels while the other tribes wavered. Young Johnson was a dedicated Tory but, thank God, not the magnet for royalist support that his father would have been.

Dashing, dynamic, hard-drinking William Johnson had essentially settled this region of the New York colony – waging ferocious war against the French three decades earlier in Mohawk buckskin and with his comely Mohawk mistress at his side, which had earned him his knighthood. He'd been a justly revered figure in this critical region west of Albany, and if he'd lived his fierce loyalty to the king might have constituted a genuine problem for the rebels. Luckily for the revolution, Sir William's overworked liver had betrayed him at age sixty and insipid John, son of Sir William's legal white wife, had inherited the family fortune rather than any of the great man's many Mohawk sons or daughters.

"It might not be too late, General," Arnold said. "If a respected figure like you were to write General Washington, then he might be moved to urge Congress to correct this error."

Herkimer pondered the proposition. "Possibly," he said at last, "but probably not. I'll write if I can muster the strength before my time comes, but the truth is that General Washington has much to occupy his attention at the moment. For that matter, General, so, too, have I."

Arnold nodded solemnly. Herkimer was right. Even with a deathbed plea from a fallen hero, and that's what Herkimer was after routing the English invasion force, Washington was unlikely to take on the Adamses at such a moment. After the disaster of the English invasion of New York and Long Island, the commanding general's own position was not entirely secure, Arnold suspected. Washington did not have an army that could carry off complex, coordinated maneuvers. His officers and sergeants had little or no military experience. His generals were, for the most part, more politicians than soldiers. Washington had yet to win a major engagement against the English, and Arnold had heard tales that the taciturn Virginia planter often occupied himself in his tent at night studying military texts by candlelight. For his own part, Arnold had never opened a military text. He led men into battle to win or die, inspiring them with his own courage in the face of enemy fire. He made strategic decisions based on logic and common sense. That was all he knew or cared about classic military tactics. Thus far, those techniques had made Benedict Arnold the most successful field commander in the Army of the United States.

"I understand, General," Arnold said. "My most profound sympathies on your wound."

"Ah," Herkimer said disgustedly, "I wouldn't have minded dying out there on the field, but this business of dying in bed is a drawn-out, undignified affair. Left with only one leg, though, perhaps this is best. My new young wife was willing to marry an old widower, but she bargained on getting a man in his entirety, at least. When do you go back, General?"

"As soon as this visit ends. I've already sent a message to General Gates that St. Leger has been repelled and that Fort Stanwix is secure, and I'm leaving a relief garrison of seven hundred to ensure that it stays that way. I'll need to give General Gates the full story in the report I compose tonight in camp on the way back to Saratoga. So, please tell me your version of the battle, General, so I can include that in my report."

Silently, Herkimer grimaced in pain and clutched at the swollen stump of his leg beneath the blanket – through which no small amount of blood was seeping, Arnold noted. Then, finally catching what was left of his breath, Herkimer said, "I'll try to be brief ..."

The hardy, forty-year-old Colonel Barry St. Leger had left Montreal in late June as the western prong of Burgoyne's invasion. St. Leger had crossed Lake Ontario by boat and had approached Fort Stanwix in early August. A veteran of heavy battle in Europe, St. Leger had brought with him a mixed force of English regulars, Tory volunteers under the command of the exiled John Johnson and nearly one thousand Senecas and Mohawks led by the Mohawk chief Thayendanega, better known to whites as Joseph Brant. Brant was the brother of Sir William Johnson's beloved Mohawk mistress. St. Leger's force also contained eight cannon. With the English was

Herkimer's own loyalist brother, Johan. Many Mohawk Valley families were so divided in their loyalties, the milita general told Arnold.

Fort Stanwix, on the banks of the Mohawk River, was a ramshackle log structure built during the war against the French and garrisoned by six hundred Army of the United States troops. Rather than attempt a direct assault on the fort, St. Leger laid siege to it and employed Johnson and other Tories to rouse the citizenry of the region to aid him in capturing it. Herkimer, a prosperous farmer who commanded the regional militia, called out all men between the ages of sixteen and sixty and marched to attack St. Leger from the rear with a volunteer force of eight hundred. Only six miles from the fort, while crossing a marshy stream, Herkimer's volunteers were deftly ambushed by St. Leger's Indian forces.

"There was blood aplenty," Herkimer told Arnold, "and rattle of the muskets and the war whoops of the Mohawks and the Senecas. They were chilling, ya, those cries. I was at the head of the column. When I heard firing, I swung my horse about and rode back and took a musket ball in my leg. The shot killed my horse. Unable at that point to walk or move well, I sliced free the saddle and dragged it while I crawled on my belly beneath a tree. Then I sat up on the saddle and began firing."

"And smoking your pipe all the while," Arnold said. "That's what I was told at Fort Stanwix. They said you refused to take cover – that you told your troops, "I will face the enemy!'"

Herkimer shrugged slightly. "A leader must lead through personal example – but you know that, General. Of all our generals, you know that best, and that's why your troops love you and would follow you into the flames of Hell. When that battle began, I but pretended to be Benedict Arnold. I could think of no better example to follow."

"You humble me, Sir," Arnold said.

Despite his agony, the dying man laughed aloud. "No one humbles you, General Arnold. Not you, of all men."

Summer rains poured down on the creek, Herkimer recalled. He and his militiamen formed a circle around a small hill, but the rain hampered the firing of their flintlocks, and the Indians came in with hatchets and knives. As they'd been trained to do, Herkimer's men paired off. One would aim and fire while his vulnerable comrade reloaded. After a while – Herkimer was unable to estimate the time for Arnold — the opposition faded away amid the thick smoke of battle, and the Tryon County Militia counted their losses. They'd suffered two hundred dead, more than two hundred and fifty wounded and another two hundred missing and, presumably, taken prisoner. But they were masters of the field, the victors in a spectacular bloodbath at a place the Indians called Oriskany. Just after the engagement, the Army of the United States forces holding Fort Stanwix had flooded from behind their walls and attacked St. Leger's camp, scattering what remained of the exhausted English forces and either destroying or commandeering all the English supplies and much of their weaponry. After gathering together his scattered forces, St. Leger had later sent a message to the fort demanding its surrender and threatening to loose his Indians on the countryside, but his demand was rejected as no more than a hollow bluff. Herkimer's volunteers and the sally from the fort had left St. Leger's forces too badly damaged to be effective.

"You know the rest," a clearly exhausted Herkimer got out. "You did the rest, after all."

Arnold had, indeed, done the rest. Thirty miles east of Fort Stanwix, Arnold had stumbled across a captive half-breed named Hon Yost Schuyler, a prisoner of the rebel forces. Schuyler was supposedly a distant relative of Phillip Schuyler's and, quite simply, a madman or a moron, or some combination of the two. The half-breed Schuyler was scheduled for hanging by Army of the United States troops as a Tory soldier. Arnold had set the nitwit free to alert St. Leger's Indian warriors that Arnold was en route at the head of a huge army to slay all who opposed him. When word reached St. Leger through the warnings of his Indian allies that Arnold was roaring westward with a huge force, the English officer abandoned his siege and fled north with his battered force. Arnold and his relatively small force of fewer than one thousand troops pursued St. Leger to Lake Ontario and spotted the last English boat on the watery horizon paddling frantically for the northern shore and Canada beyond.

"And, so, the thing is done," Herkimer got out. "And now you and Gates must stop the others – that dandy Burgoyne and his army."

"We'll stop him," Arnold quietly assured the dying general.

"God help you, General," Herkimer choked out. "I'll make that request when I see Him. It won't be long now."

Fraser. 1777

Under gray afternoon skies pregnant with summer rain, Simon

Fraser heard the sounds of Burgoyne's column long before he saw it. An army of thousands on the move is not a stealthy enterprise. Many minutes before he spotted troops coming through the forest that bordered Fort Edward, Fraser's ears caught the clunk of big guns as they rolled over ruts in the road. He could hear also the clop of hooves as they struck stones in the roadway, the lowing of oxen pulling the supply carts, the creak of leather harness under stress, the clink of bayonets against the barrels of Brown Bess muskets, the snapped orders of the sergeants, the muttered curses of sweating, straining men.

All were familiar, reassuring sounds to the general of Burgoyne's hard-edged advance troops. Fraser reveled in military life. It had saved him, he knew, from a dreary, soul-killing existence in some commercial office or in some minor government position. Fraser was comfortable with regimentation and discipline, but he chafed under routine, and he was never happier than when he was swept up in the excitement and uncertainty of a campaign. The interludes in England between wars left him bored and sullen, drinking and eating too much and always eager for action. Luckily, the English Empire's far-reaching ambitions left it with no shortage of bellicose opponents throughout the civilized world. With the Irish rebels suitably subdued after one of their periodic uprisings against the English king, Fraser had been delighted to accept transfer to Canada to fight new rebels in new country.

The general's face was a mud-streaked forest of stubble as he sat atop his foam-specked grey gelding in front of the fine stone house at Fort Edward that Fraser had taken it upon himself to commandeer as his commander's residence and headquarters. The general was weary from the mind-numbing boredom of clearing the road. Frasier looked forward to crossing the Hudson and marching toward Schuyler's forces at Saratoga. The rugged Scot heaved a small sigh of relief that the army would arrive before darkness, when the forest would become a perilous place. The journey from Skene's estate to the Hudson was relatively brief, thanks to the efforts of Fraser's advance troops in repairing bridges and clearing the downed trees along rutted dirt road between the two points, but Burgoyne still had to move many regiments, more than one hundred cannon and many hundreds of heavily laden ox carts. With the way these rebels tended to fight, sniping from behind trees, Fraser wondered if General Phillips would ever get a chance to use his cannon to good effect.

Moreover, Fraser had known that the main's army's journey would be marked by stray rebel musket fire from the woods on both sides of the trail. His own troops and the savages had done a fine job of clearing the forest of rebel snipers, Fraser knew, but not a perfect one. Some of these colonial farmers, he'd noted, were every bit as elusive as the bloody savages when the rebels took to the woods. Luckily, their marksmanship tended to be spotty.

First out of the forest surrounding Fort Edward on three sides were the Indians, scouting ahead of Burgoyne's lengthy column and warily entering this town of white man's houses. Shortly behind them came the first element of the main column with Burgoyne leading the way on his showy, snowy charger and with Clerke on his own mount at the commanding general's side. Fraser dug his spurs into the gelding and trotted forward to greet Burgoyne.

"A pleasant journey, I trust," Fraser said to his commander as he saluted smartly.

"Nothing that a congenial evening with comrades won't rectify," Burgoyne said. "I presume you've found us suitable quarters."

"The stone house at the end of this lane. It's not Skene's mansion, Jack, but it should serve your purposes nicely until we cross the river."

"We won't be here long, I hope," Burgoyne said, gazing at the gray-green waters of the Hudson at the far end of the town. "The rebels await us at Saratoga, and it would be a shame to disappoint them. I received word from a loyalist informant, by the way, Simon, that Schuyler has been replaced by a General Gates. Do you know him?"

"I do," Fraser said. "A former English major – a supplies man rather than a fighting soldier. We served with him against the French. Don't you recall the fellow?"

"I recall the name in a vague fashion, but not a face," Burgoyne said. "We can only hope that his performance at Saratoga turns out to be equally memorable. I hope, too, that General Gates has had the good grace to commandeer a gracious house for me to use as a headquarters once we defeat his troops."

"I never cease to be amazed at all the lovely homes we've stumbled across in this wretched wilderness," Clerke observed. "Some of these colonials seem to live quite comfortably."

"These colonies are uniquely prosperous, Sir Francis," Burgoyne said. "That's why the rebels believe they can survive without the empire even though they have no real national government, no national taxes and no credit with which to buy arms abroad for their pitiful army – all of which they desperately need. No one in these colonies even knows how to make gunpowder or cast cannon."

"Which, thus far," Fraser said, "they haven't seemed to need."

"Well, the empire needs the taxes they so resent paying us," Burgoyne said to Fraser. "Simon, you'll join us for dinner, I trust."

Fraser frowned slightly. He enjoyed his commander's company and wit, but Fraser was far less at home at one of his friend's fancy dinners than in his tent surrounded by the campfires of his troops. Moreover, he continued to feel that the tone of this campaign was more than a touch too casual, especially after that disastrous clash with the rebels outside Bennington. Still, he understood that his commander was a uniquely social creature. Fraser understood, too, that Burgoyne's skittish mistress was unaccustomed to the rigors of a combat force on the move in rugged terrain and that Burgoyne's instinct with women had always been to attend scrupulously to their comfort. Fraser's own wife, Margaretta, had refused to leave Europe to campaign in the colonies with her husband. Fraser, as delighted as he was with the rich widow he'd married only a few years earlier, did not miss the obligations that her presence here would have imposed upon him.

Clerke said, "Colonel Skene had a fine steer butchered for us, General Fraser. It was a colonial cow, but I'm assured it will taste precisely like our own fine English beef."

"You must join us, Simon," Burgoyne insisted. "You've been out here for weeks chopping away at those trees. The other senior officers miss your companionship – as do the ladies, I might add, although I can't imagine why."

Fraser shrugged. "Very well. I'll see to my troops and then, of course, scrub off this muck and sweat. I'll be along directly."

As the two generals spoke, Skene, who sat atop a prancing chestnut mare from the wealthy landowner's own stables, emerged from the forest at the head of his green-clad Tory regiment. At Skene's side on another of Skene's fine horses was his youthful aide, David Jones. The two trotted their mounts to the assembly of English officers. Skene saluted Burgoyne.

Skene said, "There's a fine stone house at the end of this lane, General, that should be suitable for your needs. Young Master Jones here is from Fort Edward, and he recommends that dwelling."

"I was from Fort Edward before the rebels among my friends and neighbors drove me out," Jones said. "That house belongs to a colonel of militia who's now with Schuyler, I imagine. I'm certain, General, that he would be suitably appalled at your commandeering his home for a headquarters"

Burgoyne responded with a hearty laugh. "It has already been appropriated by our good General Fraser here, a gentleman of stellar taste, as we all know. I trust that you two gentlemen will be joining us for dinner."

"We greatly appreciate the invitation," Skene said. "I'll be delighted to attend. You should know, General, that I can consume half that steer all by myself. Lieutenant Jones, however, is on a quest for his lady, who's supposed to be somewhere in the neighborhood of Fort Edward."

"Your lady love will be joining us, then?" Burgoyne asked Jones.

"She will, Sir," Jones replied. "Reverend Brudenell has pledged to marry us in camp as soon as she arrives. I'm certain that Jane made her way to this vicinity as soon as she heard that we'd taken Ticonderoga. I need but to find her. If I manage that chore this evening, we'll be delighted to join you for dinner. You'll be much impressed with my Jane, Sir, I assure you."

"I look forward to meeting her," Burgyone said.

"First, though," Skene said, "we need to attend to our regiment. General Fraser, do you have a preference as to where we should make camp?"

"Since we'll begin preparing tomorrow to move across the river," Fraser said, "I would prefer all the troops as close in as possible. The Germans will take the southern position. My own advance troops will take the east, and the rest of our English forces will camp to the north of Fort Edward. Your regiment, Colonel, can form a semi circle from the south to the north around the regulars and the eastern edge of the line. We'll leave the red men to take the outer ring to stand sentry duty."

"That'll put my men in close proximity to the savages," Skene warned. "That could provoke some friction, Sir. These local troops know the Indians, and they don't care for them."

Weary and annoyed, Fraser was in no mood for debate. He said, "Familiarity, I should imagine, will breed more caution than friction, Colonel Skene. Moreover, I would prefer to have the red men outside the main body of the encampment. They're always coming in and out as they scout about the woods. I would prefer not to have them traipsing through our ranks and disturbing our troops any more than necessary."

"Good thinking," said Burgoyne, putting a quick end to the discussion. Then the commanding general's eyes lit as he watched his troops continue to pour out of the forest into the town. "Ah, marvelous. There are our musicians."

Fraser glanced back along the dirt road to see the ox cart bearing Burgoyne's string quartet. All four men were in ill-fitting uniforms and tightly clutching their instruments as they rocked in the cart behind the oxen. Their only job was to play for the commanding general's dinner guests. Short on supplies for his own fighting troops, Fraser actively resented the musicians. They served no military purpose and ate every bit as much as a quartet of vastly more useful infantrymen.

"Thank God they made it safely," Fraser said dryly.

"Sarcasm hardly becomes you, Simon," Burgoyne said with a smile. "You'll feel vastly better, however, with some wine and some of Colonel Skene's beef in your gullet – and with some music to soothe the savage beast that is your soul."

Burgoyne's dinner party was, of course, a predictably elegant affair. The commanding general's woman and the other ladies were decked out in gowns that would have been entirely in place in the finest of London's salons. Lady Acland in particular, Fraser noted, looked especially lovely even with her swelling belly. Both her husband, Major Acland, and the youthful Earl of Balcarres were clad in full dress uniforms while Burgoyne, the baron and Fraser were in clean field uniforms, along with the other senior officers. The noblemen, Fraser noted to himself, seemed more at home at such gatherings than in the field, although he could fault neither man for his performance in getting the road from Skenesboro cleared. Burgoyne's lady was uniquely gorgeous, Fraser couldn't help but note. He could understand his friend's seemingly mindless passion for this creature, who exuded an earthy sexuality in a way the other women did not.

In honor of the baron, the string quartet was playing something from Mozart – Fraser lacked the cultural background to identify the precise piece of music — when the trouble began. It was heralded by a Tory officer bursting into the dining room and whispering into Skene's ear. The Tory colonel immediately stood.

"Forgive me, General," Skene said to Burgoyne, "I must excuse myself. We have some trouble in the camp."

"What sort of problem?" Fraser asked immediately.

"My aide, Master Jones, is in some sort of dispute with the savages."

Burgoyne stood. "We'll attend to this together, Colonel. Master Jones is too valuable a commodity to end up roasting over some fire in the savages' camp."

The three of them – Skene, Burgoyne and Fraser – strode through the darkened encampment of Fraser's troops to the east of the village and then through the nearly deserted Tory camp to what obviously was a rowdy disturbance on the eastern edge of the stronghold of logs that the English forces had created to fend off rebel attacks. Following the sound of shouting, swearing men through the darkness, the officers eventually arrived at a ring of several hundred Tories and Indians alternately cheering and cursing in various languages.

Without ceremony, Skene pushed his way through the ring. Burgyone and Fraser followed, being given a wide berth by all. In the center of the circle they found young David Jones, his officer's saber in one hand and a hatchet in the other, circling in what was obviously a death dance with a large, muscular Ottawa who held a tomahawk in one hand and an ugly-looking knife in the other. Each man was naked to the waist in the moist swelter of the summer night, and each dripped sweat and blood from various wounds. Obviously, this clash had gone on for a while. Jones' chest was heaving with exertion. The Indian still seemed fresh, however, despite the blood dripping from his injuries. Without hesitation, Skene stepped between the combatants.

"Enough," the Tory colonel snapped out. Then, arms still outstretched to keep the men apart, he turned to Jones. "Kill this man, David, and there'll be hell to pay. What is this? What prompted it?"

Jones' face was a contorted mess of sweat, blood and rage.

"Show him, you bastard," he bellowed at the Indian. "Show him what you've done, you hellspawn."

Mystified at the command in English, the Indian stood unmoving, his weapons raised. His eyes were pure murder, Fraser noted quickly.

"Where's Le Loup?" Fraser shouted out at the now subdued crowd. "Le Loup, show yourself now. That's an order."

From behind the first ring of onlookers, the chevalier St. Luc stepped forward into the flicker of the fire. From a dozen feet away, Fraser could smell the stink of rum radiating off the man.

"What generated this disturbance?" Fraser demanded as Burgoyne stepped to his side.

St. Luc's expression was grim. From behind his back, he produced a shimmering mass of tangled, red-gold hair. "This, mon general," he said. "Panther brought it to me."

"That's Jane's scalp," Jones roared in the dim flicker of firelight. "This savage bastard killed my Jane. And God knows what else he did to her first."

Then Jones once again lunged at the Indian, who danced back with his weapons ready as Skene stepped in and dragged Jones to the ground.

"David," Skene ordered, "leave it alone now. This will be dealt with. It will, I promise you."

Burgoyne stepped forward then. He glared first at St. Luc and then at the Indian. The silence from the ring of men around them was testament to the power of the commanding general's disapproving gaze. "Ask him what happened, Le Loup," Burgyone ordered. "Did he kill this girl and take her scalp?"

St. Luc stuck the flowing sea of copper hair behind his back and approached the Indian, whose weapons were still at the ready. The chevalier rattled off a few sentences in a language none of the other whites could decipher. Never taking his eyes off Jones or the other whites, the Indian responded quietly and tersely.

"She was a captive taken the other day here at Fort Edward," St. Luc said to Burgoyne. "I know this is true. I saw him take her and another white woman. I told him to protect them both."

Burgoyne nodded slowly. "And, of course, he ignored your

command. That much is obvious."

St. Luc shook his head frantically. "No, no, mon general. He says she was killed by a musket shot from one of the rebel pickets. The shot went high and hit the girl as she sat atop a horse while Panther led her away toward our camp."

"It's possible, I suppose," Fraser whispered to Burgoyne. "Much of the rebel fire has been high, thank God."

"Then why did he scalp her?" Burgoyne demanded of the Frenchman. "If he was not responsible for her death, then why take her hair?"

St. Luc shrugged, a uniquely Gallic gesture. "Mon general proclaimed a bounty on scalps. Once she was dead, she no longer had use for the hair, so Panther took it."

For a long moment, Burgoyne said nothing. Then, his eyes blazing, the commanding general said to St. Luc, "And what became of the other white woman? Did she also conveniently fall victim to enemy fire?"

St. Luc snapped a quick question to the Indian, who responded in a low voice. St. Luc then fired out a command to a nearby brave, who immediately slipped away into the darkness.

"She is alive and well in the camp of my children, mon General," St. Luc said. "She will be with us presently."

By this time, Jones had gained his feet, but he was being held firmly in place by Skene and two of Skene's Tory officers.

"Lies," Jones cried out in a tortured voice. "The lying, heathen demons. They butchered my Jane, General. Hang this bastard, Sir. Please hang him."

"Momentarily, I expect," Burgoyne said quietly.

In only a few moments, during which both the English officers and the hundreds of armed Tories and Indians stood in silence in the flicker of the camp fires, the brave returned with a shockingly naked Mrs. McNeil in tow. At the sight of her, Fraser audibly gasped. Despite the years that had passed since they'd last laid eyes on one another, Fraser immediately recognized this fat, filthy, hysterical woman as his cousin. Immediately, the general stepped forward to wrap her in the coat of his field uniform. He then held his cousin in his arms as she sobbed loudly.

"Tell us what happened, Sarah," Fraser said softly.

Through deep sobs and ragged sighs, Mrs. McNeil struggled to get out her story. The Indians had broken into her cabin and grabbed both her and Jane. She had spotted Jane being led away on a horse, but she'd paid more attention to her own plight. Certain that she would be raped and murdered, Mrs. McNeil had been surprised and relieved to have been dragged to the Indians' camp and put to work cooking and tending to the warriors' housekeeping needs. They'd only laughed or cuffed her, though, when she'd begged for some clothing.

"So, you didn't see the girl killed, then?" Burgoyne demanded.

Mrs. McNeil fought to respond, but the tears and sobs choked off her words. Clearly, the woman was distressed to the point of incoherency. She buried her face in Fraser's chest and let loose a muffled howl.

"There'll be nothing useful from this woman tonight," Fraser said, patting his cousin's tousled gray hair.

Burgoyne's brow furrowed. For a long moment, he said nothing. Then, to Fraser, the commanding general said quietly, "What do you think?"

Holding his weeping cousin in his arms, Fraser said, "Jones is right; hang the savage. If he didn't murder the girl, it's only because he hadn't gotten around to it before she was struck by stray fire."

Instantly, St. Luc stepped forward. "You cannot, mon General. Hang this man and my children will go back to Canada, and God help those they come across in their rage on their journey northward. They will lay waste to everything they encounter."

"Colonel Skene?" Burgoyne asked softly.

Skene stepped quickly away from the raging David Jones, who was held firmly by two other officers, and moved to Burgoyne's side.

"The savage is lying," the Tory colonel muttered.

"I very much suspect that to be the case," Burgoyne said. "I cannot, however, prove that to be the case at this precise moment. In addition, the loss of the savages would be difficult for us."

"My men can take over the scouting, General," Skene said. "Let the red bastards go."

"Their first stop on the way north, Colonel, would be Skenesboro. You do understand that, I trust. And, after Bennington, I can afford no troops to escort the savages out of this country and to protect your people there."

Red-faced, Skene offered no response. After a long moment, he said quietly, "I still say hang him. If one of these savages can with impunity murder the betrothed of a loyalist officer, then no one is safe."

"The sight of this man dangling from a tree limb would warm my heart immeasurably," Burgoyne said finally. "I would rather lose every savage in this command than connive in their atrocities, but I came here to function as a soldier, not as an executioner of the state, and I lack sufficient proof at this juncture to invoke a hanging in the state's name."

Burgoyne turned to St. Luc. "There is one I shall gladly hang, however – and on a moment's notice — if there's any repetition of this incident, and you know precisely, Le Loup, who that victim shall be."

St. Luc nodded his head frantically. "I do, mon General, I do. Nothing like this will occur in the future. I pledge my honor on that."

"How immensely reassuring," Burgone said. "Take the savage into custody. A court of inquiry will be conducted at noon tomorrow in front of my headquarters. At that point, I trust, this other woman will be recovered sufficiently from her ordeal to testify."

"She will, Jack," Fraser assured his commander. "I'll see to that."

Burgoyne. 1777

The knock on Burgoyne's door came nearly two hours past midnight. Babette lay unmoving in the dim candlelight next to him, sated with both wine and lovemaking. Burgoyne had not slept. The episode at the Indian camp – and its implications — lingered in his mind. Even after a pleasant evening with his comrades and their ladies, and even with his passion slaked, the commanding general's brain had been too full of fretful concerns to permit him to drift off successfully. At the rap on the door, Burgoyne quickly rose, wrapped himself in a robe and opened the door a crack. A sentry outside snapped off a quick salute.

"A courier just brought this in, Sir," he said, offering Burgoyne a cloth packet.

Burgoyne took the packet, nodded silently to the guard and moved back into the spacious master bedroom of the fine stone house Fraser had selected for him. In the gloom of the bedroom, with Babette snoring slightly in the bed, Burgyone opened the packet and placed his decoding template over the scrap of paper it contained. The message was from St. Leger. In only a few sentences, the junior officer proclaimed his mission east along the Mohawk River a failure. He wrote that he'd headed back to Canada and would attempt to lead what remained of his force along Burgoyne's path down Lake Champlain and then through the woods to Fort Edward.

Burgoyne pondered the message. I can't wait here for him, the commanding general concluded. I could use the troops, but we've been a full month getting this far from Champlain.

"Damn," Gentleman Johnny Burgoyne said aloud.

In her bed, Babette stirred. In just a moment, she'd sat up, glorious in her sleepy nakedness. Burgoyne watched her in the shadows. What a goddess this woman was, he reflected.

"Jack ..." she said.

"It's a message from St. Leger. He'll be along directly, he assures me, but I need to move this force south before he's likely to arrive.

We're still several weeks from Saratoga, my darling, and my orders require me to be in Albany before the snow flies. "

"Oh," Babette said sleepily as she sank back into the covers. She was silent for a moment. Then she said, "Come back to bed, Jack. I miss you. I'm lonely here."

Burgoyne chuckled and stood. He said. "We can do without St. Leger, if need be. It's Clinton's delay that nettles me. I surmise that Lord Howe, in his own charming fashion, is making a timely departure difficult for him."

Babette did not respond. Burgoyne was well aware that, unlike the Baroness von Riedesel, Babette grasped little of military tactics and cared even less for discussion of them. Moreover, it mattered little to Burgoyne what she understood beyond the need to polish her manners, a task she was accomplishing nicely through exposure to both the baroness and, especially, to Lady Acland. Babette had proven surprisingly charming and adept at ladylike small talk at dinner this evening. Her lover was pleased with her progress. After a moment, Burgoyne stood, dropped the robe to the floor and settled back into bed beside his mistress in the moist heat of the summer night. Tenderly, he wrapped his arms around Babette and gathered her close to him.

"If I were but the emperor instead of a mere general," he said, "then all would unfold flawlessly in crushing this troublesome rebellion."

"First minister to the king," Babette mumbled against his bare shoulder. "That's what you'll be."

Burgoyne squeezed his woman. "And you, my love, will be the

prime minister's shockingly, scandalously lovely lady."

In response, Babette snored.

℘

"All rise for the court of inquiry," Clerke called out as Burgoyne, Fraser and General Phillips, the artillery commander, emerged from the big stone house and moved to their seats at a table that had been placed on the porch. The day was gray and the air thick with the threat of rain – eternal rain, it seems, Fraser thought.

"Actually, Sir Francis, they're already standing," Burgoyne pointed out quietly to Clerke as the commanding general gestured to the hundreds of English and German regulars mixed in with the loyalists and the Indians gathered on the rolling, green front yard and in the dirt street in front of the house. They were glaring at one another with open menace. It was a solemn, surly group, Burgoyne noted.

"Yes, Sir," Clerke said as the officers took their seats behind the dining room table that had been moved outside. "Merely observing the formalities."

Burgoyne, in his powdered white wig and full dress uniform, glanced up at the crowd. A chair facing the officers had been placed on the lawn a dozen feet in front of the table. It would serve as a witness's dock.

"The court of inquiry into the death of His Majesty's subject Jane McCrea is now in session," the commanding general announced forcefully to the group. "This is not a formal criminal proceeding. In the absence of an appropriate prosecutor and legal counsel for the defendant, one Wyandot Panther, questioning will be conducted by the court itself. The Chevalier St. Luc is commanded to approach this court."

Le Loup emerged from a mob of milling Indians. Despite the heat he had added a long, flowing black coat to his attire of greasy buckskin. His wild, whitish scalp lock was tied in an incongruous pink silk ribbon, but he remained unshaven and still reeked of rum even all these hours after the sun's rise. Studying the degree of the man's dishevelment, Burgoyne doubted that the chevalier had slept. He found that realization satisfying. He wanted Le Loup as frightened of him as both the Tories and the rebels were of the savages.

"You will translate for the court," Burgoyne instructed Le Loup. "Bring forth the prisoner."

His arms tightly bound behind him with stout rope, Wyandot Panther was brought forward and seated in the chair. After his bonds were severed, he flexed his muscular arms and powerful hands. Panther eyed the court and the assemblage of hostile whites with open suspicion. Questions were asked by Burgoyne and Fraser. As translated by St. Luc, the Ottawa warrior's testimony was precisely the story the Indian had told the night before – that Jane McCrea had been killed by rebel pickets firing wildly and haphazardly in the heat of combat. The army's chief surgeon, having examined the girl's exhumed corpse that morning, testified that that her body had been struck by at least one musket ball, and possibly two more, and that the girl had been rudely scalped. Because of decomposition of the young woman's body in the fierce summer heat, the surgeon had been unable to determine if she had been sexually assaulted either before or after her death. Sarah McNeil, wrapped in a blanket and questioned gently by her cousin, was notably calmer than she had been the night before. Her terror of the previous evening had transformed itself into anger and outrage, but she could provide no illuminating details concerning Jane's death. Mrs. McNeil's only vivid recollections of the incident were her horror at being captured by the Indians, her fears that she would be raped and slaughtered and her hysterical relief after the brave who'd come storming into the Indian camp the previous evening had dragged her before Burgoyne. She'd witnessed Jane taken and led away on the horse, Mrs. McNeil testified, but she'd seen nothing of the girl after that, and Mrs. McNeil had been preoccupied beyond the point of capture with thoughts of her own unpleasant and impending demise. A still raging, weeping David Jones testified to having spotted Panther with what was obviously Jane's hair hanging from his breechclout and the Indian's immediate attack on Jones when the young officer had approached him with drawn saber. After two hours of testimony, Burgoyne, convinced that all available information on the incident had been ferreted out, called a halt to the proceeding. He then retired with his deputies to deliberate in the dining room of the big stone house as the crowd milled around out front.

"If we're fortunate, they'll refrain from slaughtering one another until we finish our conversation here," Fraser commented as he gazed through the window at the milling crowd.

"That's nothing I would count on," Phillips observed. "Both the loyalist troops and the savages yearn for a festival of butchery against one another."

"Wouldn't it be delightful if each side were to succeed?" Burgoyne said, "But only after we're finished with our business at Saratoga. Well, gentlemen, what course of action do you recommend?"

"Clearly, the savage did it," Fraser said without hesitation. "Execution is the only appropriate remedy."

"I agree," Phillips said. "Word of this incident is certain to inflame the citizenry against us, Jack. A prompt public hanging could conceivably mitigate that circumstance."

Burgoyne absorbed the advice, saying nothing for a long moment as his generals studied his impassive face. Then the commanding general said, "I have little doubt that Jane McCrea was cruelly and maliciously murdered by Wyandot Panther. What I do not have, however, is proof of that act sufficient to justify the savage's execution."

"Jack," Fraser said, "the proof is in the man's eyes and manner."

"There's little question, Simon, that if I hang this man the savages will immediately desert and wreak destruction on His Majesty's subjects here in the colonies and in Canada beyond. Moreover, I received disturbing news last night after I'd retired. Colonel St. Leger's advance down the Mohawk was halted at Fort Stanwix. He suffered substantial losses and has retreated back to Canada. St. Leger plans to join us after he regroups, but we cannot count on him arriving before we reach Saratoga. That means I'll be confronting this Gates chap with nearly two thousand fewer men – savages, loyalists and regulars – than we'd counted on."

"We'll still outnumber them by a hefty margin," Phillips pointed out.

"So, we will," Burgoyne conceded. "As near as I can determine from our loyalist spies, Gates will be fortunate to muster five thousand effectives, mostly untrained militia. Moreover, I retain every hope that General Clinton will arrive from New York City in time to aid us in this coming clash. We won't, I shouldn't imagine, arrive at Saratoga for perhaps another month."

"Then why does St. Leger's setback carry such weight in your decision on this matter?" Fraser asked.

Burgoyne said, "Simple prudence, Simon. The loss of the savages we have with us would constitute an undeniable blow to our efforts. They're maddeningly difficult to control, it's true, but they're profoundly useful as scouts and as advance forces. Given that reality and the fact that it has taken us more than a month to make our way only this far from Ticonderoga – and given that unfortunate, hugely costly bit of business at Bennington — I see no way to avoid the distasteful necessity of setting Wyandot Panther free. The consequences of doing otherwise would be unduly detrimental to our noble efforts in this campaign."

Fraser and Phillips exchanged worrisome glances.

"We'll lose many of the loyalists, at the very least," Fraser warned.

"No doubt," Burgoyne responded, frowning. "Colonel Skene is an able leader, but he most assuredly will be incapable of holding all his men. How many of them will desert us, however, remains to be seen, and we can surmise beyond all doubt that virtually all the Indian forces will depart if we indulge ourselves by giving this demon the hanging he so richly deserves."

"A devilish predicament," Phillips muttered.

"Indeed, Will," Burgoyne said, "but, as is often the case in life and nearly always the case in military matters, we face no flawless alternatives. We are compelled to abandon the quest for perfection without despair and to select the course of action with the smallest warts."

"These warts seem more like mountains, Jack," Fraser said.

Burgoyne rose from his chair, ending the discussion. "Mountains exist for the purpose of being climbed, Simon. Come, let us now go back outside and announce our findings."

ℰᴑ

Response to the court of inquiry's verdict was more rudely received than Burgoyne had expected. At the announcement that Wyandot Panther was a free man, a unified howl of protest rose up from the throats of the assembled Tory troops. Men swore and shouted. Several scuffles immediately broke out between the loyalists and the Indians that were quelled, and not without difficulty, by Fraser's regular troops weighing in with the butts of their Brown Bess muskets to restore order. As the melee died down, Skene burst from the mob and rushed to the table where Burgoyne, Fraser and Phillips sat.

"You can't do this, General," the red-faced Skene bellowed. "I won't be able to hold my men. They'll run back home to protect their women and children."

"The evidence is what the evidence is," Burgoyne responded. "You and your men, Colonel, have your sacred duty to the Crown to consider."

"And what of the Crown's duty to us as free Englishmen?" Skene demanded. "Do we not have a right to protection from the ravages of these barbarians?"

"Those protections are assured you," Burgoyne said in a low voice.

As Burgoyne spoke, a wide-eyed Le Loup, an English regular clutching each of his thick arms, was dragged unceremoniously before the table. His eyes rolling, the chevalier sank to his knees before Burgoyne.

"Mon General ..." he began.

"Silence," Burgoyne snapped. "Know this, Le Loup: if another atrocity occurs – just one more – you can be certain that you will decorate the nearest tree limb as soon as news of the violation reaches my ears. Moreover, my troops will then immediately turn their fire not on the rebels but on your children, as you refer to them. Do you understand me, Sir?"

Le Loup nodded his head frantically. "I do, mon General. I do understand."

"Then make certain that your children also understand. Get off your knees and speak to them. Do it now, Le Loup."

Le Loup immediately clambered to his feet and climbed atop the witness chair. He was shouting ineffectually for the attention of the mob of milling, brawling Indians and loyalist troops when Burgoyne rose to his feet, pulled his pistol from his waistband, cocked it and fired it into the air. The result was a sudden silence descending on the scene. Le Loup gazed over his shoulder at Burgoyne, whose eyes had narrowed to slits.

"Speak to them," Burgoyne hissed out, jamming the pistol back into his sash. "Tell them."

Le Loup spoke at the top of his lungs for a solid minute, first in one language and then in another, and all the while gesticulating wildly in sign language. Burgoyne studied the grim expressions of the Indians as their handler conveyed the commanding general's instructions to them. Their dark faces were impassive masks of stone. This time, none of the Indians spoke in response. Instead, in utter silence, they began to move away from the headquarters building and back toward their own camp. The loyalist troops did likewise. Le Loup dropped down from the chair and gestured helplessly, his hands beating the empty air, to Burgoyne.

"I have told them, mon General," he said. "I have told them they must without fail obey the will of our common father across the sea."

"And will they do that, you renegade spawn?" Skene snarled.

Le Loup shrugged. "If it is the will of God, yes, they will."

"My men will leave, General," Skene said. "I'll do what I can, but I'm not hopeful."

"And you, Colonel?" Burgoyne asked softly.

Skene stiffened. "I'm a loyal subject of the king, Sir. My life, my honor and my fortune are his."

Burgoyne nodded. "I expected no less of you, Colonel. Please rejoin your troops and do what you can to ease their fears."

"It's not their fears that concern me, General; it's their anger. But I'll do what I can."

Wearily, Burgoyne returned Skene's departing salute. He turned to go back into the headquarters building only to find Fraser on the porch stairs holding a bottle of the commanding general's fine French wine and two glasses.

"I just spoke privately to my cousin," Fraser said. "For what it may be worth, it's her belief that the unfortunate young woman probably was shot by rebel troops. In any event, I deem this a propitious moment for a drink. Join me, please."

Burgoyne smiled slightly. "So I shall, Simon. This quite likely will be the most easily defensible decision I shall make all day."

Morgan. 1777

"Well now," said Tim Murphy, gesturing with the muzzle of his Pennsylvania rifle through the bushes along the river, "what might we have here, I wonder?"

Both Murphy and Morgan dropped to their leather-clad knees, shielding themselves from view. Across the Hudson, more than a hundred yards of water away and a bit to the south of the two Army of the United States rangers, a mounted man clad in a dark green Tory uniform coat and clutching a Brown Bess musket had whipped a large, muscular horse into the water and was swimming the animal across the gray-green water. The big bay was low to the ground and thickly built, more designed for hauling than cavalry work.

"A Tory scout just prancin' into our embrace," Murphy whispered, the Donegal roots of his father's brogue thick in his speech despite his own birth in the colonies. "Should I spend a bit of lead on him, Colonel darlin', or should we wait here to politely slice the bastard's throat?"

Colonel Daniel Morgan laughed softly. "As if I didn't know what you'd prefer." Burly Tim Murphy shrugged. "My preference is the knife, y'know. Quieter."

"It's quieter," Morgan agreed. "Bloodier, though. The man might yowl on you."

"I'd rather save my bullets for the lobsterbacks," Murphy argued.

Morgan glanced at his comrade. Tim Murphy was a uniquely dangerous man, Morgan's favorite kind of ranger. In the woods, rugged, swarthy Tim Murphy was as silent as any Indian and, as the best shot in Morgan's command of extraordinary sharpshooters, far deadlier than most. At forty one, the tall, wide shouldered, thick limbed Morgan was a profoundly dangerous man himself. A hardened veteran of guerrilla combat both in the French and Indian War and in this conflict, the Virginia-born Morgan radiated an immense and easy strength. Morgan had developed a ferocious hatred of the English during the French and Indian War. That had occurred when a Morgan blow to the chin of a bullying English officer – in a unit commanded by a young John Burgoyne, coincidentally — had earned the youthful teamster five hundred lashes. Years later, Morgan had fought the English at Quebec in just a breechclout, armed with a knife and tomahawk and one of the precisely accurate Pennsylvania rifles that he insisted be issued to each of his rangers. The standard-issue, smooth-bore military musket was dependably lethal at fifty yards, more or less accurate at a hundred yards and sadly useless beyond that distance. Morgan and almost all his men could kill a squirrel at three hundred yards with their expensive, hand-crafted Pennsylvania rifles. Murphy had a special gift with that weapon. Morgan knew. At such a distance, Tim Murphy could place a slug squarely in the squirrel's eye.

"Let's just pull him down off his big, ugly horse and see if he has anything interesting to tell us," Morgan said in a low grunt. "Looks like he'll come out of the water down around there. Come along, Tim; let's you and me form a suitable welcoming committee."

The two rangers moved low and as silently as shadows behind the brush just above the river's rocky shore. Under orders from Gates to do what they could to slow Burgoyne's progress, Morgan and his men had moved north from Gates' Saratoga encampment to spend the past two weeks harrying Fraser's English advance troops as they cleared the road from Skenesboro to Fort Edward. While many of the Continental militia members had fired hurriedly at the laboring troops from hiding spots relatively close to the road – and were routinely cut down by returning English fire after they'd revealed their positions with their own spotty sniper fire — Morgan and Murphy and their comrades had taken up positions high in trees hundreds of yards off the road. From such distant, lofty perches they had casually picked off members of Fraser's corps with well-placed shots more or less at will and had vanished from their firing spots by the time the angry English troops arrived. With the road now clear and Burgoyne's army finally in place at the Hudson's eastern shore, Morgan's rangers were low on powder and shot and were filtering back to Saratoga in groups of two or three, hoping to repeat their success as snipers when the English forces resumed their march southward on the western bank.

First, though, it would be useful to pick off Burgoyne's Indian and Tory scouts in advance of the main column, as Morgan and Murphy planned to do with this man, whose horse was just emerging from the water snorting and breathing hard after the exertion of swimming the Hudson. As the Tory scout swung down from his mount to lead the animal up the steep bank to the path along the river's western shore, Murphy burst forth from the bushes, slammed into the man and drove him down into the mud. They rolled and grappled for a moment as Morgan stepped almost casually from the trees to watch the clash. Morgan laughed aloud as Murphy's knife was knocked from the ranger's hand by the scout's frantic struggle.

"Don't let him hurt you now, Tim," Morgan said mockingly. "He already has your skirts dirty."

The Tory was a big man, no more than thirty, and Murphy was struggling to subdue him. The contest struck Morgan as more or less a draw. Morgan gazed at the pair for a long moment and then swung the barrel of his rifle toward the Tory as he broke free of Murphy's grasp and gained his feet.

"Hands in the air," Morgan ordered in a low voice, "or I'll kill you where you stand."

Wide-eyed, the Tory raised his hands and shook his head. "Don't fire. I surrender. I'm deserting."

"Deserting, is it?" Murphy gasped as he clambered out of the mud at the water's edge. "Cowardly royalist bastard. Go on and shoot him, Colonel darlin'."

"Don't shoot me, please," the Tory begged. "I've got a wife and child on a farm near Saratoga. I have to get back there to keep them safe from Gentleman Johnny's bloody savages. Kill me and you'll be killing them, too. I'm no threat to you. My days of fighting for the Crown are over."

Morgan and Murphy exchanged glances. Morgan eyed the big man, who now had his hands firmly above his head as Morgan had ordered, as Murphy retrieved his knife.

"Who's your commander?" Morgan asked.

"Lieutenant Jones commanded my cohort," the Tory said. "He's a good man, but the savages butchered his bride to be, and Burgoyne let the murderer go. Not a living soul is safe while those devils run wild, as Burgoyne is permitting them to do. We're all leaving, all us loyalist troops. We have families to protect, either here or in Canada. Gentleman Johnny won't keep the savages in check – or maybe he can't; I don't know, and I don't care. All I know is that my wife and child are dearer to me than any king ever was. I'm going home if you'll let me, and I beg you to do so. I'm no danger to any rebel – only to any red devil I see come near my farm."

Morgan and Murphy exchanged glances. Morgan's rifle was aimed squarely at the Tory's middle, only a few paces away.

"What do you think, Tim?" Morgan asked. "Is he really going home or will he race back to Burgoyne to take his place back beside his comrades?"

"I can't be sure," Murphy admitted. "To remove all doubt, Colonel darlin', we really should kill the man. It would be only prudent."

"I have no comrades left with Burgoyne," the Tory said. "In the past few days we've all left – most of us, at least, all but Colonel Skene and a few dozen more who care more for king than for loved ones. I'm just one of the few deserters heading south. Most of the others have families north of Fort Edward and up into Quebec."

"You were what – a thousand loyalists or so?" Morgan demanded.

"About," the Tory said. "But we're loyalists no more. If they won't protect our families against the savages, then what is there to be loyal to?"

Morgan eyed the man and thought about it. Then he said, "Begone with you, then. Go on ahead of us on this trail. Try to double back, and we'll know and hunt you down. And leave the horse."

"Please," the Tory said. "I need the mare for plowing and harvesting."

Murphy brandished his knife. "You heard the colonel. Begone, and leave the horse."

The Tory grasped at the reins of the animal, which was standing near him. "I need the mare to feed my family," he insisted.

Morgan lowered his rifle. "Let him take the beast," he told Murphy. "Any man so eager to risk death to keep a plow horse is not a man on his way back to fight for the English."

Morgan and Murphy and the other rangers, moving along different trails and joining up only periodically, took nearly a week to make their way back to Saratoga for more powder and shot. Along the way they ambushed several other Tory deserters and killed only the ones who insisted on resisting capture and questioning. As the rangers drew nearer the encampment they joined one another finally in ragged groups along the trail down the west side of the Hudson. Morgan moved his men only in single file or two abreast.

The contrast with the precision marching of the English and German forces was both striking and purposeful. Morgan had learned early on in the last war against the French that European-trained officers insisted that their troops move almost trancelike in slow, ungainly formations developed for troop movements along the country roads and in the open fields of the Continent. His own military tactics developed from fighting both beside and against Indians. Morgan viewed such formal marching formations as slow, ungainly and perilous in the heavily wooded terrain of the colonies. The bigger the mass of men, he knew, the sweeter the target for snipers and for sneak, hit-and-run attackers from the forest, a favorite Indian tactic.

At the same time, though, Morgan was aware, engaging English forces in mass battle formation was a risky business on open ground. Under the iron discipline of their lieutenants and sergeants, English troops not on the march spent as many as six hours a day in drill, physical exercise and weapons training. A European-style musket volley followed by a tightly controlled bayonet charge was a fearsome thing to confront. While the rebel troops were farmers and shopkeepers first and poorly trained soldiers only temporarily, the English soldier was a lifetime enlistee whose only work was the unquestioning, businesslike slaughter of enemies of the king, and the typical English soldier had nearly a decade in the ranks. Luckily, Washington had once remarked to Morgan, the English Empire had not fought a major war in a dozen years, so only its older soldiers had direct combat experience. Nonetheless, Washington was in no hurry to engage the royal forces in the open field, and neither was

Morgan.

It was late in the afternoon on the sixth day after Burgoyne had arrived at Fort Edward that Morgan and his rangers arrived back at Gates' position at Saratoga. They scaled the hill from the river, gave the password to the pickets and then made their way into the camp past the recently erected earthen bulwarks and the few pieces of cannon Schuyler had managed to scrounge up before Gates took over command. Morgan dismissed his men under their officers and sergeants to find food and a place to sleep. The ranger colonel then made his way through surging throngs of men in leather and homespun to the small log house that Gates had selected as his headquarters. Morgan was amazed at the size of the camp. Sprawling now over several large farm fields, the encampment had grown conspicuously since Morgan had led his men out of it and to the north. Literally thousands of local militiamen had made their way to Gates' banner, it seemed. He found Gates at his desk, scribbling furiously on scraps of paper. The commanding general greeted Morgan warmly and listened intently to his report about the harassment rebel troops had inflicted upon the English as they cleared the road to Fort Edward.

"That's the best we can hope for, then," Gates said. "We've delayed them, and we reduced their forces somewhat with the victory we enjoyed at Bennington, but they're on their way now, and we must be ready to stop them here. I'm beginning to actually believe we can do that, Colonel."

"I share your optimism only to a certain degree, General," Morgan said. "Most assuredly, this is good ground to defend, but the problem with it is that warfare on the open field can't be avoided once Burgoyne manages to make his way up the bluff, as he surely will. You realize, Sir, I'm sure, that this will be our first open field clash with the king's army in this entire rebellion. It is, in short, precisely the circumstance they've been waiting for."

Gates nodded. "I know. General Washington has avoided such open field combat, and wisely so. The Royal Army has fifty thousand highly disciplined regulars throughout the empire, and we've never managed to raise more than eighteen thousand regulars at any one time."

"And that number is closer to six thousand at the moment," Morgan pointed out, "throughout the whole of the colonies."

"Luckily," Gates said, "Burgoyne has no more than eight thousand with him on this campaign — and, at this point, probably less."

"Certainly less. We came across a number of Tory deserters on our way back from Fort Edward. It seems that the Tories are leaving Burgoyne because the woman of some Tory officer was murdered by the savages."

For a moment, Gates treated his ranger chief to a broad smile, a rare expression for the taciturn commanding general. "I heard about that. For several days, we've had militiamen from this region and from New England flooding into camp with the tale. She was a local girl named McCrea, and this development seems to be working in our favor in recruiting."

"It has certainly worked in our favor in terms of demoralizing the Tories."

"If we're lucky," Gates said, "they'll all desert Burgoyne by the time he arrives here. More importantly, though, this unfortunate incident seems to be bringing us the militiamen we so desperately need to swell our numbers. I've been writing letters to each town and village for miles around and well into New England. I'm begging for militiamen to join us here to help stop the savages in their depredations. That's what I'm doing at the moment, actually. I also sent a message to Burgoyne reprimanding him for permitting this murder. He has not responded to me as of yet, but the purpose of that letter was not to persuade him to mend his ways; it was to spur enlistments. We desperately need the militia, Colonel, and now we seem to be getting them."

Morgan nodded. He well understood the difficulties in recruiting volunteers to the rebel cause. It was hardly popular with most of the colonists, whose primary goal was to be left alone by both sides. Many of the regular Army of the United States soldiers had volunteered only for one-year enlistments, and the militiamen came and went as they pleased, paying scant attention to military training or discipline but willing to fight surprisingly effectively beside the regulars when sufficiently aroused. If the McCrea woman's murder had aroused them, then fine. Schuyler's inability to persuade the militia to fight the English at Saratoga had been his great leadership failure, which was why Morgan was reporting to Gates in the first place, as both men well knew. Unlike Schuyler, whose presence was off-putting but commanding, Gates was not an inspiring leadership figure to say the least. But he had a keen eye for opportunity, and he had no intention of letting this tragedy pass without taking full and complete advantage of it for his own purposes.

Gates took his place back behind his field desk, taking his quill pen in hand once more. "I have more letters to send out, Colonel," he said. "I'm most grateful to you for both the thoroughness of your report and for the fine soldiering you and your men displayed on the route to Fort Edward. But these words on paper may turn out to be more valuable weapons for us than powder and shot. You are dismissed, Sir."

Morgan stiffened slightly at the abrupt dismissal, another display of the commanding general's dismal social skills, but Morgan saluted without a word and exited the cabin. As he moved through the now darkened camp, past the campfires of the newly arrived militiamen, he strained to hear their conversations around the flames. A born leader in stark contrast to the perpetually tone-deaf Gates, Morgan was always tightly attuned to the mood of the men. Their chatter tonight, he noted, seemed to be more or less exclusively about Burgoyne and Jane McCrea and the colonists' fears for their own communities as the English drew near with their Indian allies. By nature, Morgan was a realistic man, recklessly courageous but almost fatalistic. He accepted his mortality stoically and did not number a desire for advanced old age among his ambitions. A drinker and a gambler and a soldier mainly because of his passion for adventure and his distaste for boredom, Morgan harbored only pallid hope of surviving the rebellion and virtually no hope of escaping hanging if it failed. Still, he found himself buoyed tonight by his talk with his commander and by the buzz of conversation he was catching from around the campfires.

It's really possible, I suppose, Morgan thought as he snaked his way through the crowded, bustling camp toward his own troops. We could win this little dust-up after all.

Babette. 1777

Babette sat up in bed and yawned. The sun was high, and the room was empty. She had expected that. By privilege and inclination, Babette was not an early riser. Each morning, well before dawn, Burgoyne habitually rose from the bed they shared to garb himself in a field uniform and descend the stairs to study maps and confer with his officers over tea. This was his unswerving routine no matter how late he and his lady had entertained their guests in the big stone house near the river and no matter how many hours the commanding general and his lady had devoted to lovemaking after the guests had departed.

Burgoyne's desire for Babette seemed unquenchable, she'd noted to herself many times. Despite the nearly thirty years between them, Jack displayed not only a degree of virility sufficient to exhaust Babette in their bed at night, he also pounded against her with such spirited, relentless vigor and penetrated her so deeply that Babette often came awake mornings with a sweet soreness in her loins to stir her memories of their passions of the night before. Jack possessed many virtues, she thought to herself each morning as she came awake alone in the bed they shared, but none more conspicuous than his gifts as a lover. She was acutely aware that the valet in the hall outside their door had often heard Babette's shrill voice as Jack brought her to the height of lustful joy, but she didn't care. Peter had only rarely stirred her passion in such powerful fashion, and, deep in her heart, she understood that pleasing the general in such a manner was the bedrock of her hold on him.

Babette wasn't as thoughtful or as worldly as Burgoyne, and she occupied a station in life well below his, but she well understood that she could touch him in the very depth of his being through lovemaking. She knew, too, that Jack took satisfaction and pride in his ability to provoke such sounds of abandon from his youthful bedmate. It was a relationship in which Burgoyne — like all men in relationships with women, Babette often pondered — held all the power. But not in this — not in this one, crucially important area. In the shadows of the bedroom, Babette could render Burgoyne virtually helpless, stripping away from him not only his clothing but also his casual, self-possessed dignity. She could reduce him to the essential man he truly was — with none of the grandeur of his lofty rank, with none of the smooth artifice or charming sophistication that was his hallmark at all other times.

And Babette knew, deep in her soul, that it was critical for him to be able to fan the fires of her lust as well as her adoring, totally approving love. She understood Burgoyne's deep need to be able to satisfy her desire in clear, unambiguous terms. So, let the valet who slept on the floor outside the bedroom hear her grunt and groan and shout and scream. Let the sound of her voice slice through the thick wooden door and into the hall where the valet lay, no doubt wide-eyed, in the night. If anything, Babette knew, the whispered, chuckling tales of the commanding general's prowess as a lover only enhanced his stature with the men he led. Burgoyne knew that, too, she understood, which probably was why he never attempted to muffle her soaring cries in the night.

Rising from the cover nude – Burgoyne insisted that they always sleep unclothed – Babette made her way to one of the bedroom's front windows. Down at the river bank, she could see Burgoyne and several other officers conferring as a large, milling mob of men labored at some mysterious task beside the water. Babette made appropriate use of the chamber pot, scrubbed in the wash basin atop the dresser, clad herself in a breezy summer dress and made her way to the first floor of the large house. After tea and a bite of muffin – Babette always ate lightly in the morning after those heavy meals amid the perpetual round of evening entertaining – she made her way down the soft dirt of the main road to where the commanding general stood, deep in conversation with several other officers. Under the direction of Lieutenant Twiss, Burgoyne's engineering officer and perhaps a dozen sergeants, the soldiers were sweating and straining in the rising summer heat, hauling tree limbs and sawing at them, unfolding sheets of canvas from the ox carts and restraining themselves from their habitual stream of vulgarities and obscenities at the approach of the general's lady.

Babette accepted with a dazzling smile the slight bows of Burgoyne and his subordinates. "What are you building this morning?" she asked.

"A bridge, Madam," Burgoyne explained. "An army with cannon and supply wagons cannot cross a river without a bridge. And, where no bridge exists, one must necessarily be created."

Babette gazed across the broad expanse of gray-green water. She was a strong swimmer, but she wasn't sure she could have paddled successfully all the way to the distant western shore. "It's a great distance. Won't it take a considerable amount of time to erect such a large bridge?"

"Far less than one might think, my love," Burgoyne said, smiling. "The bridge our canny young Lieutenant Twiss will erect for us will be only a temporary floating structure with a tightly bound roadway of logs resting upon pontoons. The pontoons will be fashioned from wooden frameworks covered with the large sheets of canvas we brought with us on ox-carts from Canada – after all that canvas has been bathed in oil and grease, that is, to prevent the water from gushing through it."

For a long moment, Babette watched the men work. Already the logs for the roadway were being trimmed to a length of no more than a dozen feet, and a squad of men were fashioning the frames of what looked like crude rowboats. Yes, she could see how this would work – a string of canvas-hulled boats lashed together, floating all the way across the wide expanse of the river, with a log roadway over them..

"It's exceedingly clever, Jack," she said. "I would never have thought of such a thing."

"I must confess that I didn't think of it, either, my darling," Burgoyne said. "For the concept we can offer our profound thanks to the memory of Xerxes, the long-ago king of Persia. Twelve centuries ago, he invaded Greece with an army of one hundred thousand. He had to transport his army across the Hellespont where it joins the Black Sea, and to accomplish that the king required a bridge. This design is what he came up with — although he used a sturdy, ocean-going ship to anchor each end of the structure. We'll have to make do with a few stout trees along each shoreline."

"I've never heard of Xerxes," Babette admitted. "Did his invasion go successfully?"

"Well," Burgoyne explained, "Xerxes' first effort at bridge-building failed rather dismally, so Xerxes beheaded his engineers and appointed new ones to complete the chore more effectively. You are listening, I trust, Lieutenant Twiss."

"I am, Sir," Twiss called back from the shoreline, where he was directing the work of the frame builders. "This will function rather nicely, I assure you. As I recall, Sir, Xerxes ultimately failed in his invasion and was himself beheaded by his palace guard."

"Yes," Burgoyne said, "that's precisely what happened, poor chap. My hopes for this invasion, however, remain cheerfully high. Like you, Lieutenant, I'm also rather attached to my head."

Burgoyne's remarks produced a titter of laughter from his officers, as often happened. Babette never knew for sure if the laughter generated among Burgoyne's officers by his airy remarks was a product of flattery or genuine amusement. Both, she had concluded early on in her love affair with the commanding general. Jack was always cynically witty and dependably entertaining in conversation, but he also was the commander. As each of Burgoyne's subordinates was well aware, he held the fates of these officers squarely in his hands.

Babette slid her arm around Burgoyne's. "Walk with me along the river for a while — unless you plan to saw a log or two for the roadway yourself, that is."

"My lady has identified my weakness," Burgoyne said to his officers. "I'm insufficiently skilled with a saw to be of any further use here. Good day, gentlemen. Carry on."

His officers snapped to attention and saluted. Casually, Burgoyne returned the salutes and began to stroll with his mistress along the river's shore. In marked contrast to the dismal gray skies that had been so conspicuous throughout the campaign, this was a dazzling day in late August with a gentle, warming sun showering down on the Hudson. Burgoyne and Babette had made only a few hundred yards under the tall trees at the water's edge, occupying themselves with flirting small talk, when they caught the sound of hoof beats behind them. They turned simultaneously as Frasier, his face grim atop his gray gelding, reined in his mount and slipped from the saddle, issuing his commander a perfunctory salute.

"Simon," Burgoyne said expansively, "why such a dark expression? I do hope that no harm has befallen my chamber musicians. I know how grievously such a disaster would distress you."

"It's the loyalist troops," Fraser responded. "I've just received a report from Colonel Skene. As of this morning, his command was down to fewer than fifty men. It's his prediction that most of those now remaining will be gone by tomorrow morning."

Burgoyne's expression never changed, but the tone of his voice lowered. "The Jane McCrea business, without doubt."

"That's Skene's view, Jack. Young David Jones was one of the early deserters. He was highly regarded by his men, and others followed his lead. Colonel Skene, of course, entreats me to report that he personally will be with us until the end, but he essentially has no command left."

"A good man, Skene. Well, he did warn us, did he not?"

"That leaves us down nearly another five hundred men," Fraser said. "Moreover, Le Loup says that many of his savages seem to have departed as well. They go into the woods to scout and then simply never return to camp. He counts more than a hundred and fifty of them gone now. Frankly, I'm not sure the old renegade won't join them before we cross the river."

"What's the savages' complaint?" Burgoyne demanded, a touch of anger in his voice. "No one was punished for the McCrea incident."

Fraser shrugged. "Le Loup says they complained that the campaign is taking too much time. They have harvests to attend to at home. Moreover, he told me, they were wounded by the disapproval of their white father. He means you, Jack. They complained to him that you've refused to let them fight for our common father across the sea in their most effective manner."

"Yes, well, I damned well did disapprove, Simon, and rightly so. And not nearly enough, it would seem. You were right, you know, we should have hanged that chap – Panther, or whatever the fellow's name was. Well, the loss of the loyalists can damage us in the long run ..."

"... but the loss of the savages has a more immediate impact," Fraser said quietly, finishing his commander's thought.

Burgoyne merely nodded silently. Babette studied the faces of both men. Fraser lost his easy smile and became habitually glum, she'd noticed; whenever military matters were discussed — always fretting over this operational detail or that one. This was the first time, however, that she'd witnessed anything that even resembled a crack in Burgoyne's generally carefree demeanor.

"Why is the loss of the savages such a problem?" Babette demanded. "Aren't we better off without them and their bloody ways?"

Fraser and Burgoyne exchanged glances. This was the first time Babette had indicated the slightest interest in the business of the campaign, and neither general was accustomed to responding to the questions of the women accompanying the army.

"It's the bridge, my love," Burgoyne explained. "The pontoons are vulnerable to sniper fire from the forest – the rebels' specialty. The savages could easily keep the forest clear for us. Without them, building and protecting the bridge will take longer as we dispatch our regulars into the woods to hunt down the snipers. That'll cost us valuable time."

"Couldn't General Phillips move cannon to the river shore and fire grapeshot into the forest?" Babette asked. "That's what he did to protect the landing at Ticonderoga. I'll never forget that racket. Wouldn't that help protect the bridge?"

Again, Burgoyne and Fraser exchanged glances, and then the commanding general burst into spirited laughter.

"A new military strategist in our midst, Simon," Burgoyne said, "and her idea is a sound one."

"Indeed," Fraser said, chuckling.

. "That's precisely what General Phillips did, my love," Burgoyne said, "and it's what he'll do here as well. Once again, we'll release what Sir Francis so delights in calling the thunder of captains."

"The bridge will still take longer to build than it should without the savages rummaging about the forest hunting snipers," Fraser told his commander, "but the lady is correct. The big guns should eventually be able to buy us our passage to the western shore. Congratulations, Madame. Your plan shall be adopted."

"And instantly," Burgoyne said. "Phillips and his artillery men have had too easy a time of it thus far. Now we shall make them work. Simon, please inform General Phillips that he must bring his guns forward immediately."

"And so I shall, Jack," Fraser said, saluting smartly.

After Fraser had galloped off down the shoreline on his gray gelding, Burgoyne took Babette's hand.

"A capital idea, my love. Had you been born a man, Bab, you'd have made a fine military thinker."

"Had I been born a man," Babette replied, "I would be in the forests of Quebec trapping beaver like my father."

"And my life would be left desolate and immeasurably impoverished," the commanding general told his mistress as he planted a kiss on her cheek.

"You'd thought of it already, hadn't you?" Babette said, somewhat accusingly.

Burgoyne stopped and gazed out over the sun-drenched river. His expression was uncharacteristically sheepish. "Grapeshot through the trees is a more or less standard tactic against irregulars in forested regions, my love. Yes, we would have preferred to have used the savages – not merely to protect the bridge but also to spread an appropriate level of terror among the rebels. Now, however, we'll make do nearly as well with General Phillips' guns, I suspect. It was quite clever of you to think of it, though. It's not as though you're a seasoned military campaigner."

"You and Simon were merely humoring me," Babette said.

"We were attempting to treat both you and your shrewdly intuitive suggestion with due respect. My most sincere apologies if we were somewhat awkward in that well-intentioned effort. Both Simon and I are better soldiers than diplomats, after all."

Babette did not immediately respond. Life with Burgoyne had taught her the virtues of restraint, but her experience with men from the gentle classes of Europe was severely limited, so she never knew for sure when she was being condescended to or being accorded an appropriate level of regard. Despite Babette's fondness for Lady Acland, she often felt the same in her company and, especially, in the company of the baroness, although Jack insisted relentlessly that Babette study their ways and manners and learn to emulate them. Deep inside, Babette feared that, unlike a real lady, she would never master the skill to present more than one face to anyone – and that face, though lovely, would always offer a painfully transparent window into what was genuinely in her mind at any given moment. Sometimes she despaired that she was condemned for all eternity to be only who she was, no more and no less, no matter whose arm she decorated. Therefore, when confronted with uncertainty about whether she was being subtly ridiculed, it had become Babette's habit to dismiss the entire matter and change the subject. That's what she did now.

"What about the loyalists, Jack?" Babette asked. "How will you replace them?"

"Clinton," the commanding general said. "If he leaves New York quickly enough, we shall have more than sufficient forces for a quick and decisive victory over the rebels at Saratoga. If Clinton fails to join me in a timely fashion, we still should be able to win the day without undue difficulty."

"Will there be more of them than of us?" she asked.

"It's irrelevant, Bab," Burgoyne told his lady with uncharacteristic curtness. "The mob can't stand successfully against the English soldier in the open field. They know that; it's why they've never tried. The entire rebel strategy depends on outlasting us, not on defeating us man to man. At Saratoga, they'll have no choice but to engage us on our own terms, and Saratoga will pave the way for total victory for His Majesty's army."

"The Grand Strategy," Babette said.

"It's taking shape," Burgoyne said, patting her hand. "And you've now helped it along in more ways than one."

Fraser. 1777

Construction of the pontoon bridge, as Fraser had predicted, turned out to be a lengthy and arduous affair, even with literally thousands of hard-laboring soldiers thrown into the task under the command of the energetic and assiduous Lieutenant Twiss. As the forests along the river's eastern shore were denuded of trees to create the roadway and the sounds of axes and saws biting into wood filled the village just outside the sagging stockade of logs that constituted Fort Edward, the piles of material for the structure slowly began to pile up on the river's shore. Sniper fire had been a persistent annoyance throughout the early stages of the task, but the moment the English introduced the canvas-covered pontoons to the water sniper fire from the woods on both sides of the river intensified markedly. Roughly twelve to fourteen feet in length and riding as high as four feet above the water line, the pontoons presented tempting targets for rebel snipers who'd been awaiting the opportunity to destroy them.

Each time a pontoon was perforated by a musket ball it had to be pulled from the river and its canvas covering either repaired or replaced. And, all the while, General Phillips' big, booming guns responded to the sniper fire by propelling jagged, metal death into the forests on both sides of the Hudson all around the construction site. The sound of the artillery was deafening, but the effect of Phillip's beloved cannon fire was mixed. Often both cannon fire and construction were halted for hours at a time while the few remaining Indian warriors, mainly a separate party of Mohawks who'd traveled in from the west after St. Leger's defeat, joined Fraser's sullenly grumbling advance troops in scouring the woods on both sides of the river for rebel marksmen, who displayed a maddening capacity to melt into the forest and then return with more sniper fire when the English troops had abandoned the scene.

"It's all attrition," Fraser explained to Babette and the other ladies at one of Burgoyne's elegant dinner parties. "We're managing to build and deploy pontoons on the river more quickly than they can damage them. We have literally thousands of men at work on the task. And now our brilliant young Lieutenant Twiss has come up with a canny mechanism for protecting the pontoons from the snipers. Each goes into the water with an armored shell made of logs than hangs off either side of the canvas boat."

"How are the armored shells of logs attached?" asked Lady Acland.

"Ropes," Fraser explained. "Each side of log armor hangs from several stout lines across the open top of the pontoon. The logs can't be more than a few inches thick, however. Otherwise, the weight of the arrangement would sink the pontoon, especially after we place the log roadway atop the entire structure and try to move carts and cannon over it. But the armor catches most of the musket balls. A clever chap, our Lieutenant Twiss. He says he must be, or the commanding general will chop off his head."

"Zis is slow going," the baroness said sourly. "Too slow. Ve haff taken too long to reach zis point."

"Yes," Fraser agreed. He liked the baroness and had come to respect her judgment in military matters. She seldom asked a foolish question, and her observations were unerringly on the mark. "But we'll get it done soon enough now. Before we capture Albany and settle in for a winter's rest in advance of sweeping into New England in the spring, we must subdue that rebel position on the western shore. This is the only way to get there."

"Schuyler was shrewd to take a position so far north of ze town," the baroness said. "Freddie says it is good for us zat he vas replaced."

"Most assuredly, Madame," Fraser said. "General Gates is a

supply man and a bureaucrat — not a fighting commander. And fight he will have to do once we descend upon him."

"Vunce ve get across zis river," the baroness von Riedesel said.

Work on the bridge progressed at a quicker pace once the moist heat of the summer began to evaporate. When construction was complete in mid-September, Burgoyne moved his army to the river's western shore in only two days, working from dawn to dusk. From the start, with the army's band on the river's shoreline playing stirring music to buoy the spirits of the invading force, the crossing was predictably precarious. At any one time, the pontoon bridge was able to bear the weight only of a few supply carts and cannon and only a few dozen troops, well spread out in single file. It bobbed and swayed ominously in the water as the oxen-powered supply carts, disturbingly exposed to the fire of any rebel snipers on either shoreline, were driven gingerly across the vast expanse of the Hudson.

Fraser took the lead position for the crossing, slowly guiding his gray gelding over the uneven log roadway, letting the animal place its hooves as it deemed fit. Horses were particularly fussy on the topic of footing, Fraser knew. The dull-witted oxen hauling the supply carts were far less graceful, and several of the carts slipped off the roadway during the two-day crossing, dragging the lowing oxen into the water. When that happened, the carts and oxen had to be hauled out of the water on the western shore by swearing, frustrated soldiers. At the end of the second day, after Riedesel's Germans had crossed, the elegant calash carrying Babette, Lady Acland and the baroness and her children was taken across the bridge on its own, to minimize any prospect of mishap. The final officer across the bridge was Burgoyne, riding alone and with agonizing slowness in full dress uniform atop his showy white charger and making a great display of it all. The commanding general arrived on the Hudson's western shore to the spirited, rowdy cheers of his men. Fraser breathed a sigh of relief as the hooves of his commander's horse touched the dirt at the bridge's terminus.

"You made a lovely target out there for any sniper," Fraser whispered in Burgoyne's ear.

"Courage, Simon," Burgoyne said. "Always courage."

"I well understand the virtue of a display of the commander's disregard for danger," Fraser said, "but that was a bit of a chance, Jack."

"The troops needed it. This bridge was soul-killing work for fighting men. An extra ration of rum for all this evening, Simon. We're now about the genuine business of war rather than mere preparation. I want their spirits high. Have your advance troops found for me a suitable headquarters?"

"They have. I inspected it myself. It's a conspicuously luxurious farmhouse atop a bluff slightly downriver that commands a lofty view of the Hudson. And you'll never guess who owns it – General Schuyler. It's his country home. It's the sort of place I wouldn't mind owning myself, actually."

Burgoyne smiled. "Your taste has yet to fail me, General Fraser. Please take your rightful place at the front of the column and guide us to our new headquarters."

As soon as it had served its purpose, and far more quickly than it had been constructed, the bridge was broken apart. Supplies were loaded into the canvas-covered pontoons, which had now become cargo boats, and the floating supply train began to move southward down the river, pulled by soldiers with oars in wooden boats that had been hauled overland from Lake Champlain. By nightfall, the army and its followers were taking up positions and pitching tents around the gracious house Fraser had selected as his commander's new base of operations. Fraser ordered the placement of pickets and muskets loaded and held ready all around the encampment. Phillips placed his big guns in strategic locations. Now that they had crossed the river, Fraser knew, the rebel scouts would be probing the English camp for weakness at every opportunity. Fraser inspected the camp in detail as the men settled in around the building and in the fields atop the bluff.

For most of his men, Fraser knew, dinner would be sparse that evening, although the extra rum ration Burgoyne had approved would dull the rumblings of their stomachs. So much time and effort had been devoted to the river crossing over the past week that foraging had been necessarily neglected and food supplies were running disturbingly low. Fraser was conferring with the army's chief commissary officer when a headquarters courier arrived with a hand-scrawled message from Burgoyne. The senior officers and their ladies were invited once again to dine with the commanding general and his lady. Chamber musicians would entertain. Could Fraser possibly attend?

Simon Fraser rolled his eyes. The battle was now at hand. After many months of hardship, tortured troop movements and unexpected setbacks, the army had crossed the Hudson and was now within striking distance of its enemy, right down the road. And Burgoyne still persisted in this frivolous entertaining, night after night. Fraser had figured out long ago that the parties were designed less to raise the spirits of the senior officers and their ladies and more for the benefit of Burgoyne's Canadian woman, who clearly loved the glitter of such elegant evenings.

It was not that Burgoyne was blinded to reality by love, Fraser understood, nor was the commanding general inattentive to the needs of the campaign. But his steadfast fixation on this woman, as lovely as she was, struck Fraser as unseemly under circumstances so grave and immediate. Men would die soon, many hundreds of them – probably thousands, actually — and horribly. Fraser remained confident about the outcome of the coming clash. Like Burgoyne, Fraser well understood that the English army massed in field formation and firing in disciplined volleys at short range had no equal on the planet. And no army on Earth could stand against an English bayonet charge in the open field, a tactic that Gates could not avoid confronting if he were to prevent the invading force from taking Albany. No, Fraser had no doubt about the coming victory, but he felt strongly that it was past time for Burgoyne to focus all his energy and attention on the battle and only on the battle. As he scrubbed himself in his spacious tent, shaved in the tiny mirror that hung from the main tent pole and dressed in a clean field uniform, Fraser determined to tell that to his friend that evening.

The party was in full sway when Fraser made his way to Schuyler's house as the sun was setting over the forests at the western end of the departed gentleman farmer's charred fields – fields meticulously burned to cinders by the property's owner to deny food to the invading English troops. Still, Burgoyne's personal commissary staff had managed to locate a hapless pig, a half dozen chickens and a store of vegetables from a section of field too wet from the endless summer rain for Schuyler to successfully set afire before fleeing south in advance of the advancing English army. These foodstuffs, deftly prepared in the mansion's kitchens behind the main building, occupied the center of a gigantic table in a dining room so large it could qualify as a banquet hall. Senior officers and their ladies juggling full plates and glasses of fine wine milled about the grand house as Burgoyne's chamber musicians played in a corner of Schuyler's sweeping ballroom. Fraser found Clerke pouring from a bottle of good burgundy into one of Schuyler's delicate crystal glasses.

"Good evening, Sir Francis," Fraser said jovially to the commanding general's aide. "Any where might our noble commander be?"

"Outside," Clerke said. "He's taking in the view of the river from atop the bluff out front while awaiting his lady's appearance. She's taking her time coming down to dinner this evening. I presume that the day's journey has wearied her ladyship unacceptably."

"You seem to be just a trifle drunk rather early in the evening, Sir Francis," Fraser said with a smile but in a firm voice. "I would advise you as a friend I hold in high regard to avoid using the term 'her ladyship' in Jack's presence."

Clerke laughed. "I know better than to do that, of course. But thank you for your advice, General. I shall strive harder to curb my acid tongue. It's so difficult, though. Lady Charlotte was such a marvelous, gracious lady. And this Canadian girl, well .."

"Caution and prudence, Sir Francis," Fraser said, raising his eyebrows and relieving the commanding general's chief aide of the bottle of wine. Moving away with the smile still plastered on his face and grabbing two glasses from the table near the roast pig, Fraser moved outside the house and spotted Burgoyne, still in his dress uniform, standing atop the bluff overlooking the river. Simon Fraser approached his commander holding the bottle high in one hand and the glasses in the other.

"I saw you standing there," he told Burgoyne, "and I thought to myself, 'There's a man who might benefit from a drink.'"

"Your perception is both flawless and laudable, Simon, as always. Are our troops properly settled in for the night?"

"Oh, yes," Fraser said. "The extra rum ration is being warmly received, but they're keeping their muskets handy. General Phillips has placed an iron ring of cannon about the south end of the encampment."

"Good," Burgoyne said, sipping at the wine Fraser had poured for him. "We're now but days away from Gates' position at Saratoga. I need the men relaxed and happy tonight and then properly primed for battle by week's end."

"Will we be attacking that quickly?"

"It's not inconceivable that they'll attack us now that we've crossed the Hudson," Burgoyne said. "General Arnold is reportedly among their leadership, and you know his reputation for aggressive action. This afternoon, a party of some two hundred rebel irregulars was spotted along the road ahead. You were in the field, so I ordered some of the baron's troops to engage them, but the rebels faded away at the approach of the Germans. They fled like rabbits into the woods atop the heights."

"That's what they do," Fraser said. I've had General Phillips assess our current readiness for battle. We seem to be at about five thousand effectives at the moment, Jack – twenty-five hundred of our own troops, eighteen hundred Germans and the rest assorted remnants of Skene's men, some new loyalist recruits and still nearly eighty savages, for which Le Loup was taking full credit when last I saw him."

"You'll not see him again, I fear," Burgoyne responded. "The baron reported to me that Le Loup headed out north with a few of our braves just after we'd completed the crossing. My guess is that he won't stop until he's back in Canada."

"Carleton should hang him, then."

"He won't, though," Burgoyne said. "Le Loup is a civilian, after all. Still, what we have left should be enough, I imagine. It's less than I'd hoped for at this stage of the campaign, and we're down to fewer than one hundred cannon after that Bennington business, so we might seem weak enough now to stir Gates into a display of overconfidence. One can only hope he would be so foolhardy."

"Any word from Clinton?" Fraser asked.

"None yet," Burgoyne said. "He must have moved north along the river by now, but I have no clue to his whereabouts at the moment, and I would prefer to attack Gates with Clinton at the rebels' back from the south."

"A pincer movement?"

"More like the crude work of a blacksmith, Simon, with General Clinton as the anvil and our army as the moving hammer. I'll give Clinton another week. Then, if I still don't hear from him, we'll take on Gates by ourselves. Despite our reduced numbers, I expect no major difficulties in that chore. The men must be ready, however. I want them at work at dawn digging trenches for the defense of our encampment here. We'll resume drill as soon as the fortifications are complete and continue it daily until we move south for the final clash before marching into Albany. Beginning tomorrow, the ladies and their servants will move to the back of the column and bring up the rear of our advance."

Fraser glanced out over the river. In the pinkish light of the fading sun behind the two men, the river below had taken on its own greenish-golden glow. Scattered leaves in a few of the trees along the water, mainly the oaks and maples, had begun to burn red and yellow from the coolness of the nights.

"The advance might be slower than you care for," Fraser said, gazing at the scenery. "The rebels are up to their old tricks on this side of the river. They've destroyed all the bridges over streams along the road – the ones that flow into the Hudson from the heights. I already have Twiss out front, felling trees and erecting new bridges."

"Under heavy guard, I trust," Burgoyne said.

"Indeed. It wouldn't do at all to lose our good Lieutenant Twiss. Isn't this is a stunningly gorgeous part of the world, Jack? It's lovelier by far than anything I've ever seen on the Continent or in primitive, frozen Canada. Too much pine and birch up there; no color in the fall. I would very much like my final resting place to occupy a bluff such as this overlooking the water, as this spot does."

"The Hudson has a thousand such bluffs, I would imagine," Burgoyne said. "They're highest near the tight bend of the river at West Point, well south of here. That's why the rebels built their forts there – to command ship traffic on the river with cannon positioned up high. Howe should have moved the navy up there long ago and taken those damned forts. Instead, the bloody fool invaded Philadelphia with most of his army, and now Clinton has to get past those forts to aid us, and he'll probably have to manage the chore with too small a force to accomplish that goal with the ease the task deserves."

"How much of that do you think occurred by accident?" Fraser asked.

Burgoyne hesitated before answering. Then he said, "None at all, of course. This expedition has enemies in London. I have enemies in London, for that matter – Lord Germain chief among them. As we defeat Gates at Saratoga, we'll also be defeating bitter enemies across the Atlantic for whom the buffoonish Lord Howe is but a hapless pawn. But defeat them all we shall, Simon – and soon."

"Forgive me for my candor, Jack," Fraser said. "I speak not only as your advisor but also as your friend. It is, in my view, time for a more serious tone to this campaign. Thus far, these rebels have fought better than anyone had expected – certainly better than I'd expected. It's my conviction that this endless round of entertaining by the commanding general transmits to our senior officers a message that Saratoga will be an easy engagement for us. I must confide – and I've said this only to you — that I'm not entirely certain that will be the case."

"Riedesel has said much the same thing to me – although I suspect the counsel he offered is more his wife's than his own. The baroness does not think highly of Madame, as I'm sure you've noticed."

"It's not about Madame …" Fraser began.

"Of course it's about Madame, Simon. Sir Francis despises her as well, as do the lords and their ladies – with the possible exception of Lady Harriet, that is, whose soul is too gentle to despise anyone. They resent being compelled to socialize with Madame as an equal. Any advice I receive on the topic of my entertaining must be viewed in that context."

"Not mine," Fraser said simply.

Burgoyne, who had been gazing out over the river, glanced at his friend. "No, of course, not yours, Simon. Your advice I trust implicitly. You should know that I'm not unaware of the daunting nature of the challenges now immediately confronting us. Now that we're across the river, we've severed our supply and communication lines with Canada. The nights are marked by chill, and our winter uniforms are in storage at Ticonderoga. We now must move quickly – Clinton or no Clinton. I well understand the gravity of our circumstance. Left to my own devices, I might well have retreated back to Canada or Ticonderoga after that disaster at Bennington."

"That was the fault of the Germans," Fraser said.

"That was the fault of the commanding general," Burgoyne corrected. "It was I who dispatched the Germans and not you to the Hampshire Grants with our own troops. That's what made retreat back to Ticonderoga an untenable option. Had I tried to winter there, and re-launch the campaign in the spring, Lord Germain would have had many months to convince Lord North and the king that we're on a fool's errand in this operation. By then, Howe might even have managed to run down Washington and vanquish the main body of the rebel army, blunderer though Lord Howe might be. No, the only way to protect the Grand Strategy was to continue moving forward. And now that we've crossed the Hudson, the only way to protect it is to win at Saratoga, which we shall accomplish within a week to ten days."

"And the entertaining?" Fraser asked cautiously.

Burgoyne sighed. "I shall endeavor to find other ways to buoy spirits among the senior officers and their ladies. Madame can read by candlelight at night. I've been teaching her how to read, you know, Simon. She's doing quite well with it. My new lady has a sharp mind."

"And a good heart, too," Fraser said. "I'm aware of that. I do very much like her, Jack. It's just …"

"I understand," Burgoyne said. "We're here to fight, and the fight is now near. I'm grateful for the guidance of a fast, faithful friend in a world awash with enemies."

"There she is now," Fraser said, nodding toward the house.

Babette stood alone on the vast porch of Philip Schuyler's stately mansion, flanked by soaring Doric columns. She wore a sweeping gown of deep blue silk, one of a half dozen such dresses Burgoyne had commissioned to have created in Madame's behalf by a talented Canadian seamstress. Burgoyne's eyes washed over the image of Babette for a long moment as she stood against the splendorous background of Schuyler's grand house.

"Madame never knew it before we met, but she was born to live amid such lush and lavish surroundings," Burgoyne told his friend quietly. "By the time I'm through with her, she'll be fully at home among them."

Lady Harriet. 1777

Jack's snoring hadn't been bad enough, Harriet Acland thought. Not only had the big dog's noise stirred her unwillingly to wakefulness, now he was drooling again.

He's dreaming of eating, she thought.

In the dim light of the flickering candle atop a small table on the other side of Lord Acland's large tent, Lady Harriet lifted her head from the plush feather pillow she had brought from England and watched as saliva gushed like a fountain from the animal's jaws directly onto her husband's shoulder. John slept on, peacefully semi-drunk after Burgoyne's most recent dinner party and snoring blissfully himself as Jack, in his usual sleeping position between the Aclands on their field cot, continued to snore and slobber in placid, canine contentment. Harriet nudged the huge Newfoundland, who was roughly the size, shape and color of a yearling black bear. Jack lifted his massive head and panted good-naturedly – hot, moist, fetid dog breath – directly into her face.

"Get down, Jack!" she hissed at the gigantic dog, nudging him roughly once again.

Jack grunted and sighed. Slowly, the big animal rose to his feet on the canvas, turned ponderously on the cot and slipped off the foot of the cot to the tent's grassy floor. John stirred slightly as Jack moved to the other side of the large tent and dropped heavily to the ground directly beside to the small table that supported a flickering candle. Lady Harriet took the big dog's place in the center of the cot and rolled up against her husband's warm back. Her eyes closed again. Lady Harriet loved Jack dearly, but she was not fond of trying to sleep beside the big, clumsy beast except on the coldest nights. This night in Lord Acland's tent was steeped in fall chill, but it had been John, pleasantly tipsy, who'd invited the Newfoundland into their cot after the commanding general's sparkling party at Philip Schuyler's country mansion. Harriet had been willing to tolerate Jack's warm, furry bulk, but not his incessant canine snoring and most assuredly not the sea of dog spit he'd been generating as he'd dreamed, no doubt, of consuming some heroic meal, which was Jack's idea of Heaven.

Pressed against her husband's back, Lady Harriet drifted off once again to sleep. She had no idea how long she had been in deep slumber when she suddenly came awake in a frenzy of thick smoke and panicked excitement as men moved frantically in the thick fog around her. Instantly, she became aware of swirling, billowing smoke and of dim shapes moving beside the cot and of orange-yellow flames licking evilly at the tent's canvas top. She felt John pulled rudely from the cot amid a burst of muttered cockney oaths and curses from soldiers milling around inside the tent.

The rebels have attacked! Lady Harriet Acland thought as she struggled to clamber out from beneath the blankets. With distinct alarm, she felt the smoke fill her lungs and assault her eyes. She could see nothing, could find no air to breathe. For the briefest of moments, Lady Harriet felt herself swept up in panic, but her natural coolness under pressure – the determined steel that lay at the core of her character – took over more or less instantly.

The baby, she thought. The baby must survive.

Without hesitation, Lady Harriet rolled out of the cot and onto the tent's grass floor. She began instantly to crawl on the swelling belly that contained her unborn child. The wall of flames that had consumed the tent's far wall was at her feet, and Harriet crawled with determination through the smoke and away from the fire. Down here on the grass, she could find blessed air. She knew she had to get to the far wall of the tent, crawl beneath the canvas and make her way to safety.

John, she thought. Where's my John?

The smoke was so thick now that she couldn't see more than an inch in front of her face. She reached forward with her hands as she crawled until – There! There was the tent wall! – she was able to grasp the tent's canvas skirt in her eager fingers, lift it up and scuttle beneath it into the cold night air. Once outside, Lady Harriet scrambled to her bare feet, coughing violently to clear her lungs of the smoke, and lurched awkwardly away from the burning tent. Her baby was safe, thank God. But John?

Where is my husband? Lady Harriet Acland thought.

Burgoyne, 1777

"The burns are about his face and upper body," Sir Francis Clerke was saying, "but he's eager to resume command of the grenadiers as soon as the surgeons finish with him."

At the long, gleaming table in Philip Schuyler's vast dining room, with the sun not yet slipping up over the river at the front of the house, Burgoyne sipped his tea and said, "Lord Acland seems not a lucky soldier, Sir Francis – first the wound from the sniper on the road to Fort Edward and now this. And Lady Harriet?"

"Shaken but unharmed," Clerke responded.

"That's gratifying news."

"After she managed to escape the burning tent she turned to find Lord Acland amid the flames, struggling to rescue her. He'd already been pulled from the tent by several alert grenadiers, but he'd gone back in to save his wife. That's how he was burned. Her ladyship ended up rushing back into the flames and rescuing him instead."

"Do we know yet how this mishap came to be?"

"Their dog, Sir. The animal apparently overturned a table with a lit candle atop it, and the flame from the candle set the tent afire."

"We should shoot the damned dog and feed it to the men," Burgoyne said.

"Well, they're hungry enough to eat it. Upon awakening this morning I learned that a party from the Twentieth Foot, along with a few of Riedesel's dismounted dragoons, went through the sentries at the southern end of the encampment to go foraging just before sundown yesterday in a potato field down the road. They were attacked by a rebel reconnaissance party. We suffered roughly thirty dead or wounded."

"Damn!" Burgoyne shouted, slamming a hand down hard on the tabletop. "Thirty more men down? We can't afford that sort of pointless erosion of strength. Put out an order, Sir Francis, in the name of the commanding general. The men must be reminded that a soldier's life is the exclusive property of his king. I will, with great reluctance but with absolute certainty, hang the first man who again crosses the southern sentry line. Have the order promulgated throughout the encampment. Do that immediately before more fools go foraging for more potatoes."

"I will," Clerke said, standing. "Are we moving forward today, Sir?"

"We are. Send out that order, too. We'll break camp and form up on the road at daybreak."

"We're not waiting for Clinton, then."

Burgoyne shook his head. "We can afford no more time. The men's bellies are empty, and my own humor is growing distinctly dark. We need a fight, Sir Francis."

As Clerke and Burgoyne exchanged salutes and Clerke moved smartly out the door, Babette appeared in the other door at the far end of the room clad in the heavy nightgown she had not worn to bed at the end of the previous evening's festivities. She and the commanding general's aide exchanged silent nods as Clerke exited the room. Babette sensed the usual chill in Clerke's manner toward her, but Burgoyne's grim expression brightened as he spotted his mistress.

"You're up early today," he noted.

"Your valet told me that Lord Acland was injured overnight," she said. "How is Lady Harriet?"

"Uninjured, thankfully. Simon informs me that she's in the infirmary, nursing her charred husband."

"I should go to her," Babette said. "Lady Harriet is my only friend, Jack – the only one who can abide me except for you and Simon."

"And so you should," Burgoyne said, rising, moving to Babette's side and taking her in his arms. "She would appreciate the gesture, I'm sure, but then hurry back and pack. We're moving forward today. You and the other ladies will move this morning to the rear of the column."

"And tonight?" Babette asked. "Where will I sleep tonight?"

Burgoyne sighed and smiled ruefully. "Unfortunately, with the other ladies in a tent at the northern end of the encampment. The burden of command will henceforth require me to sleep near my senior officers in my own tent near the southern boundary."

"The battle is finally at hand, then."

Burgoyne laced his hand into the fingers of his mistress. "Victory is at hand, my love – victory for me and victory for you as well. A glorious victory awaits for both of us."

Arnold. 1777

"Good fighting weather," Benedict Arnold said to his waiting aide, Richard Varick, as Arnold emerged shirtless from his tent in the crisp September air.

The general's tent, only slightly larger than those of less exalted soldiers, had been erected at the eastern edge of his command's encampment. Arnold's troops were arrayed in a small city of such tents ringing the western rim of the vast expanse of plateau overlooking the Hudson. Still flushed from a night of drinking, a form of recreation and relaxation Arnold treasured to ease his constant nervousness, the general gazed up at the sun peeping over the horizon of the endless stretch of woodland on the far side of the grayish-green river.

Unshaven and dressed only in his uniform pants and boots, Arnold drew in a deep breath and stretched his arms wide. "The morning air has an invigorating snap to it, Dirk. That means we won't sweat to death when the carnage begins – as it must, and soon."

"Which explains your sunny mood, then," Varick said.

"Haven't you sat around long enough?" Arnold demanded with a smile. "Isn't your arse sore? Mine is, certainly. Come along, Burgoyne. I long to make your acquaintance – and have you make mine as well."

Varick laughed as Arnold slipped back into his tent and emerged again, this time in his blouse and field uniform coat to ward off the mid-September morning chill. Varick's commander was seldom in so high a humor, at daybreak or any other time. When he wasn't furious over something – pretty much anything at all, Varick had often noted — Arnold tended to brood, sulk, pace and twitch; it was his nature. But the prospect of imminent bloodshed always seemed to cheer him. Arnold had confided to Varick that he'd deeply regretted St. Leger's flight back to Canada. Arnold had hoped fervently for a gratifyingly hellish clash at Fort Stanwix — had actually prayed for one, in fact, in the privacy of his tent at night — but St. Leger's annoying caution had robbed him of the joy of combat, and Arnold had been left with a strong feeling of unease ever since.

Arnold gazed out over the field. Already, in the dim light of dawn, his men were at work at the edge of the plateau – at the eastern end of this sprawling farm field owned by a man named Freeman, who'd either fled south to Albany or was milling about the encampment somewhere as an ad hoc member of one of the New York militias. The troops were a combination of Army of the United States regulars and militiamen from around the region. They were putting the final touches on heavy wooden and earthen fortifications erected atop the hill up from the road than ran along the river. They also were constructing the last of the log breastworks and thick dirt walls from which they could fire down on the English and Germans as they charged up the hill — as they would be forced to do to take this position and clear the river road below for safe passage to Albany to the south.

"It's good ground Schuyler chose for this, Dirk," Arnold said as he surveyed the scene. "Damned good ground he selected."

"It seems to be," Varick agreed. "What I still don't understand is why Burgoyne insisted on crossing the river and coming down this side of the Hudson when he could have marched unimpeded down the eastern shore and ended up directly across the Hudson from Albany. He must have considered that plan"

"No doubt he did," Arnold said, gesturing toward the river. "But he would then have had to build a bridge under fire from Albany

and then cross the river under even heavier fire. Also, the river is
far wider at Albany than at the spot he did select to the north for the
construction of his bridge – probably too wide for any such bridge
to be successfully erected, actually. This way, if he can fight his way
past this point, he can approach the town from the high ground to the
west and crush any defenders left there against the river itself. No,
Burgoyne did the right thing to cross the Hudson north of here. Only
now he has to get past us at this tight spot where our guns control
passage along the road on this side of the river. And to do that he
has to get through the deep ravine at the bottom of the heights. Then,
under fire from us above him, he has to get up that high, steep hill
out there to reach open ground up here. He has to do all that before
he can finally face us on open ground and fight us the way he so
longs to fight us."

"Now I understand," Varick said.

Arnold responded, "Schuyler saw it all in his mind – saw it
perfectly — and he picked the perfect spot. And then Congress
sacked him and we have this damned fool –" Arnold gestured with
his hand toward the horseback figure of Gates, accompanied by the
ever-present Wilkinson, riding up the hill from the road below and
onto the plateau – "commanding the entire venture. God help the
rebellion, is all I can say."

"He'll hear you, you know," Varick muttered as Gates and
Wilkinson drew nearer.

"The hell with him if he does," Arnold said with a broad smile.
"The bastard needs me, and he knows it. That's why I'm in this
location commanding the northernmost wing — the portion of our

force that Burgoyne will have to face first when he arrives here. Good morning, General Gates. A fine day for unfettered violence, don't you agree?"

The officers exchanged salutes and Wilkinson swung down from his mount to greet Arnold and Varick eye-to-eye, on equal terms. Gates remained atop his horse, gazing down solemnly on the three. Arnold interpreted the move as just another petty, transparent effort on Gates's part to assert silent dominance over the commanding general's subordinates. That Gates would do such a thing, and he did so many such things in all his dealings with Arnold and others, was just one reason Arnold despised the man so thoroughly. Whatever the commanding general's gifts as a politician manipulating the petty princes of Congress, Arnold had concluded early on, Granny Gates was a dismal incompetent as a military leadership figure. Gates couldn't lead a horse to water, Arnold often told Varick — and anyone else who happened to be in the vicinity when Arnold launched into one of his regular, oath-laden rants against the new commanding general.

"They're quite near now, General," Gates said. "Colonel Wilkinson here brought back three prisoners from an English foraging party – men from the Twentieth regiment. They confirmed our suspicion that Burgoyne is but a few miles north now and bent on marching on Albany as a winter headquarters. It's my best estimate that we'll be attacked as early as tomorrow."

"Good work, Wilkinson," Arnold said. "I trust you took the time to kill a few of the royalist bastards during your foray."

"Several dozen, actually," Wilkinson said evenly. "They were south of their own line digging potatoes out of a field."

"So, they're hungry, then," Arnold said cheerily. "Excellent. Hungry men are generally eager for a fight. Well, so are we. What is our strength at the moment, General Gates?"

"With the newly arrived militia from New England, the New York colony volunteers and Morgan's Rangers, we're now at about five thousand effectives. You're here on the left, General Arnold. I have General Learned commanding the center and General Glover commanding the right wing above that tavern along the road – the one operated by that Bemis fellow. My belief is that Burgoyne commands about the same number at this time."

"Marvelous," Arnold said. "Then I'll take a portion of my left wing today and move north on the river road to provide our guests a proper welcome."

"You shall not do that, Sir," Gate snapped out. "We'll broach no foolhardiness at this juncture. Reinforcements flood into this camp daily, and we have this good ground as a crucial ally. We shall not abandon it."

His eyes narrowing, Arnold said, "The ground will go nowhere, General Gates. It'll stay right here whether Burgoyne has five thousand men or whether I can reduce that number somewhat before he reaches this location. My desire is to make him bleed a bit as he meanders our way."

"It is my plan that we will follow, General Arnold," Gates said, his voice rising. "You, General Arnold, will follow orders. Do I make myself understood?"

For a long moment, Arnold was silent, although his face reddened

Burgoyne. 1777

The commanding general's sweeping, silk-lined tent was more like a pavilion. It was easily a half dozen times the size of the tents that housed ordinary officers, and the pennant that fluttered from its pyramidal summit was the banner of his own regiment. When Burgoyne emerged from the tent at dawn, he found the air thick with fog. Rain gushed from the skies in a steady drumbeat of drizzle on the sea of tents around him. In the moist chill, amid a churning swirl of activity in the camp, Burgoyne found Generals Fraser and Phillips awaiting him with Sir Francis Clerke at their side. The three senior officers stood beneath the awning that stretched out from the tent's entrance.

"A distinctly unpleasant day," Simon Fraser said to his commander.

"For now," Burgoyne agreed, "but this mist will lift as the sun climbs higher. This is all from the river, you know, gentlemen. This is September nineteenth. This time of year the Hudson this far north begins to lose its warmth well in advance of the coming winter. The heat evaporates from the water in the form of morning fog, but it always clears up later on. As it is, the fog should be our friend. It'll shield our advance along the river road this morning and foil the rebel snipers."

"Yes," Phillips said, "but the rain will make our charge up the open hillside to the heights slow and slippery."

Burgoyne clasped his artillery commander firmly on his shoulder. This, the commanding general knew, was a time to instill confidence and enthusiasm in his senior officers. He would accomplish that by radiating an abundant supply of confidence of his own. That calm assurance, combined with the warm and genial wit that was the key implement in Burgoyne's ample kit of leadership tools, would be on conspicuous display at this meeting.

"That assessment would be correct if we were to actually charge with mad abandon up the open hillside to the heights," Burgoyne told Phillips, "but I have no intention of being quite so accommodating to General Gates – not with this reduced force at my back. If we had two or three times more men, we could go right up the slope, Will. We could engage the rebels in the open field and crush them in fairly short order. Now, however, our task must be accomplished with more stealth and prudence but with no less resolve and no less assurance of success."

Fraser studied his commander with approval. This was vintage Burgoyne, he knew. Fraser was minutely alert to everything around him this morning, his nerves tense and his own blood high as the battle loomed. The long-awaited clash was near, and he was anxious to hear Burgoyne's plan.

"What do you have in mind, Jack?" Fraser asked.

In his long, dark blue cloak, Burgoyne strode to the table of maps that Clerke, having moved next to the table shielded by the tent's front awning, had arranged for the commanding general. The key map sat on top of the pile amid a half dozen candles flickering in the pre-dawn light. Burgoyne said, "Unfortunately, we know too little of the positions Gates has established atop the heights. The loss of the savages has impeded us in that regard, gentlemen, but we can presume that the fortified positions are along the hillside, which we shall avoid, and largely in and beyond the open farmland at the southern end of this thick forest. You will note that the forest extends down from this position to their fortifications along the top of that hillside up from the river road. Instead of climbing that open hillside from the road while under fire, as Gates clearly hopes we'll do, it is my plan to ascend the hillside further north, through the thick woods along the slope here, and then proceed atop the heights to the south through the forest itself. Once we reach this open area at the northern end of their position, here, we'll gather into battle formation and advance properly."

The two generals and Clerke studied the map intently.

"That'll be slow going for our thousands of troops," Phillips noted. "It'll take many hours amid the trees for us to fight our way through those thick woods and reach that open ground."

"It'll be a hellish chore, General, getting all your big guns up there and then down through the woods to the open ground," Clerke told Phillips. "There are a few rugged roads up there, but no true pathway for our cannon."

"Indeed," Burgoyne broke in. "I'm afraid, Will, that your precious cannon will be of only limited utility to us in today's engagement. A few of them can be employed from the road to destroy some rebel fortifications atop the heights, I suppose, but only a few others can be hauled up the wooded hillside to be available for use in the open field to support our troops. The ground the rebels have chosen to defend has robbed us of the option of utilizing our big guns as I would prefer."

"It's good ground to defend and nasty ground to assault," Phillips grumbled. "How do you prefer us to deploy – and when?"

Burgoyne gazed around at the fog and at his troops loading their packs. Each man had been assigned sixty rounds of powder and ball, and their packs would be both heavy and bulky, Burgoyne knew – weighty loads on that long march through the woods.

"We'll wait a few hours until the fog clears a bit and we can see our way properly," Burgoyne said. "We'll then move out in three columns. Simon, I would prefer that you take command of the right wing. Your troops will have to cover the longest distance to reach the battlefield. I shall take the center, which will be under the nominal command of General Hamilton. Will, the left wing shall be under the formal command of the baron. The Germans must feel that their commander has a central role in this engagement, but I would prefer that you accompany him as my agent and as the baron's mentor. He'll be in the woods and you will be on the river road below, but you'll remain in close touch."

Phillips nodded. He understood that he would be in actual command of the army's left wing, and he would see that Riedesel understood this as well. Phillips was an austere, taciturn man and an eminently capable general. He and the equally austere, equally taciturn, equally capable baron understood one another perfectly, which was why Burgoyne had joined them together in harness for this engagement.

"And my guns?" Phillips asked. Clearly, he was annoyed at the limited role for his cannon in Burgoyne's plan while, equally clearly, he could see the plan's wisdom. Phillips had been worried about that open slope up from the river road.

"Ah, yes," Burgoyne smiled, "your beloved guns. They'll be split up, I'm afraid. The terrain will be too challenging for any other course of action. Six six-pounders and three three-pounders will go with you and Riedesel along the river road to fire upward and assault the rebel fortifications. Four six-pounders and four three-pounders will go with Simon on the right. They'll be beastly to get up that wooded hillside and through all that length of forest, Simon, but they'll provide you with at least some limited firepower once you finally reach the open ground to the south. I'll take six six-pounders with me in the center. As for all the other big guns, it would simply take us too long to move them into position."

"Then where will they be?" Phillips demanded.

"They'll remain here in camp under heavy guard," Burgoyne said, "along with our baggage, what meager supplies we have remaining and, of course, our ladies."

"Troop deployment?" Fraser asked simply.

"On the right," Burgoyne said, "you'll take the light infantry battalion, the grenadier battalion and the twenty-fourth regiment. You'll also take the German advance troops and what's left of Skene's loyalist regiment."

"Roughly a thousand men," Fraser said, totaling the forces in his head.

"Closer to nine hundred effectives," said Burgoyne, who'd done his own accounting the night before as he'd worked out his battle plan. "Will, your force will consist of the three German regiments and an English crew for each cannon. My own center will be made up of the twentieth regiment, the sixty-second, the twenty-first and the ninth. In all, my center will consist of about eleven hundred effectives."

"And that leaves what in camp to guard my guns?" Phillips asked.

"Roughly two thousand men," Burgoyne said, "most in reasonable health. We'll leave behind the forty-seventh and Riedesel's regiment from Hesse-Hanau. They're mostly gunners anyway. Without their cherished cannon the poor chaps would feel lost in the field."

Burgoyne turned to Fraser. "Simon, since you have the greatest distance to cover to gain your position, you'll move out first on the river road, select what you deem an appropriate spot and climb from there into the forest atop the heights. You'll then move west while my own center successfully completes its climb to take its position on your left, and we'll then move southward in tandem upon my firing of three cannon, one after the other, in rapid succession. Will, the column led by you and the baron will leave this encampment last. From the river road, just north of where the woods meet the open ground at the rebel position, the baron can climb the hill on the wooded side to the north with a few cannon while you continue south on the road with the rest of the cannon and your gunners. From that position you can direct your fire upward to assault the rebel fortifications. You may lead your men up the hillside at such time as you decide your fire has wreaked sufficient havoc on the rebel emplacements. Any questions, gentlemen?"

Both Fraser and Phillips studied the maps in silence for a long moment. They understood the plan well enough and could come up with no improvements.

"Where do you want me, Sir," Clerke asked.

Burgoyne reached out a hand and placed it on his aide's shoulder. With his usual engaging and confident smile, Burgoyne said, "At my side, of course, Sir Francis. Without you close at hand as I brave such arduous terrain, I should be both heartsick and abjectly forlorn."

Arnold. 1777

"Here comes General Gates," Varick said.

Varick and Arnold stood at a fortification overlooking the river road, supervising the placement of one of the few cannon Gates had allotted to Arnold's wing of the defense. Arnold spun about and spotted Gates galloping across the field directly in his direction. The man was alone and moving quickly. Whatever his other failings, Arnold noted, the commanding general could sit a horse.

Something's afoot, Arnold thought.

As Gates pulled his mount to a sudden halt, Arnold snapped off a salute. The men were watching, Arnold knew, and he was determined to display proper respect in front of the troops for the commanding general for whom he personally could muster no shred of respect whatever.

"They're on the move toward us," Gates snapped out. "Scouts report that they struck most of their tents on that plain up near Schuyler's home and have moved into the woods north of us. The last report I received is that they've crossed the great gorge in the forest up there."

Arnold broke into a broad grin. "So, they won't come up the open hill in front of us after all. How charmingly respectful of General Burgoyne. Well then, let's go get them in the woods, General. They're no damned good in the woods; we are."

"No!" Gates bellowed. "We'll stand behind our fortifications, General Arnold. That's what they're for. I'm merely alerting you to make ready to be attacked."

Varick watched as Arnold's face predictably turned beet-red.

"Did they haul up cannon with them?" Arnold demanded.

"Some, I'm told," Gates said. "Not many, apparently."

"Then, damn it, we can't just sit here, General Gates. Let them bring those guns within artillery range and they'll reduce these flimsy log redoubts to slivers, and then we'll be against them in the open field. We must go and fight them now on our own terms. For God's sake, man, let me at least send Morgan and his rangers to meet them in the woods before they can deploy those cannon. You must do that, Sir. The move is essential."

For a long moment, Gates was silent, clearly weighing the advice despite his decidedly defensive instincts.

"You could send Dearborn and his light infantry, too," Arnold pressed. "We must retard their advance and reduce their numbers before they clear the forest. I implore you, General Gates, do not permit them to reach this open ground with their ranks and cannon intact. If you do that, they'll slaughter us like sheep."

Gates hesitated only a moment longer. Then he said, "All right, General Arnold. Order Colonel Morgan and his riflemen to take to the woods. I'll get word to Dearborn."

Satisfied, Arnold nodded. "Thank you, General Gates. A wise

decision."

But by then Gates had already whirled about on his horse and was galloping to the center of the line to Arnold's left.

"He didn't hear you," Varick said.

"It doesn't matter," Arnold told his aide. "The bastard is cheerfully indifferent to my approval or disdain. Well, come, Dirk. Send word to Morgan to move forward. Meanwhile, we now have nine regiments to make ready for a fight today."

Fraser. 1777

Burgoyne had been right about the fog. It was still thick but beginning to lift. Nor had the commanding general exaggerated the difficulty of the ground. Dodging musket balls from stray snipers, Fraser drove his men relentlessly as they hauled their small supply of cannon up the steep, soft, muddy, heavily wooded slope from the river road and then westward across spongy ground through the thick forest. It was not a quiet procession. Any attempt at stealth was pointless with thousands of swearing, sweating, heavily armed men, packs weighing heavily on their backs. The troops loudly snapped dry tree branches underfoot as they moved along amid the sharp clink of steel and the squeak of leather through the dim, mist-shrouded woods.

Deep into the forest, Fraser and his men found an overgrown road and followed it as they used their compasses to move into proper position. The road led directly into a deep, wide ravine and out again on the other side. The cannon wheels moved easily down the slippery slope and then dug in on the far side. Two hundred soldiers hauling on ropes finally dragged the big guns back up to level ground. The sun was almost overhead when Fraser halted his forces and then spread them out in a thin line well back from the edge of the open ground he could just barely discern through the woods to the south. He dispatched a courier to Burgoyne to inform the commanding general that Fraser had attained his position. Fraser feared, however, that the courier might not make it through the rebel scouts in the forest. For more than a half hour, he rode his gray gelding among his men, making jokes with the weary, winded soldiers who had settled on the leaf-strewn dirt as Fraser urged them to ready their weapons.

"The time is near," Fraser told his men as he rode among them, wondering if Burgoyne's troops had yet taken up their position to his left in the center of the attack line. Just after noon, Fraser heard the sound. From his left, through the thickly forested area, came three quick, astonishingly loud cannon blasts, one after the other. He drew his saber as the men in the forest around him clambered to their feet. Fraser raised the blade high above his head.

"Forward," General Simon Fraser called out through the woods.

Morgan. 1777

It's too damned bright, Morgan thought as his force of five hundred men, bent at the waist and running low to the ground, crossed the open fields of Freeman's farm and gathered in a ragged line along the southern fringe of the thick woods.

Morgan knew that his rangers, clad in buckskin and mostly greenish-gray-brown garments of homespun fabric, would be harder to see in the fall woods than Major Dearborn's blue-and-buff clad infantrymen, who were forming up noisily to Morgan's right. Morgan's rangers most assuredly would be less conspicuous targets than the mostly red-clad English troops Morgan knew lay directly ahead through the trees. But Morgan silently cursed the evaporating fog for its rapidly quickening departure. The moist canopy of sky above the field and forest remained dull and gray, but it still generated more intense light than Morgan cared for in a large-scale confrontation in the forest. The light was especially hazardous if his men were to face Indians, whom Morgan suspected would pave the way for the advancing Royal Army.

Moreover, Morgan knew that the density of the woods would negate the greater range of his rangers' Pennsylvania rifles. They would have to engage the advancing English at relatively close range, where the English Brown Bess muskets would be more effective at killing than they would have been at greater distance. As a result, Morgan was approaching this task with intense vigilance and a certain degree of trepidation. He was always happier sniping. So were his rangers. At long range, through thinner woods, Morgan's men were uniquely deadly. This would be fighting in denser woods – if the Army of the United States could prevent the English from breaking through to the open field, that was – but it would be head-on, face to face combat at relatively close range. Morgan's men had tomahawks and knives. The English, he knew, would wield bayonets, and they were trained to use them to blood-chilling effect.

First, Morgan knew, would come the Indians – at least as many as Burgoyne could still muster. He knew from Tory deserters who'd defected to Gates' side after the Jane McCrea debacle that Burgoyne's savages had largely deserted the royal forces – supposedly, anyway, unless those deserters had been sent into the rebel camp specifically to mislead the Army of the United States leadership. Morgan knew, too, however, that those remaining savages would serve as the cutting edge of the advancing English line and could slither through the tree trunks like murderous ghosts. Morgan's own men had that ability. They'd learned to do it as frontier hunters, and Morgan himself had further trained them to move in the forest like shadows. Only the Indians would do it better, he knew. While his rangers were the most capable deep woods troops on either side, Morgan was aware, they remained markedly less stealthy than the red men, although the rangers were generally superior marksmen.

Morgan was aware also that his rangers were justifiably wary of the Indians' capability in such circumstances and that the very presence of those elusive, profoundly dangerous figures in the woods ahead would instill a degree of caution in his troops that Morgan feared would hamper their effectiveness. He felt that wariness himself, which was why he was on foot today instead of on horseback, and he couldn't fault his men for their concerns. He wished the fog had clung to the ground longer, lending his rangers a greater degree of equity against the red men. As it was, Morgan was delighted that Burgoyne had so few of them left – if, in fact, that was actually the case.

"There's nothing ahead of us that I can see, Colonel darlin',"

Tim Murphy said, peering intently into the forest. Murphy always tried to hang close to Morgan in battle. Each man had an instinctive grasp of the other's moves. With Murphy near, Morgan knew, he was free to abandon cover periodically, stand upright and bellow out instructions to his men up and down the line. Or, as he often did, Morgan would be free to communicate to his men by using a turkey call – a woodsman's bugle. And all the while sure-shot Tim Murphy would be scanning the woods to pick off any enemy who'd been waiting for a clear chance to kill the ranger commander. Sniping enemy commanders was one of Morgan's favorite battle tactics, even though he knew that he himself was a prime target for the opposition.

"They must still be back a ways, Tim," Morgan said. "It won't be long now, though. We need to get in there, take up positions in the trees and behind trees and be ready to fire when we begin to hear their great racket as they march toward us."

"Wait!" Murphy hissed out, ducking to his knees. "I saw some movement – there."

Morgan held out his arms and silently motioned to his line of men with arms out and palms down to flatten on the ground at the edge of the woods. Morgan himself was one of the last men down. He settled his belly on the wet earth beside Tim Murphy.

"I see one of them back there through the trees," Murphy whispered. "It's one of the damned savages."

"Kill him," Morgan ordered.

"My pleasure, Colonel darlin'," Murphy said as he quickly rose, raised his Pennsylvania rifle, draw a bead on his target and fired in less than a single second. Snap shooting with deadly accuracy was a specialty of Morgan's Rangers. It was a skill born of the hunting of deer and honed in defensive warfare. In a heartbeat, Murphy was back on the ground, reloading.

"The man is now but a memory," Murphy muttered, biting the stopper off his powder horn and pouring a fresh charge down the barrel of his still-smoking Pennsylvania rifle.

Morgan raised his head as sputters of fire spat out from along the line of his men at the forest's edge. Tim Murphy had not been the only ranger to spot movement in the woods. As the powder smoke poured from rifle barrels and wafted upward above the heads of Morgan's rangers, they also could hear the crackle of new musket fire from their right among Dearborn's light infantry. The English were here. Finally, after all these months, the battle had been joined.

Instantly, Morgan was up, Murphy following close behind, moving into the woods and keeping his head low. At his wordless move, Morgan knew, his men would follow, slipping into the woods as their commander advanced silently. The battle still was not yet fully in motion, Morgan sensed. The main force of the Indians was still back, now moving through the trees as silently and elusively as tendrils of mist. He located what had been Murphy's target only forty yards in, stretched out beneath a towering oak, the left quarter of his skull blown away. Morgan gazed down at the fallen enemy in surprise.

"No savage after all," Murphy whispered. "It's a Tory in Indian garb. What the hell are they doing, do you think?"

"Trying to fool us," Morgan said.

As Morgan spoke, both men flattened to the ground at the sounds of something large crashing through the woods at their rear. Each ranger had rolled on his back, rifle lifted quickly to firing position when Arnold, atop his big bay mount, came thundering up to their position at a full gallop through the trees.

What a beautiful target he makes atop that horse, Morgan thought. And the lunatic couldn't care less, God bless him.

Morgan and Arnold had fought side-by-side at Quebec and shared both a mutual affection and respect. From his saddle, Arnold glanced down on the wide-eyed corpse of the English irregular and smiled broadly.

"So the deserters told the truth; they're low on Indians," Arnold said. "Colonel Morgan, you and I have seen too many redskins to be deceived by that garb of paint and feathers. They sent out Tories dressed like savages for the purpose of slowing your advance. Move your men forward now and slice through this fraud."

Morgan clambered to his feet, still amazed that Arnold would gallop headlong into the woods and then simply sit there atop his horse, high in his saddle in the woods, as if challenging the enemy to fire on him.

"Are you coming with us, General?" Morgan asked.

"General Gates has sent me instructions to move to his headquarters to advise him as the engagement unfolds. I'll obey my orders, Colonel. That's where I'll be."

As Arnold spoke, stray shots rang out through the forest on both sides of the tall oak tree. His lips pressed tightly together, Arnold gazed around the woods, his eyes shining as though a fire was blazing in his brain behind them. His expression was one of pure, ferocious longing.

"I would rather by far to be with you, Dan," the general said in a low, hoarse voice. "Good fortune to you this day."

Then, without another word, Benedict Arnold spun the big bay about and galloped through the woods into the open field beyond. Morgan and Murphy watched as Arnold, reaching the field beyond the line of trees, dug his spurs into the animal's sides and tore off over the open ground toward Gates' headquarters.

"Touched in the head, he is," Tim Murphy said, shaking his head. "A wild man."

"Yes," Dan Morgan said, rising slowly to his feet. "A pure warrior, though – through and through. Come now, Tim, we have killing to be about."

Babette. 1777

The three-room building was tiny — no more than a hut, really. It squatted in the forest near the Hudson just off the river road slightly north of the action on the battlefield. That morning, after Burgoyne's army had moved forward to the forest north of Freeman's farm, Babette and the other officers' women were gathered up from their assemblage of tents at the camp on Schuyler's fields, just south of the mansion, and instructed to pack their bags. The women were being moved closer to the action, since the English army contemplated no move back to the north. This was the building in which they would spend the day in relative shelter from the violence ahead.

Babette had shared a tent the night before with Baroness von Riedesel and her two young daughters. The children had spent the night swaddled in their mother's thick Bavarian blankets, alternately coughing, sneezing and crying while Frederika von Riedesel calmed them soothingly or snapped at them, as the occasion required. In general, though, the girls were notably well behaved, and Babette mentioned this to the baroness.

"Ya," Frederika said. "Zey are good children."

"It must be so hard for them on a journey like this," Babette said.

Frederika said, "My father vas a general like my husband. Many a time as a child my mother and I accompanied him on campaigns like zis. Children are always children. Zey complain and cry and play. Zat is vat children do."

Babette had put on a bright, summery dress of pale blue, one of many Burgoyne had bought her in Quebec as they'd prepared for this campaign. She noted that the baroness, who tended to dress more casually except on the occasions when Burgoyne entertained his officers and their ladies, today wore only a shirt of homespun and an old, faded skirt, clothing of exceptional ordinariness. Babette said nothing, but she was surprised. Baroness Frederika was generally quite attentive to her own appearance. When the calash and the ox carts arrived at the hut and Babette stepped down in the fog, she realized that this small building was to be more than merely a shelter for the officers' women. Already in place were several regimental surgeons, laying out their medical instruments.

"This is a hospital," Babette said to the baroness in surprise.

"Ya," Frederika said, lifting her children down to the ground. "Go play. Stay near ze building." Then she turned to Babette. "Zere vill be casualties zis day. Ze men fight. Ve women help vis ze wounded. Come, I vill show you vat ve do."

For a long moment, Babette gazed at the tiny building with trepidation. From the south, she suddenly caught the distant, muffled sound of three rapid cannon blasts, one after the other.

"Come," Frederika said briskly. "Ve vill haff much to occupy us."

Burgoyne. 1777

The drums set the pace. Ahead of the commanding general, who sat wrapped in his long blue cloak high atop his white horse, the ranks of Burgoyne's center had begun their advance through the forest in perfect attack formation. More than one thousand men were stretched out on either side of Burgoyne throughout the rugged, thickly treed landscape. He knew that similar forces were on the move through the woods to both his right and left, stretching out several miles. At the end of each row, a drummer beat out the cadence – ba-dump! Ba-dump! Ba-dump! — as the red-clad troops marched to the relentless rhythm in stoic, machine-like unison.

"They know we're coming now, Sir," Clerke called out from atop his mount to Burgoyne's right.

"Indeed they do, Sir Francis," Burgoyne agreed with a smile.

In his saddle, Burgoyne was otherwise silent as he studied the scene ahead. As of yet, he could spot no light from beyond the trees

– no sign of open ground ahead yet. Burgoyne issued no commands, snapped no orders. His regimental commanders, their saber-wielding officers and their bellowing sergeants understood perfectly what was to be done from here – to march steadily forward, slowly and inexorably, like a force of nature, like a tidal wave of death. They would continue their move forward against enemy fire from the trees ahead, periodically halting to fire en mass from formation, sending tightly bunched showers of lead into the trees ahead. Then, when the opportunity presented itself by the appearance of enough enemy soldiers in a single spot, to lower their bayonet-tipped muskets, drive the blades through the guts of the opposition and continue the methodical, shoulder-to-shoulder march over the bloody corpses of opponents.

It was what the Romans had done with their large, square shields and short swords – weapons especially designed for combat at close quarters. Painted blue and waving their axes and bulky long swords above their heads, the fur-clad barbarians had sent vast, screaming mobs racing with wild abandon into those rigid Roman ranks. The legionnaires had maintained their tight discipline — slicing, chopping, stabbing and disemboweling the shrieking fools before them as the Romans, unstoppable, had marched steadily from Italy to Scotland, leaving a broad path of blood and bodies behind them. So, too, it would be here, Burgoyne knew. So it had always been when the king's troops had marched as one to their drums into battle against any hapless, doomed force that had dared stand in their way.

Now, as the English force moved forward, pausing periodically to direct a volley of fire into the woods ahead, Burgoyne could spot a stray English or German soldier fall, the victim of a sniper's shot. They lay where they fell, their comrades never breaking ranks as they stepped over their fallen fellows and continued the advance. It was the discipline, Burgoyne knew – the iron discipline that was the hallmark of the king's military. The Germans in their high metal helmets and dark green jackets with red facings might break at some point, he knew, if the opposing fire grew heavy and deadly enough. They were, after all, only hired hands fighting for the fortunes of their princes back in the Fatherland but not for king and country in the same sense as were the English troops. No, Burgoyne knew, his men would continue the forward march in the face of any opposition, with the last man standing perfectly willing to stride purposefully into the fires of Hell if duty demanded it of him.

For his own part, sitting high atop his showy mount just behind the advancing English ranks, Burgoyne knew he made a tempting target for any rebel sniper, as did Sir Francis riding beside him. He also knew, however, that this display of personal courage on his part – his cool, casual disregard for his own safety, however heavy the opposing fire – was his duty to the men who would die so gallantly this day at Burgoyne's orders. He knew, too, that any sniper likely to fire on him would be far more likely to take the quicker, easier shot at the more immediate danger to that sniper's life – the thick ranks of English and German infantrymen marching toward that sniper at closer, deadlier range.

As the rate of fire increased, both from his own troops and from the rebels ahead in the forest who were beginning to dig in now against the English advance, Burgoyne felt the breeze of a musket ball whipping by within just a few inches of his head. Burgoyne immediately sat up straighter in his saddle. The dense tree growth and difficult terrain was impeding the forward march more than he'd expected. He watched his troops break ranks again and again to clamber up hills or to get around clumps of bushes and tree growth. Periodically, his ears caught the blast of cannon to each side as the few gunners he'd brought along on this engagement blasted flurries of grapeshot into the woods ahead.

Each time they fired, Burgoyne knew, the cannon had to be reloaded and then dragged at a furious pace back to the front of the assault. Increasingly, Burgoyne noted with annoyance, this was slow going. Once they pushed the rebels into open ground, though, beyond the woods, the pace of the attack would step up immeasurably. To his right, from the corner of his eye, Burgoyne caught the sight of Clerke's hat popping high into the air – caught, no doubt, by a stray musket ball. Burgoyne's own gloriously plumed uniform hat remained firmly in place. He turned to Clerke, who now sat his horse bare-headed and white-faced, as the general's aide, like Burgyone, stiffened his spine to sit even straighter in his saddle.

"Courage now, Sir Francis," Burgoyne called out.

Ashen, Clerke merely nodded to his commander. "That's the second hat I've lost on this campaign, Sir. A damned annoyance."

Riedesel. 1777

The baron heard the sound of fighting – the gunfire and the

cannon blasts through the woods off to his right. He had put his forces into motion upon hearing the three cannon blasts from Burgoyne's command, ordering his troops to march southward through the thick woods toward the open ground. Unfortunately, his men were moving only slowly in the forest, and the stray sniping into Riedesel's right front from the trees ahead did little to speed up matters. From the saddle of the horse the portly baron sat so expertly, Riedesel called out to his most trusted deputy, Colonel Nicholas von Breymann, who rode beside him about thirty yards away.

"Do you see anything?" Riedesel called out in German.

Breymann shook his head. "No, Sir. I think there are only a few of them, and they're all ahead to our right. The center is having a rough time of it, I would venture."

"And perhaps the right wing, too," the baron called out. "But we're apparently on a picnic today, Colonel – a picnic on difficult ground, but a picnic to be sure."

"So far," Breymann shouted back.

"I should have some chicken legs brought with me," Riedesel muttered to himself.

Gates. 1777

Wilkinson was a muddy mess – hatless and splattered with wet dirt and with the right side of his uniform coat soaked and smeared thickly with filth.

"What the hell happened to you?" Arnold demanded as Gates' aide burst through the door of the commanding general's headquarters.

Gates was at his desk studying a map through his spectacles. Arnold stood just behind him, peering over the commanding general's shoulder. Arnold's aide, Varick, stood silently just inside the door. As Wilkinson burst into the small building, Gates glanced up, seemingly baffled.

"Horse slipped and fell in the mud," Wilkinson got out with a sheepish smile.

"Are you injured?" Arnold asked.

"Only in my pride, Sir," Wilkinson said.

"What have you to report?" Gates demanded. His tone was curt, his expression grim.

Wilkinson's smile vanished as he strode across the small room and pointed to the map. "Morgan and Dearborn have the enemy center halted – halted for now, at any rate — in the woods right about here. The English sent out an advance party to explore a bit, and they reconnoitered in the open around a small cabin in Freeman's fields. That's when some of Morgan's men opened fire and killed a number of the English officers and a respectable number of their enlisted. I saw the scene, General Gates. The entire cabin is ringed with dead. When the English fled back into the forest, Morgan's men chased after them and ran directly into the main body of the English center. They got a bayonet charge for their trouble, but Colonel Morgan regrouped them. Burgoyne is in personal command at their center, I was told, Sir. Some of Morgan's men saw him with their own eyes."

Gates' eyes widened in wonderment. "The commanding general is in the center of the line itself?"

"He is, Sir," Wilkinson said.

"We should kill him," Arnold said quickly. "I'll go myself, General Gates. I'll take care of Gentleman Johnny Burgoyne for you."

Gates gazed at Arnold in slack-jawed astonishment. "Target an officer? General Arnold, the rules of war—"

"—Sweet Jesus, war has no rules," Arnold snapped angrily. "Morgan targets officers every chance he gets, and God bless him for his noble work."

"He does, Sir," Wilkinson said. "I saw his work at the cabin. Every other corpse was an officer."

"If we target Burgoyne and actually manage to kill him," Arnold said, "then all this comes to a halt, General Gates. And now we know where he is."

Gates rose, red-faced. "We shall take no such action, General Arnold. And you shall stay in this headquarters to advise me. Do you understand me, Sir?"

For a long moment, Arnold said nothing. He merely glared at Gates. Then he said, almost in a whisper, "As you wish, General Gates."

"All right, then," Gates said, turning back to Wilkinson. "Where are Burgoyne's other wings?"

"He has forces on the river road at the bottom of the fortified hillside, under our guns, and at the wooded area north of the heights. That's his left wing. He has his right wing in the forest well to our left. Those on the road have some cannon with them. They're tearing up our hillside fortifications with some fury, Sir. We believe that the other wings have a few big guns as well. Their right wing has yet to be confronted or even examined from ground level, although some of Morgan's men have climbed trees and believe they've slowed its progress with their sharp shooting."

Arnold said, "If their right wing reaches open ground and then swings left the English can attack Morgan and Dearborn from two sides, Sir. If we fail to hold the heights and they make their way up that hill, they'll then have our men on a third side as well."

Gates ignored his subordinate general, focusing his attention exclusively on his aide and his maps. "Do we have an estimate of the strength of those three wings?"

Wilkinson said, "Morgan estimates about a thousand troops in each, not counting what are now their dead and wounded in the center. Between both Morgan and Dearborn we have only about half that number in the field, and we're losing manpower even as we take prisoners."

"We have too few men in this fight," Arnold cautioned. "We need to empty out the camp and push the bastards back into the trees."

'This is a defensive position we hold here," Gates argued. "You were correct, General Arnold, about sending troops to slow their advance through the forest, but I can spare no more men from our fortifications."

"Let the English get their cannon into the open, and we'll soon enough have no fortifications left to defend."

"We will hold here!" Gates bellowed suddenly. "We will hold, I say! Colonel Wilkinson, go get me more information. I need to know in more detail where their right wing is."

"Very good, Sir," Wilkinson said, saluting. He was out the door and beginning to mount his muddy, skittish horse when he felt

Varick's hand on his shoulder.

"Down some of this," Varick offered, holding out a metal flask. "Rum. It boosts the spirit."

Wilkinson took the flask and poured a good measure of its contents down his throat. It burned as it struck his gullet. Wilkinson welcomed the sensation.

"Have the two of them have been like that all day?" Wilkinson asked.

"More or less. The senior officers not in the field are making excuses for leaving the command post and then for staying away as long as they can manage. Gates won't let Arnold leave at all. It's not a warm relationship, you understand."

"Oh, I understand," Wilkinson said, swinging up and into his saddle as the distant din of musket fire sounded, punctuated by the occasional cannon blast. "What I don't understand is why General Arnold is so eager to get out there needlessly and quite possibly get himself killed."

"He doesn't believe it's needless," Varick said, shrugging. "Besides, you know, he doesn't care if he lives or dies. When his wife got sick and died after he left New Haven to fight in this rebellion, he lost all interest in living. I think General Arnold's real goal is to die gloriously on the battlefield. That's why he's so damned fearless in battle."

"The men love him for that," Wilkinson said. "They see him as the most gallant general in the army. General Gates believes that he's seriously demented."

Varick laughed. "And they're all completely correct in their assessments, aren't they?"

Fraser. 1777

The sniper fire was too heavy and too accurate. For the moment, the English could move no farther. It was no more than a temporary halt to the advance, Fraser knew, but the lack of progress left him furious anyway. He had no idea what was happening to Burgoyne on his left or with Phillips and the baron on Burgoyne's left, but for now Fraser was preoccupied with his own difficulties.

The thick and distressingly deadly musket fire from the trees was taking down Fraser's men in complete ranks every time they tried to march forward, and they couldn't even see the opposition yet. In response, the English fired disciplined volleys into the woods ahead from their Brown Bess muskets – inflicting some damage, Fraser was sure, but he couldn't determine how much. And each time the English rose and formed up for an advance, the sniper fire intensified, forcing them back into cover behind the trees.

Moreover, the fog had returned, only now it was fog not from the river but from smoke created by gunfire from both forces. Visibility amid these trees was wretched. Fraser was red-faced with frustration when Lieutenant Dunbar, who was commanding Fraser's small supply of cannon, approached the general through the smoke-shrouded tree trunks. Dunbar had with him, under the control of his pistol, a young Army of the United States captain clad in the garb of a woodsman — a prisoner who'd been taken by the savages, Dunbar explained.

Fraser questioned the man himself.

"What's your name?"

"I'm Captain Van Swearingham of Morgan's Rangers."

"Where's the main body of your forces?" Fraser demanded.

"Back there," the captain said, gesturing over his shoulder.

"How many men? What strength?"

"I don't know for sure."

That was a lie, Fraser knew. "Who commands?"

"General Gates. General Arnold is second in command."

"Where are they?"

"I don't know."

Fraser studied the rebel captain. The man was visibly scraped up and bloodied. The savages did not tend toward gentleness with their captives. But the man seemed in an annoyingly fine humor. Fraser said, "Unless you inform me of your force's precise strength and positions, I'll hang you immediately. You do understand that, I trust."

The young captain shrugged. "You may if you please. There are many hundreds in the woods around us. Beyond the fact that you'll have business aplenty on this day, I have no information for you."

The man's obvious bravery both impressed and irritated Fraser, who grabbed the reins of his gray gelding and swung up into his saddle.

"There's a small cabin a short distance to the west," Fraser told Dunbar. "We're keeping prisoners there. Get this man into proper custody."

"Do you want him hanged, Sir?" Dunbar asked.

"It's a towering temptation," Fraser replied, "but, for the moment, I'll resist it"

Then the general galloped off through the thick, smoky woods to survey his stalled line.

Varick. 1777

Slightly drunk – ever so slightly, actually, given the gravity of the situation – Dirk Varick was standing just outside the Army of the United States's headquarters, taking in the growing sounds of battle to the north, when Arnold stepped outside the building. Arnold's face was a conspicuously bright pink, and his brow was furrowed.

He was close to exploding, Varick knew. He had seen this before.

"Sir?" Varick said.

"No," Arnold said quietly, "I haven't killed him yet, although I find the urge very nearly overpowering. Find a mount, Dirk; you're going for a ride. Send out the New Hampshire Continentals and the regiments of Scammel and Cilley. Tell them to move to Morgan's left to confront Burgoyne's right directly. We can't let those bastards out of the woods, and sooner or later they'll break into the open unless we throw more troops at them."

"So, he's finally listening to you," Varick said.

"If he hadn't I'd have strangled him at his desk, as he well understands by now. While you're out, identify for me five more regiments that can move into action on short notice. They'll go in as reserves as soon as these new troops are in position and properly engaged."

"Very good, General," Varick said.

"And Dirk ..." Arnold said.

"Yes, General?"

"No more rum, Dirk – not until we've settled today's bloody business. Then I'll drink with you."

Varick saluted smartly. "Very good, Sir."

Burgoyne. 1777

The full English line, Burgoyne understood, now stretched several miles on either side of his position in the center as his troops approached the southern edge of the forest ahead and the vast, oblong-shaped clearing of farm fields beyond. As Burgoyne had expected, his ranks had been thinned by sniper fire during the arduous advance through the woods, but in the open the rebels would find no hiding places. Grapeshot from Burgoyne's cannon would decimate them. All he had to do was to get those big guns properly in position. The grapeshot combined with volleys of gunfire from his infantry would do the job nicely.

"I can see daylight ahead, Sir," Clerke called out.

"Blessed daylight, Sir Francis," Burgoyne called out in response. "God's own daylight. It's time now to move the cannon forward and into position."

Babette. 1777

All the officers' women were in place when the first casualties began arriving. Babette had been assigned the task of preparing bandages – of ripping into pieces Philip Schuyler's elegant linen sheets, of which there was a gigantic pile at her feet. Babette preferred to perform the chore outdoors, on a bench just outside the hut that overlooked the river. In the cool, crisp morning air, the fog was slowly lifting. Inside the hut, Babette had noticed – with all the surgeons and orderlies and the other women all buzzing about, the air was already stifling.

After those first cannon blasts, the sounds of gunfire from the south had begun to blossom. It now existed as a more or less constant din off in the distance – staccato bursts of musketry punctuated by the boom of cannon. If she looked closely, she could see the powder smoke rise above the trees far to the south. As time wore on, and the noise became a fairly constant crackle off in the distance, Babette was surprised to find herself growing accustomed to it.

All the officers' wives were on hand now, having arrived one after the other in ox-carts and carriages, some with their servants, some completely alone. Lady Harriet Acland arrived in a calash with her gigantic Newfoundland, Jack, at her side. The huge dog was romping with the children of the baroness in the small yard behind the building. Babette had met all of these women at one time or another during Burgoyne's elegant evenings of entertaining on the campaign trail to the north. Now she saw them in a totally different light. Instead of fine gowns, the women now wore old clothing. Their hair was tied back from their faces with scarves or even bits of rag. They spoke little and went about their various chores with cool, practiced precision. All these gentle-born women, she realized, had performed these nursing chores many times before. Each knew precisely what was required of her.

The first casualties were brought in as morning faded. A wagon bearing eight wounded men moved north on the road and stopped in front of the building. The mud-caked men were bloodied and moaning. Two were already dead. Babette watched as their corpses were carried around to the back of the building, where the baroness's children played with the huge Newfoundland.

From her position on the bench in front of the hut, where she kept her hands busy ripping up sheets, Babette could hear the laughter of the children continue unabated.

Morgan. 1777

"They're coming through," Tim Murphy called out to Morgan as the rangers backed cautiously out of the smoke-choked woods into the open ground of Freeman's fields. The English had drawn too near now for Morgan to try to maintain his position in the trees.

The relentless beat of their drums was almost deafening.

"Get the men away from the edge of the woods here," Morgan bellowed, "and get them down on their bellies in the field about a hundred and twenty yards back. That's beyond the effective range of the enemy muskets. We can fire from flat down on the dirt. Tell all the men to reload while on their backs. I want no man standing up to reload and becoming a tall target for musket ball or grapeshot. And tell them to shoot the artillerymen first, if they can – and the officers, too. Now, spread the word, Tim."

Without a sound, Murphy faded back into the forest to pass along the order. As his rangers poured from the woods, Morgan assessed his strength. He had less than his original five hundred now, but his force remained essentially intact, as far as he could determine. In just a few moments, Morgan had his men lying prone in the dirt well back from the forest's edge, Pennsylvania rifles ready, listening to the English drums as they drew ever closer inside the tree line. As the first red coats came into view through the trees, Morgan put his turkey call to his lips and sounded the command to fire. What resulted was a sharp rattle of gunfire as a thick, billowing cloud of black powder smoke rose up from the dirt of Freeman's farm. As the smoke cleared, Morgan noted with satisfaction, the red coats were no longer visible in the trees. That first rank had been cut down where they'd been marching.

"Reload in teams and fire at will," Morgan called out. "We have to get those damned artillerymen before they can get us. Pick off the bastards as soon as they're in sight."

Gates. 1777

A messenger from Morgan burst through the door as Arnold, Gates and several other senior commanders studied their maps. The courier was a smallish, dirt-streaked man in buckskin who didn't even bother to salute.

"Colonel Morgan's compliments," the courier gasped out, still winded from his run across the fields. "We have their forces stopped at the tree line on the north side of the fields. The colonel believes we might have gotten Burgoyne with a well-placed shot."

Arnold slapped the desktop vigorously. "Good. Now we have the bastards."

"If it was really Burgoyne," Gates said quietly.

"Yes, General," Arnold said. "If it was really him."

Burgoyne. 1777

The southern edge of the woods was marked by a thin strip of wispy pines. As each marching rank of English infantry reached that position, a storm of fire from the open ground tore it completely apart. Now the power smoke was a blinding cloak over the entire area, blotting out the pallid sunlight. Burgoyne, on his white mount only a few yards back in the trees from the edge of the woods, could see nothing beyond. Nor could any of his troops, he knew. Nor could the rebel marksmen, Burgoyne was certain, but their fire continued unabated. The rebels were simply aiming into the smoke, hoping to hit something – pretty much anything, it seemed – and enjoying a disturbing degree of success in that task. Four times Burgoyne's officers ordered bayonet charges into the smoky fields. Four times the English troops vanished into the billows of smoke as the rebel rifles spat out lead. Four times no English soldiers returned.

"We're halted here," Clerke said needlessly. "We're blind in this damnable smoke."

"So are they," Burgoyne pointed out.

"Not completely, it seems," Clerke said. "They're getting the gunners and some of our officers, Sir, every time the smoke clears for even a moment. Captain Green went down not long ago from his white horse. They must know by now that you're here at the center. They might figure now that they've gotten you."

"Let us hope fervently," Burgoyne said through the surrounding din of musket fire and cannon blasts, "that their disappointment continues unabated."

Phillips. 1777

At the bottom of the fortified hill along the river road, well to the left of both Burgoyne's position at the edge of the forest and the left wing commanded by Riedesel, Will Phillips was in a tightly controlled rage. His troops and guns were arrayed along the road, amply shielded by heavy volleys of fire from his protective infantrymen from capture or interference. In his royal artillery officer's coat of dark blue, Phillips raced atop his horse back and forth behind the guns, directing their relentless loading and firing. But once the log hillside fortifications had been reduced to kindling and the earthen breastworks along the hillside had been converted to piles of loose dirt, Phillips had been reduced to blindly firing high over the hilltop. He was simply hoping that his shells were doing some damage to the rebel forces beyond but unable, in the thick, rolling fog of gunpowder smoke that had consumed the entire field of battle, to determine if his beloved guns were having any positive effect whatever.

From atop the hill and across the field, he could clearly hear the intermittent boom of cannon blasts, which he assumed issued from the big guns hauled into the woods that morning by his comrades. But the English cannon fire from the main battlefield was only spotty – not the continuous roar of doom that Phillips knew would be necessary to clear the field of rebel marksmen. Phillips simply couldn't tell what was happening up there, and the courier system between the various commands was undependable this day, as it often was under heavy battle conditions. The rebel sharpshooters, Phillips surmised, were simply picking off most of the English couriers as they moved along the line.

"I'm going up there," Phillips finally told Lieutenant Twiss, who had accompanied the artillery force along the road to supervise the repair of bridges as Phillips and his big guns moved south that morning. "I'm going to haul four of these guns up that hillside and across the field to where General Burgoyne is positioned and give him some more firepower."

Twiss, safely positioned behind a cannon, immediately stood up and gazed up into his commander's stern face. "General, we don't know what's going on up there – what you'll be riding into."

Phillips shook his head dismissively. "I know that our work here is well enough done. All we're doing here now is making the rubble bounce — blasting log splinters and showers of dirt into the air. This hillside is clear, Lieutenant. I'm now taking the guns to where they might do more good."

"I urge caution, Sir," Twiss said.

"Caution be damned," Phillips said tersely. "Our people up there have too little artillery. You can hear from all the way down here how seldom we're getting off the sort of fire we should be offering the rebels. Order up four guns harnessed to horses and a party of men to escort them. I'm going up the hill to the real battle, Lieutenant."

"Very good, Sir," Twiss said, saluting.

In just a few minutes, Phillips — along with his men, his four cannon and his horses — were gathered at the bottom on the hillside, the river at their backs. From the back of his mount, the general drew his saber and pointed it up the smoke-choked hillside.

"Forward," Will Phillips bellowed out, digging his spurs into the flanks of his mount and driving the animal into a mad gallop up the incline.

Behind him, his officers and infantrymen began their climb as the horses dragging the four cannon dug their hooves into the soft dirt of the badly battered hillside overlooking the gray-green waters of the Hudson River.

Babette. 1777

Wounded and dying soldiers lay all over the yard now, literally hundreds of them stretched out in and between the hospital tents that had been erected around the hut by the river. They had begun as a trickle. Then their arrival had become a stream, and now it was a virtual tidal wave. The ravaged soldiers gushed blood by the gallon as they were tended to or as they moaned or screamed beneath the care of officers' wives or more earthy women from the contingent of several hundred wives, girlfriends and whores that had accompanied the rank and file army south from Canada. Inside the tiny building, as they dispensed rum and laudanum liberally to the wounded, blood-splattered surgeons sewed or chopped or sawed and swore horribly. No niceties were observed here, Babette noted early on, especially as the wounded began arriving by the score. One particularly surly and hard-pressed Irish surgeon, annoyed that Babette had bumped into him in the doorway as she'd hustled inside with more torn-up sheets as bandages, had snarled at the commanding general's lady to, "Stay the fook out of me way."

The next wagon contained three men. Babette was horrified to realize that she knew them all. All were officers. All had, at one time or another, made her acquaintance at one of the commanding general's galas at either Skene's mansion to the north, in the big house in Fort Edward or at Schuyler's Saratoga mansion just to the north along the river road.

One was a Major Harnage, whose wife was among the nurses laboring at the side of the baroness. Without even a hint of distress on her face, the businesslike Madame Harnage took immediate command of her husband's care. Another was a youthful lieutenant whose name Babette could not recall. His wife, whom Babette had also met, immediately rushed to his side. The lieutenant had suffered a grievous head wound. As did all present, Babette understood this to mean that the wife would soon be a widow. So, too, did the lieutenant's lady understand this, but she betrayed no emotion. Instead, she remained stoically calm, holding her husband's hand in the side yard as she awaited his trip inside to the surgeon, who would surely be able to accomplish nothing with so immense an injury.

These English women, Babette thought. Do they have no blood in their veins?

The worst, though, was Captain Young, a handsome young man of no more than nineteen who'd captivated Babette with his boyish charm only a few nights before at the most recent dinner party Burgoyne had thrown at Schuyler's estate. Captain Young had two wounds, one in the left leg that bled heavily and another in his lower abdomen, which bled hardly at all. Babette helped carry his stretcher into the hut. The Irish surgeon immediately tied off the leg wound with a tourniquet.

"You'll be losing that leg, lad," the surgeon said as Babette stood next to the blood-soaked table on which Captain Young had been stretched out. "I'll not be able to save it for you."

For a moment, Captain Young said nothing. Then, in a voice as thin as paper, he said, "The gut wound will likely kill me anyway, am I not correct?"

"Aye," the surgeon snapped out. "But if it doesn't, and if I don't take this leg, gangrene will poison you in just a few days. Give yourself a chance, lad."

"Tend to someone else," Captain Young said dismissively.

Wordlessly, the surgeon moved to another table. Babette leaned down over the young officer.

"They might be able to save you," she said.

Young shook his head. "If they can't save all of me, Madame, then there's no point in being saved. Tell General Burgoyne to let my father know that I died bravely in the king's service. I'm an only son. My father will need to know that."

"Woman!" the surgeon snapped out from the next table. "Come here and help these other ladies hold this man down."

"I have to go," Babette said to the youthful officer.

"As do I," Captain Young responded.

Morgan. 1777

The trees. Morgan loved them – or, at least, he harbored vastly more affection for trees than for open ground.

And that's where most of his rangers were now, settled back in the relative safety of a tight row of trees along the southern edge of Freeman's farm. From high branches or from behind tree trunks, Morgan's men were pouring fire into the expanse of Freeman's fields as the English moved out from the tree line on the north side. Even with the dense field of fire Morgan's Rangers had brought to bear on the English at the tree line, the periodic blasts of grapeshot from their cannon had driven Morgan's men back, tripping in the thick smoke over the bloodied, mangled corpses of their less fortunate comrades. Now, though, back in the cover of the trees while the English moved about in the open ground just outside the northern tree line — fine targets despite the intense visibility problems for each side — Morgan's confidence was returning. He had no firm idea of how much of his command remained. With his own eyes he'd seen a distressing number of good men fall. But the steady rattle of fire the remaining rangers produced indicated that there were enough of them left to continue inflicting real damage on the English cannon squads.

And the English officers, of course. Morgan's men were managing to bring down the officers with both glee and deadly dependability. That was important not because the English troops needed officers to direct their actions in battle. The tough, well-trained English infantrymen fought fiercely enough with only sergeants to guide their aggression. But if the lobsterbacks were to break under heavy fire from Morgan's men there would be too few officers left standing just behind the front lines to effectively drive them at saber point back into combat position.

With cool precision and from the shelter of a thick maple tree, Dan Morgan directed a shot from his own Pennsylvania rifle into the smoke-shrouded field before him. Several hundred yards away, through a break in the thick powder smoke, he spotted a red-clad figure on the English side go down. That resulted from his own shot, Morgan hoped, although there was no way of knowing. His troops could dependably load and get off three to four shots every minute, and the field of fire being put up by his remaining rangers was both steady and impressive. Some, he knew, had to be low on powder and lead at this point, but he'd spotted rangers retreating from the open ground scavenging for ammunition from the corpses of their fallen fellows, as they'd been trained to do, and he'd watched them also retrieving the invaluable Pennsylvania rifles that helped Morgan's rangers fight so effectively.

As Morgan rolled back behind his tree to reload, he became aware of Wilkinson moving, bent at the waist, through the trees to Morgan's side as Wilkinson scoured the battlefield gathering information to carry back to the commanding general.

"How goes it?" Wilkinson asked.

"We're holding our own," Morgan said, pouring powder down the barrel of his rifle. "We did miss Burgoyne, though, as it turns out. I spotted him not long ago, still alive and kicking, riding back and forth behind their front line. The man we thought was Burgoyne must have been some other royal officer."

"A pity," Wilkinson said. "Well, we still have time before sundown."

Morgan said, "We've been at this – what? – three hours now — four, maybe?"

"About," Wilkinson said as he flattened on the ground beside the ranger commander. "It's mid afternoon now. If we can hold them where they are until sundown, they'll have to withdraw back into the woods when night falls."

"Maybe," Morgan said. "They've gotten past the woods now and taken this field, and they won't give it up until the light fades completely. You're right, though; the trick will be hold them here, and we're doing what we can. We need more men out here, Colonel. Tell that to General Gates."

"I'll tell him, but I can't guarantee he'll accommodate you, Colonel Morgan."

"We've been back and forth with them on this ground," Morgan said, rolling to his right on his belly, sighting along the barrel of his rifle and firing once more as he spoke. As Morgan rolled back behind the tree and began reloading he said, "Twice, we've moved forward and grabbed a few of their big guns, but they came back and chased us away before we could use them. We've been killing their artillerymen, though. With my own eyes, I've seen a good twenty of them go down. That has kept their big guns silent for long periods, while they re-manned. If we can keep that up, we might be able to push them back a bit. Christ knows we're trying."

"I'll pass that along to General Gates," Wilkinson said.

"Assuming that General Arnold hasn't throttled him yet," Morgan said, rolling to his right and firing once more.

Phillips. 1777

Will Phillips was following the sound of the guns.

On horseback, he'd led his force up the hillside, musket balls buzzing around his ears. With his saber, chopping and stabbing from his saddle, Phillips had personally killed two of the one hundred or so rebels atop the hill. Then his own infantry, charging up the hill behind the general, caught up with him and routed the rest. Through the billowing clouds of powder smoke and the racket of musket fire all around, Phillips then galloped his mount across the field, his four cannon trailing in his path, to the spot where he supposed Burgoyne's center to be just outside the tree line to the north. Guiding his mount through the smoke, Phillips finally happened upon an English cannon emplacement about three-quarters of the way across the largest field on Freeman's farm. He found a lieutenant named Hadden in charge of the gun.

"Where's Captain Jones?" Phillips demanded, inquiring of the officer he knew to be in command of the cannon Burgoyne had brought with the center force.

"Badly wounded, Sir," Hadden said. "The sixty-second has suffered more than two hundred killed, wounded or taken prisoner. We've already lost more than thirty of our artillerymen."

Phillips spat out a curse. That meant that Burgoyne had lost two-thirds of his trained gunners. No wonder the cannon fire Phillips had heard from the river road had been so sporadic.

"Four guns are following me, Lieutenant," Phillips barked out. "I want you to spread them out along this line and direct your grapeshot into those woods over there. That's where the heaviest rebel fire is coming from. You'll need more men out here, too."

"General Burgoyne dispatched the Twentieth to the left, Sir. They're clearing the woods over there."

"Good," Phillips said. "That'll pave the way for Baron von Riedesel and his Germans to move out here into the open and hit the rebel right. I just rode right through them with only a few shots coming my way. The rebels seem sparsely manned over there."

"They're not heavy anywhere that we can see, Sir," Hadden said. "But, by God, the devils can shoot. If we could just get closer to them with our bayonets …"

As Hadden spoke, a pellet of lead came whizzing through the smoke and struck the barrel of the cannon with the force of a blacksmith's hammer on an anvil — and a clanging sound not dissimilar. Instinct prompted each officer to duck at the sound.

"Yes," Phillips said, slowly raising his head. "Well, there's an argument to be made, Lieutenant, that we might be just a trifle too close. Here come my cannon. Use them to full effect on those woods."

Hadden drew himself to full attention and snapped off a smart salute.

Digging his heels into his mount, Phillips called out over his shoulder, "Stay low, Lieutenant. There'll be ample time for military courtesy once the lead stops flying."

Wilkinson. 1777

He's out of control, Gates thought. The man is simply insane.

"We can still lose this," the red-faced Arnold was shouting. "There's daylight enough left for them to push us completely off this plateau. You must send more men, General Gates. You simply must!"

"Our fortifications must be manned …" Gate began.

"The hell with our fortifications. Morgan and Dearborn have them stopped, but they can't hold them all day. If the English get past Morgan and Dearborn and then past the troops with Cilley and Scammel, they'll use their cannon to reduce those redoubts to rubble. There'll be no stopping them then."

Gates was about to respond when Wilkinson burst through the headquarters door. Saluting in only a perfunctory manner this time, Wilkinson immediately broke into his report. The boy was excited, Gates noted. For himself, Gates felt no undue excitement. He was not an excitable man, and he viewed his calm, cool demeanor as one of his most laudable qualities as a commander. Horatio Gates always kept his head. What troubled him most deeply about Arnold was that the younger man seemed to relish the loss of self control. These petulant tantrums constituted a childish self-indulgence on Arnold's part that Gates found positively abhorrent. He viewed them as a distasteful display of total self-fixation on Arnold's part.

"Colonel Morgan is begging for more troops, Sir," Wilkinson was saying. "He's holding them back, but he and his rangers are hard-pressed. I know that's true, General Gates. I was amid them for more than an hour."

"I have none to send him," Gates said quietly.

"You have Broeck, Cook and Latimer and their Connecticut militiamen," Arnold snarled. "You have Livingstone's and Van Courtland's New Yorkers. You have General Learned's brigade. You have Marshall's regiment. You have a wealth of men in reserve behind our fortifications, General Gates. We outnumber the bastards now."

"The camp must remain secure," Gates replied.

"The entire damned rebellion must remain secure," Arnold roared, spinning about, grabbing his uniform hat off its hook near the door and storming out with a shout over his shoulder. "By God, I'll soon put an end to this."

The door slammed behind Arnold. A few seconds later, Gates and Wilkinson caught the sound of Arnold's horse galloping off.

"Find him," Gates told Wilkinson quietly. "Tell General Arnold to come back here immediately, or I'll have him hanged for desertion. I swear I will hang the man, Colonel. Tell him that."

Wilkinson located Arnold in camp, locked in intense conversation with both Varick and a mob of men from the Massachusetts line who were eager for news from the front. Wilkinson caught Arnold's arm and pulled him apart from the knot of soldiers.

"He'll have you dangling from a tree, General," Wilkinson said.

"You know I'm right," Arnold said.

"Yes, you're right; of course you're right. Between the two of us, I'm sure we can convince him of that. But I can't do it alone, General. I lack your standing, Sir."

"I'm ordering out the troops – all the ones I mentioned and more. Then I'll come back, Wilkinson – not before."

"Do it, then," Wilkinson said. "We can persuade him to approve the order after you've given it – but only if we work together. I need you, General Arnold, and the rebellion needs you – not out on the field fighting but back in that cabin, helping me make the case to General Gates for what's right."

Despite his obvious and still only barely controlled rage, Arnold smiled slightly. "You'll be a general one of these days, Wilkinson – not because you're a born warrior but because you're a born political beast. All right, I'll give the order and then I'll go back."

"You must apologize, General," Wilkinson warned. "He won't listen without an apology."

Arnold tore off his hat and gazed skyward for a long moment. He took a deep, ragged breath. Then he fixed Wilkinson with a fierce, steely stare.

"I'll do it," Benedict Arnold said finally, "but a musket ball through the heart would constitute a far gentler fate."

Fraser. 1777

Fraser bent down over the young Army of the United States officer as the woods rattled with musket fire and the powder smoke shrouded the scene. The lieutenant in his bloody uniform coat of blue and buff was no more than a boy, actually, perhaps eighteen years of age, possibly even younger. The young man had gone down in a blaze of musket fire. That had happened after Fraser had noted that his new opposition preferred the ground instead of the trees and seemed to shoot with far less precision than the rebel troops that had stopped Fraser's force earlier. In response to that observation, Fraser had ordered his men to advance behind a series of musket volleys and brutal bayonet charges. The standard English tactics had proven far more effective against conventional Army of the United States infantry than against the irregulars Fraser had confronted earlier. Fraser's force was now moving forward with relative freedom.

The young officer clutched both arms over his red-soaked middle. He was bleeding to death inside, Fraser knew. The general had seen many such wounds in the past. Gut wounds were virtually always fatal – if not immediately then within a day or two as infection set in.

"Am I dying?" the boy asked. His voice was little more than a whisper.

"You are," Fraser told him. "We'll return your body to your army with appropriate honors. To whose command do you belong?"

"I'm in General Learned's brigade."

"How long have you been on the field?"

"Not long," the boy got out. His voice was as weak as the rustle of fall leaves. "We were ordered out to bolster Colonel Morgan's forces, but we found you before we found them."

Fraser said, "Morgan was here for a while, I surmise, but he must have moved most of his men to the center after slowing us up as he did. General Learned, it would appear, led you too far left in the fog of battle. What's your name, boy?"

The young officer opened his mouth to speak, but no sound issued forth. Fraser gazed down on the fallen soldier's wide-eyed, open-mouthed face. He was dead. Slowly, wreathed in the smoke, Fraser stood up over the corpse. Dying men, he knew from experience, seldom lied. If Fraser was opposed now only by standard rebel infantry, instead of those infuriating sharpshooters, he knew he could now break through to the open ground.

Finally.

Riedesel. 1777

The baron had moved his forces steadily forward, both surprised and puzzled over the feeble resistance he'd encountered. Ahead and to his right, he could hear the sound of heavy firing. Burgoyne was seeing action, he could tell, and possibly Fraser as well in his position much further to the right. Riedesel was not surprised when the courier arrived from that direction.

"General Phillips' compliments, Sir," the courier said, saluting smartly.

Sitting in his saddle beside the baron on his own mount, Breymann translated into German for his commander as the courier delivered his message in English. Burgoyne at the center and Fraser on the right were heavily engaged, although Fraser was on the move with a renewed advance against rebel infantry. Burgoyne was especially hard pressed by sharpshooters and was making slower progress. General Phillips had moved most his forces and most of his guns from the river road and up into the open field, leaving only a skeleton force to guard the supply train, whose defense now fell to Riedesel.

Phillips now requested the use of two of the cannon that Riedesel had brought with him.

"He wants his guns?" Riedesel said to Breymann. "All right, then, give General Phillips his guns. He aches to use them, I know. Tell him also that we will stay here on the left to protect the supply train, but we will move to the right as soon as we are able to effectively bolster the commanding general's center while we protect the supplies simultaneously."

Breymann translated the baron's response. After the courier replied to the German colonel, Breymann told Riedesel, "He says we have had it easy thus far but that we will be moving into heavy fire as we advance further."

The baron smiled slightly. Then he said in German, "It's about time, I would say. Take two companies, Colonel, and the guns General Phillips requests. Have this man lead you to the point of the fiercest conflict. I shall follow with the bulk of our force and our remaining cannon. We have for our comrades who fell at Bennington some revenge to exact, do we not?"

Breymann nodded grimly. "We do indeed, Sir. Thank you."

With banners fluttering and drums booming, the baron resumed his forward march as soon as Breymann departed with his two companies and Phillips' cannon. Riedesel was careful to maintain a stout line along the road to protect the supply train, but he longed to move to his right as the enemy firing intensified from that direction. The day was growing late, he knew, and the fury of the battle was coming to his ears through the trees. The baron was eager to join it. After what seemed like an eternity of marching to drums and enduring stray sniper shots, Riedesel finally spotted the light of open ground far ahead. As he stepped up his pace, moving up on his mount to the very front of his advancing command, another courier arrived. Grabbing an English-speaking junior officer to translate, the baron listened intently as the courier informed him that the battle was raging no more than a mile and a half ahead and to the right in the open field of a farm at the bottom of a small, wooded hillside. General Burgoyne, Riedesel was told, needed his help immediately.

"Specht!" von Riedesel called to one of his senior officers. "I'm moving forward with the Rhetz regiment. You continue moving along this line with the forty-seventh and the cannon. Move right into the rebel flank when you reach open ground."

"Would you not prefer that I take the point, Sir?" Specht said.

Riedesel's face turned a vivid red. He roared, "No! There's a fight up ahead, and I'm missing it."

Fraser. 1777

When Simon Fraser's weary and somewhat mauled right wing finally managed to push Learned's infantry from the woods, Fraser instantly moved his troops left into the open ground, where they formed up in formal combat ranks, as they'd been trained to do. Assault ranks were almost impossible to maintain on heavily forested ground. Here, though, his men finally were in position to do their best, Fraser knew. The rebel infantry was backing up reluctantly under the assault of the English musket volleys and periodic bayonet charges, but even through the thick, choking powder smoke that shrouded the open ground Fraser could see that perhaps five thousand men on both sides were now locked in mortal combat in the fading light of day.

Bugles blared. Sabers and tomahawks flashed through the smoke. Men swore, screamed and moaned. Drums drummed. Cannon boomed. Muskets barked. So did hard-edged Royal Army sergeants in the varied accents of East London, Liverpool and Yorkshire. The air was thick with lead. Fraser ignored it. He well understood that his life was now in the hands of fate. Courage and calm could win the day, as foolhardiness could also lose it, but none of those qualities would necessarily keep him alive. Fraser could only keep cool and command decisively and trust for his own survival in nothing more reassuring than pure luck.

Many others had seen no luck, he could see. Corpses were strewn everywhere on the field. Fraser could see English redcoats, Germans in coats of blue and green, rebels in blue and buff and homespun and leather – all soaked in their own blood. Men of all colors – white, red and black – struggled, crawled or lay unmoving in the dirt amid the billowing smoke. The carnage was simply immense, and the firing on both sides was essentially ceaseless. It was all madness – the same scene Fraser had witnessed in every major military confrontation of his lengthy career in the king's service. It was what he had expected. This was war, and war, Simon Fraser well knew, was madness in concrete form.

From the flow of the troops on each side and from the frenzied English bugle calls to his left, Fraser understood more or less immediately that Burgoyne's center was in danger of obliteration unless Fraser could turn the rebel left flank. As he threw his troops into that task, Simon Fraser spotted Riedesel on his horse several hundred yards away at the head of a racing mob of Germans. They had arrived at the top of a small hill at the eastern edge of the clash. Between the hilltop and the battlefield lay a deep ditch from which rebel fire was issuing. Riedesel's saber flashed; then he and his troops poured down the hill into the rebel right flank and the frantic mob of battling soldiers below. Behind the baron and his forces came a second wave of Germans, this one dragging two cannon down the hillside. From his vantage point at the western edge of the battlefield, Fraser could hear the thundering blast of the German cannon and the rise of the Germanic cheers over the din of the scene before him. He knew that the baron and his men were successfully clearing both the ditch and the woods just to the south of the main conflict.

Now, perhaps, we can actually win this, Simon Fraser thought as he drew his saber, drove his spurs into his own mount and plunged into the mob.

Burgoyne. 1777

As darkness fell, firing slowly died down on both sides. The rebels were withdrawing to the woods to the south of the field, Burgoyne knew. In the stygian shelter of the trees, they would dot the woods with snipers and form a tight line behind their remaining fortifications to protect their camp. The day's engagement was over unless Burgoyne chose to send his remaining force forward into the woods for a full, frontal assault in the darkness. Burgoyne did not so choose.

Instead, he had his buglers call his commanders while a bare-headed Sir Francis Clerke moved frantically with three other officers about the English force assessing the day's damage. By the time Fraser, Phillips, Riedesel and the other senior officers made their way to Burgoyne's side at the northern edge of the field Clerke was making his report.

"We count not quite six hundred killed, wounded or missing, Sir," Clerke was saying. "Of those, about thirty five are officers, including two lieutenant colonels, three majors and nine captains. We've also lost fourteen lieutenants, a number of ensigns and twenty six sergeants."

"It was those damnable sharpshooters," Burgoyne said. "Every time the smoke cleared they targeted commanders."

"They're bloody good at that," Fraser said.

"Yes, they rather are, aren't they?" Burgoyne said. "I imagine that the sixty-second regiment was hardest hit."

Clerke nodded. "Only sixty effectives remain of the sixty-second regiment, Sir."

Burgoyne turned to Riedesel. "You saved the day for us, my good Baron," the commanding general said in French. "You turned their right flank and saved us from a horrific misfortune at the center. His Majesty and I are most grateful."

"I but performed my duty," Riedesel responded stiffly in French.

"This has been an English victory with German assistance," Phillips said stiffly as he picked up the gist of the conversation.

To Phillips' mind, too many English soldiers had died today for Burgoyne to allot so much credit to the German hired hands.

"Yes, Burgoyne said. "Well, a victory of sorts, at any rate. We do command the field. That means that we won the day, but their army remains intact, and our losses have been distressingly daunting."

"Theirs might be even higher," Fraser said. "The field is littered with their dead and wounded as well as ours."

"Perhaps," Burgoyne said, "but they can recruit more men from their colonial militias, especially since we failed today to destroy their army."

"All the more reason for us to resume the attack in the morning," Phillips said.

"I shall consider that decision overnight," Burgoyne said.

"The men are spent," Fraser said.

"So are theirs," Burgoyne pointed out.

"General Burgoyne, we most assuredly can't retreat now," Phillips said firmly.

"Nor shall we," Burgoyne said quickly. "Instead, we shall camp here for the night behind a sturdy picket line, retrieve our wounded in the morning and – unless they launch an attack against us with the rising of the sun, which I very much doubt they'll attempt – we'll bury our dead right here with appropriate honors. By then I shall have made up my mind on a future course of action, gentlemen."

"It'll be hard on our men to have to listen all night to their wounded fellows moaning and dying in the darkness only a short distance out front of our lines," Fraser said.

"Lacking firm information on the enemy's position, and with

even the possibility of a daybreak attack from them, we have no choice about that," Burgoyne told his senior commanders. "We'll also exchange prisoners tomorrow. That should settle down our troops a bit. I have no use for their men, gentlemen. Among other things, they'll consume too much of our dwindling food supply, and I very much want our own people back with us as quickly as possible. Upon the dawning, if we're not under attack, I'll dispatch a messenger under a white flag to General Gates. Then we can tend to our wounded out front who survive the night and, if I'm then so inclined, resume the attack after that."

"We should permit no fires tonight," Fraser cautioned.

"Oh, God, no," Burgoyne said. "They'd pick off our men by the firelight and chuckle amongst themselves during every second of the butchery. The troops will eat cold food from the supply train tonight, Simon. Have the word passed, Sir Francis."

"And after tomorrow, Sir?" Phillips pressed. "What then?"

Burgoyne remained silent for a long moment. Then he said, "We'll camp here while we clean up the field. At present – and subject to alteration after I duly consider all factors involved – my inclination would be then to move back a bit for a few days and rest the troops. For myself, I would prefer another brief sojourn at Schuyler's lovely estate before we resume our march forward."

"We should attack upon the dawning, Jack," Phillips advised. "They'll be as battered and as worn as we are, and they lack our discipline."

"I shall consider your counsel, Will," Burgoyne said. "You are dismissed, gentlemen. My most sincere compliments on your gallantry and on that of your commands. Stay awake tonight. I could be wrong. They might just launch an attack against us at dawn, so we must remain vigilant. And, as General Phillips argues, we might yet launch an attack of our own."

As the other senior officers moved off to see to their various commands, Simon Fraser lagged behind. He found himself troubled by Burgoyne's obvious indecision. When the other senior commanders were out of earshot, Fraser asked, "Have you heard from General Clinton since he left New York City, Jack?"

"I have not," Burgoyne said quietly.

"Worrisome," Fraser said, "especially in light of our losses today."

"Somewhat worrisome, I will concede," Burgoyne said to his friend, "but soldiering can be a worrisome business, Simon."

"They fought better than we'd anticipated," Fraser said.

Burgoyne said, "It was a different sort of warfare they practiced today – the rebel troops in clothing that made them indistinguishable from their background, the disturbingly accurate fire from long distance in flexible skirmish lines. They fought as our savages fight but with better weaponry."

"All the more reason," Fraser said, "to ensure that the savages never get their hands on a goodly supply of muskets, wouldn't you say?"

"Indeed. Our troops are trained to fight against men of similar training. That's what slowed our progress and kept us from covering ground as quickly as we needed to."

"Well, we can't change tactics," Fraser said. "The men can't be retrained now."

"No," Burgoyne agreed. "Aside from which we lack the rebels' long distance rifles, and we can be thankful that they don't have more of them. But we're in the open now, Simon and that's very much in our favor. Man to man, they still can't stand against us in open ground."

"So, you'll take General Phillips' advice? We'll attack in the morning, then?"

"I'll ponder the matter," the commanding general told his friend.

Gates. 1777

Just before dawn, with moist fall mist from the Hudson swirling in the darkness, Wilkinson guided his still mud-caked mount to the small, crowded cabin that served as Gates' headquarters. Inside, Wilkinson found the commanding general at a table, studying maps of the battlefield and locked in intense consultation with a half dozen of his senior commanders, including a conspicuously agitated Benedict Arnold. No one had slept, Wilkinson could tell. For himself, Wilkinson had grabbed only a few hours sleep in a tent before he'd been awakened just a short while before.

"We have a deserter, Sir," Wilkinson said. "The man is a corporal from the sixty-second English regiment, which he informs us was badly mauled in yesterday's action. His teeth are blackened from where he used them to uncap cartridges."

"To hell with his teeth," Arnold snapped. "Did he have anything useful to tell us?"

Wilkinson stiffened slightly. Arnold was difficult and demanding under the best of circumstances, he knew, and the general's ferocious supply of energy had been insufficiently released in the confines of this small building the day before as the actual battle had unfolded miles away.

"Just provide us with the relevant information, Colonel," Gates said more gently.

"The enemy is well supplied in terms of munitions, Sir," Wilkinson said. "The deserter told us they'd each been issued sixty rounds of ammunition going into yesterday's engagement, and he showed us his cartridge box with sixty additional rounds issued to the English troops last night."

"We can supply no more than forty rounds per man left in fighting condition," Arnold told Gates. "I received word from General Schuyler back in Albany. He knows our munitions situation, and he's sending us all the lead from the windows of his town house and lead from windows all around Albany as well."

"Would that General Schuyler had some bayonets for us, too," General Learned said. "Our infantry has no more than one bayonet for every three muskets."

"Do they plan to attack?" Gates demanded, ignoring the comments of his senior commanders.

Wilkinson nodded. "The deserter believes they do, Sir. He said the Mutiny Act was read last night at the head of every English corps to remind the troops of their duty to the Crown. That's what prompted him to desert. After yesterday, he wants no more part of this engagement."

"Yes, well," Gates said, "get that red coat off the man and place him on our front lines. He'll not avoid a fight if one is to come today any more than the rest of us will. Get the men back on their feet, gentlemen, and form up the lines behind our fortifications. If this deserter is correct and the attack comes, we must be prepared."

"We're down fully a thousand effectives from yesterday's action, General Gates," Learned said as he moved to the door to depart and gather his troops. "The men are exhausted and battered. I count our strength at just under five thousand men fit to fight – roughly what the English have now, I would imagine, and they clearly have more munitions."

No one disputed Learned's assessment. He was a capable senior commander, well respected, and his estimate of the rebel army's vulnerability was a thing to be taken seriously.

"They might not come," Gates said. "We gave them heavy resistance, and they surely are bleeding as badly as we are. But we must be ready. All are dismissed. Courage, gentlemen."

Arnold lagged behind. "If I were Burgoyne," he said to Gates, "I would attack right through the river mist as the sun rises. He knows we're worn down now, and he's in the open ground with our right badly weakened. I would feint left and then come into our right with full force. I request, General Gates, that you permit me to take Morgan and three regiments out in front of the right wing to hit the English left before they can advance in force."

"No, General Arnold," Gates said quietly, moving into the speech he'd rehearsed meticulously in his mind during the meeting with his senior commanders. "You are a fine commander and an excellent tactician, but you are unacceptably rash, and your conduct yesterday was nothing less than insubordinate. You shall command troops here no longer, General Arnold. You are relieved, Sir. Retire immediately to your tent. That is where you and Major Varick shall spend the remainder of this engagement."

For a long moment, Arnold was speechless. "General Gates ..." he began at last.

"There will be no debate over this, General Arnold. If you dispute this order, I shall have you clapped in chains and held for a court martial. I am in command here, Sir, not you. Your conduct yesterday shall be duly noted in my report of this engagement to General Washington. He can then send for you to serve at his side to the south. He can court martial you. He can hang you, if he so chooses. I shall make no recommendation in that regard, but you will, indeed, report to your tent and remain there for the balance of this engagement."

In what was nearly a whisper, and with his eyes glittering with rage, Arnold said, "If we'd sent more men into the field earlier we could have beaten them. You are a coward, Sir, and we might well lose this engagement as a result of your craven instincts."

Gates' expression darkened markedly. "And you, General Arnold, are a consummate fool – an insubordinate and perhaps mutinous fool at that. You are dismissed. Report to your tent, General Arnold. Do so now."

Arnold stood quivering for a long moment. Then he turned, grabbed his hat and cloak and stormed out the door of the little building. Wilkinson, standing wide-eyed and aghast on the other side of the small room, said, "Sir, it was General Arnold's advice on tactics that saved the day for us."

"It was," Gates admitted, "but the price of that advice came too high, Colonel. General Arnold is a severe disruption to the discipline and good order of the army. You are to watch him as my agent, Colonel, and to ensure that my orders are carried out to the letter. Place General Arnold's forces under the immediate command of General Learned, and prepare our troops for defense against an attack. I still doubt that one will come, but we must be ready for it if it does."

Wilkinson saluted and disappeared immediately out the door. Slowly, Horatio Gates moved back to the table with its littered covering of maps.

Long overdue, the commanding general thought to himself with satisfaction.

Burgoyne. 1777

The courier arrived in the misty veil of pre-dawn darkness, just as the English troops were forming up for the attack. Burgoyne had finally decided just after midnight to launch an offensive in the morning. He'd ordered the attack for first light. Escorted into the commanding general's sprawling, pavilion-like tent, the smallish, mud-splattered cavalryman snapped off a salute and handed over a leather-bound packet. Burgoyne read the message carefully. He then dismissed the courier, threw his flowing blue cloak over his shoulders and sought out Fraser, whose headquarters had been set up well to the right of the commanding general's emplacement. Burgoyne, high atop his white horse, moved briskly toward Fraser's tent in chill air swarming with thick tendrils of fog. As he passed by this regimental encampment or that one, his filthy, blood splattered troops cheered him, their breath forming billowing clouds. Burgoyne acknowledged the acclaim with a nod of his head and a tip of his plumed hat. Fraser, alerted to the commanding general's arrival by the noise, was waiting for Burgoyne outside Fraser's tent.

"Clinton is coming," Burgoyne said quickly from the back of his mount. "Call off this morning's attack. We're falling back to Schuyler's estate until Sir Henry arrives. The men need the rest, and we need our hospital tents in a more secure location further north."

"Where is Sir Henry now?" Fraser asked.

"On the lower Hudson with two thousand men in a flotilla of vessels from New York Harbor. He has to make his way to West Point and fight his way past the rebel forts there. Then he'll join us. I estimate he'll need about two weeks before he can properly subdue those forts and reach this position from the south. We do have them now, Simon."

Fraser was elated. "Bloody marvelous. With us to their north and Clinton at their rear, they'll be forced to surrender or be crushed between us. Have you received word from St. Leger as well?"

"I have not." Burgoyne said. "St. Leger might be finding the going tough as he moves south from Ticonderoga. We did, certainly, and his force is much smaller than our main body was. But Clinton is all we need to assure victory, and we must soften up the rebels before Sir Henry arrives. I'm ordering all our cannon moved to this location. General Phillips can then commence a twenty-four-hour-a-day bombardment of the rebel positions, which should sweeten his mood markedly. I want them badly dispirited by the time Clinton's force gets here."

"Well," Fraser said, "we have the powder and shot for that chore. I wish we had more food for the troops, though"

Burgoyne smiled. "We'll all dine heartily this winter in Albany, Simon. By the time we move eastward in the spring to stamp out this rebellion once and for all, we'll all be as round and rosy as our moody German baron."

Babette. 1777

From the sprawling porch of Schuyler's mansion at Saratoga, in the swirl of mist from the river, Babette watched the ragged file of red-coated troops round the bend of the river road to the south. Clearly exhausted and worn down, they moved methodically into encampment mode all across Schuyler's rain-soaked fields, which were still blackened from the crops that had been set afire when the rebel general had abandoned the property months before. Tents were erected. Backpacks were lowered wearily to the ground. Bayonet-tipped muskets were stacked, stock-down and barrel up, in pyramidal groups in front of the rising tents. Campfires were begun. The army was settling in again, and still Babette could see no sign of Burgoyne.

It was nearly an hour before he arrived, Sir Francis at his side, at the head of his own cavalry regiment. Burgoyne was swathed in his dark cloak over his field uniform. A groom took his horse as Burgoyne dismounted and strode up the steps to the mansion's porch. Babette instantly fell into his arms. The commanding general was unshaven and smelled of sweat and wood smoke.

"Did you miss me?" Burgoyne said.

"You've been gone three days – an eternity," Babette said, her face buried in his chest. Then she pulled away and gestured out to the troops milling around the charred fields. "This can't be all that's left."

"Oh, no," Burgoyne said. "A large burial detail is at work on the battlefield. The bulk of our army is now entrenched on the heights above the river. General Phillips is cheerfully placing his cannon. The Earl of Balcarres occupies the open ground with light infantry. Breymann and the Germans occupy an elevated area just to the north. We're also building fortifications there. I've ordered the construction of three huge log breastworks – one atop the heights commanding the river road and the others for the benefit of Balcarres' troops and those of Breymann. We're dug in now within a mile and a half of the enemy lines, and we need hardened positions until our reinforcements arrive from the south. I received word from General Clinton, who's on his way now from New York City. All is unfolding nicely, my love. And I trust you were suitably amused during our separation?"

Babette caught the glint of gentle mockery in Burgoyne's eye and voice. She said, "You know what I was doing while you were out playing with your soldiers. It was awful, Jack – all that blood and suffering. But I've completely revised my judgment of the baroness. She's some woman. I watched her nurse the wounded with enormous compassion. She held men down and clutched and comforted them while the surgeons sawed away their arms and legs. The baroness was covered with blood all that day, and she never hesitated and never complained – not even once."

"She's a soldier's wife," Burgoyne said simply.

Babette hesitated a long moment before she said it, but then she asked, "Was Charlotte like that, Johnny? Did Charlotte nurse the wounded with so much compassion and courage?"

"She did," Burgoyne said quietly, gazing out on the river, "and on many occasions. My Charlotte was a great and gracious lady, my love."

Then, once again, Burgoyne took Babette in his arms and held her tightly. He said, "But I'm gratified now to find myself immeasurably blessed with the loving companionship of yet another great and gracious lady. Come now and help me wash. I find on this dismal morning that I very much require the magic of your touch."

Burgoyne: Before it all began

Burgoyne's first act after purchasing the rambling old inn known as Lambert's Oaks had been to build an addition to the place – a vast banquet room beneath a soaring arched roof. His purpose was to create in his new country home an environment suitable for entertaining vast assemblages of friends from London. The sprawling, three-story brick building stood in the heart of the Surrey countryside just fifteen miles from Parliament. Burgoyne promptly renamed the place The Oaks. It could sleep nearly fifty guests, but until the addition was built it had lacked an appropriate central room in which guests could gather when the glum English weather, as it so often did, soaked the pleasure out of fox hunting and horse racing and forced everyone indoors.

It was in that room, upon his return home from St. James Palace, that Burgoyne found Charlotte in a tall chair at the end of the long dining table. She was sitting near a vibrant, crackling fire in the huge, open fireplace. Looking even more pale and wan than usual, Charlotte was wrapped in both a robe and blanket against the moist spring chill. She was sipping tea as she leafed through a slim book. Burgoyne strode into the room from behind her and kissed his wife on the cheek. Charlotte immediately shut the book and turned in her chair.

"You startled me, Jack," she said. "I didn't expect you until this evening."

"Business was completed rather early in the morning," he said, taking a chair next to her. "But I can tell you all about that later. I didn't mean to disturb you, my love. What are you reading?"

"I'm reading Candide," she said. "After us having met Voltaire all those years ago when we lived in France, I've always felt guilty at never having read it. This stay of yours in London seemed to provide a perfect opportunity. It went well with the king, then?"

"Well enough, I judge," he said. "His Majesty seems favorably disposed toward my plan. I've sufficiently discredited Germain in his eyes, I think, that the colonial minister won't be able to stand in my way. My only concern is Lord North. If he opposes the Grand Strategy the outcome of my efforts will remain in doubt. I suspect that Lord North will not oppose it, however, if he deems the king sufficiently committed."

Charlotte nodded. "I could have father speak to Lord North if you like. Father can be persuasive, as you know."

Burgoyne nodded silently. Charlotte's ancient, wealthy father, the Earl of Derby, commanded influence sufficient to command the rapt attention of anyone who might serve as the king's first minister. After a few, long-ago years of blustering outrage at the charming, gambling rake of a commoner who'd eloped with his daughter, the old man had settled down to become uniquely helpful all through Burgoyne's military and political career. That help had endured for the last thirty years.

"I do appreciate how helpful Lord Derby could be, my love," Burgoyne said, "but it's a point of pride with me that, if I'm to win the king's support in this venture, I should be able to accomplish that chore on my own without further aid from your family."

"A smart soldier makes use of every advantage," Charlotte said. "That's what you've always told me, Jack. Certainly, any assistance from your family would never be a possibility."

Burgoyne smiled. Charlotte's pride in her lineage and her accompanying disdain for her husband's never ceased to amuse him. The reality was that Burgoyne's own disdain for his family exceeded Charlotte's by far. He'd had no use for the drunken captain of dragoons whose name he bore, and he'd had even less use for the now-dead English nobleman who'd really fathered him with a married woman. Burgoyne's only gratitude to any of them was for Lord Bingley's willingness to ease his illegitimate son's admission to Westminster. Schooling in that exclusive institution had constituted a crucial start for Burgoyne. It had led to a fast friendship with Edward Stanley, who was now known as Lord Strange, and finally to Burgoyne's runaway marriage to Stanley's glorious sister, Charlotte, whose father commanded such immense walth, power and respect. Burgoyne understood also, however, that most of his success had been the product of his own charm, cunning, drive and energy.

"I'm not rejecting the earl's aid, my love," he said, patting his wife's hand. "I simply prefer not to trouble him unless it proves absolutely necessary. How goes the cough today?"

As he asked the question, Charlotte coughed. Burgoyne could hear the wheezing in her chest. She'd fought the asthma since childhood, but the grip of the disease had grown more ferocious as Charlotte's hair had grayed and as the network of fine lines had appeared about her eyes and mouth. She remained the most beautiful woman in London, Burgoyne often told her – and she knew that he truly believed that despite his chronic dalliances with other women — but they both were aware that her growing frailty was due cause for concern.

"The cough was fine until you reminded me of it," she said, smiling slightly. "It's this awful weather, Jack. Perhaps I should have stayed in town at Derby House rather than come all the way out here in this wetness."

"We should go back to France this summer – to the south this time, near the sea. It's warmer there, and dryer. It would do you a world of good, my love."

"How do we do that if you're in the colonies?"

"You're right, of course. If the king does approve my plan he's likely to dispatch me to Canada immediately. If I'm not here, though, I do insist that you make the trip to France yourself. Or, perhaps, to Italy. You need some time in a warmer, dry spot with gentle sun. In fact, we might consider a journey to Italy or Spain before I return to North America. We could pack and leave rather soon, and I could hurry back to London alone if I'm summoned."

Charlotte shook her head. "No, we should stay here in England until you know if your plan is approved. I'll be all right. I've been all right this long, haven't I?"

Burgoyne was silent for a long moment. Clearly, Charlotte realized, he'd been deep in thought since his meeting with the king and during the long journey from St. James Palace back here to The Oaks. Finally, he said, "I don't have to do this, Charlotte. If His Majesty does adopt the Grand Strategy, that might be sufficient for my purposes. Clinton could lead the actual invasion – or Gage or Cornwallis, perhaps; anyone but Howe, actually — and I could stay here in England with you. If you prefer, that's what I'll recommend."

"What would be the point of it all, then?" she asked. "This is about your career, Jack, and I've always taken pride in supporting that. What sort of soldier's wife would I be if I were to hold you back now?"

"You wouldn't be holding me back. My career means nothing to me without you. If something were to happen while I was gone ..."

She took his hand in hers. "What will happen will happen,

whether you're here or in Canada or in some other godforsaken place. It's beyond the power of either of us to control."

"If something were to happen," he said quietly, "I could not go on."

A small smile played about Charlotte's lips. She gazed at her husband for a long moment – acutely aware of both his strengths and failings and nonetheless devoted utterly to him, as she had been from the moment their eyes had first met so many years earlier. Finally, she said, "You would go on, Jack. It's what I love most about you – your talent for enduring and for always finding some way to fight your way to a better place."

"You've always ignored my shortcomings, Charlotte. Would that the rest of mankind possessed your gentle, charitable heart. More and more, as your health fades, I begin to think my proper place is here with you and not on campaign in the colonies."

Firmly, Charlotte shook her head. She said, "Gentleman Johnny Burgoyne has never known his proper place – never settled for whatever place he happened to find himself in. That, above all, Jack, has always been your greatest gift."

"You're wrong, Charlotte," Burgoyne said quietly. "My greatest gift has always been you."

Riedesel. 1777

The baron's humor was dark.

Frederika was tightly attuned to her husband's moods, which routinely ranged from silent, stoic annoyance to methodical diligence in the performance of his duty to the relatively rare display of grudging amusement. By nature, Freddie von Riedesel was a dour, taciturn man. Tonight, however, he was positively surly. Frederika could tell that from his tight-lipped facial expression as the baron surveyed the lavish dinner table before them. It groaned beneath the weight of a freshly prepared feast – two haunches of venison from a hapless deer that had wandered out of the woods that morning and been summarily executed with a Brown Bess musket by one of Burgoyne's foragers, a half dozen roast chickens and geese from Schuyler's rapidly dwindling supply of poultry that ran wild around the sprawling estate, a leg of lamb scrounged from the flocks of a nearby farmer.

Frederika knew what was troubling her husband. The food was good – skillfully prepared, as always, by Burgoyne's fussy, white-clad squad of jabbering, French-trained chefs – but the sumptuous meal inside the mansion stood in stark contrast to the rough fare being consumed by the rank and file soldiers in their tents all around the great house.

And the wine. Fully a dozen bottles of the commanding general's fine burgundy, Madeira, chardonnay and reisling had been opened and stood at attention in various locations around Philip Schuyler's huge dining room table. Already, she noted, Sir Francis had made a notable dent in one of them. The commanding general's chief aide dearly loved his wine, Frederika had noticed before.

She glanced at her husband's plate, which he had hardly touched and which he had pushed slightly away from him. She said in German, "You must eat, Freddie. Your strength you must maintain."

"We eat too well here," Riedesel grumbled. "We drink too much. Outside our troops dine on beans and salt pork and hardtack, and too little of that is left."

"The general is trying to keep our spirits high," she argued. "He wants his senior commanders cheery."

"I am famous among all for my cheeriness," Riedesel said sourly.

"Ya," his wife said to him, "as cheery as you were on our wedding night."

Riedesel turned and glared at the baroness. Frederika made an impish face at him. Despite himself, the baron smirked. "You keep me humble, my darling," he said.

Frederika shrugged. "Someone must."

At the head of the table, which seated nearly three dozen senior commanders and younger officers of noble breeding in dress uniforms and their carefully coifed ladies in jewels and shimmering gowns, Burgoyne suddenly stood. The music from the chamber group in the corner of the gigantic room died instantly.

"Good evening, ladies and gentlemen," Burgoyne said. "Thank you for the pleasure of your company this evening. I have called you together this evening for a formal report on the current status of our campaign."

Burgoyne then launched into a brief description of the battle of five days earlier and an assessment of the damage each side had sustained in the clash. From his description of the action, and his assessment of the relative positions of the opposing forces after the clash at Freeman's farm, it was clear that he viewed the event as a victory for the Royal Army. One by one, he lauded his commanders from their contributions and extended to them the gratitude of King George. Burgoyne took several minutes to glowingly describe the courage and effectiveness of the German troops led by Riedesel. Freddie sat impassive throughout the commanding general's speech, the baroness noted. Only she, she was sure, could discern her husband's dim view of this entire proceeding.

Burgoyne then shared with his commanders the contents of a message he had received only a short time before they'd convened at this table. It had come from Brigadier General Powell, a senior English officer left with two regiments at Fort Ticonderoga to protect the Royal Army's supply lines from Canada.

"Three contingents of rebels," Burgoyne told the assemblage, "each about five hundred men strong, moved two days ago against Forth Ticonderoga and the Lake George landing to the south. They drove our forces off Mount Defiance. That's the other name for Sugar Loaf Hill, where General Phillips placed his cannon and effectively captured the fort for us. The rebels burned several hundred small supply boats along the lake shore. They then demanded surrender of the fort, but General Powell vowed to defend the facility to the last man and finally managed to drive them off. We lost in excess of three hundred troops in the engagement, but our supply lines remain secure. The rebels also attacked our force at Diamond Island, some twenty-five miles south of Ticonderoga, where they were repulsed with considerable losses by two companies of the forty-second regiment under the able command of Captain Aubrey. The rebels are continuing to fight, gentlemen, and we are continuing to defeat them at every turn – as we shall soon defeat them utterly on the ground we now occupy to the south of this location. They cannot move back and thus cannot escape us."

As Burgoyne finished his remarks, Riedesel, from his chair at the far end of the sweeping table, spoke out in French. Burgoyne listened to the remarks, replied to them in French and then said to his commanders, "The baron inquires as to when we might resume our attack at Bemis Heights. My response, gentlemen, is that we shall resume our attack when General Clinton informs me that he is near with the force he's bringing up from New York City. Between the two of us, we should make quick work of the main rebel force to our south and proceed forthwith to Albany shortly thereafter."

Burgoyne's words were greeted with subdued huzzahs and cheers from his commanders. It was then that Riedesel, after glancing into the faces of his comrades, rose to his feet. He turned to his wife.

"Translate to English for me," he said to his wife in German. "My French is not good enough for what I have to say."

The baroness rose to stand beside her husband. "He asks me to translate," she explained to the group. Then she turned her eyes toward Freddie.

"I am greatly honored to serve in this command and under this notable commander," Riedesel said softly as his wife translated his words simultaneously and in a louder voice. "You all know that I am a fighting man by birth, by training and by personal inclination. I do not fear battle. Neither, however, do I embrace the concept of suicide. We lost strength on our long journey down from Canada, and we have been further weakened by our first day of real battle on the farms to the south. The rebel forces also suffered heavy losses, as we have determined, but now they are growing stronger while we are not. Our scouts report that, in the wake of their having withstood our initial assault five days ago, hundreds — perhaps even thousands — of rebel volunteers are now pouring into their camp. Already they outnumber us badly. If we do not attack immediately we will have no chance of victory. So, here is the best advice I can offer:

"If we do not attack upon the morrow – and I now deem such an act a perilous course, given the relative numbers on each side — then we should break camp and return to Fort Ticonderoga to spend the winter before renewing our campaign in the spring. If we move back now, we can get to the fort before winter weather arrives. If we wait a week or more to break camp, it is possible – even likely, I fear — that we will be caught on the trail as the snow flies in this inhospitable land, and if that happens we might not be able to reach Ticonderoga. This is my best and most deeply considered advice. Gallantry and superior skill generally wins battles, but often – when the odds grow too one-sided – those qualities are not sufficient to attain victory. It is my best judgment that luck is no longer with us on this campaign. I would be remiss in my duty to my prince in the Fatherland and to my commander and comrades in this noble venture here if I did not say this. I thank you for your patience and attentiveness."

Then Freddie von Riedesel and his wife sat down. The baroness gazed at her husband, a slight smile on her face. Her pride in her husband's candor and judgment was obvious to all. For a long moment there was silence at the great table as Burgoyne and the other senior commanders absorbed Riedesel's words. The baron's concern about the army being caught on the trail in winter had captured everyone's attention. English troops in the colonies had never adjusted to the rigors of the North American winter. The deep snow and bitter cold was utterly foreign to their European upbringings. Too many English soldiers had frozen to death on guard duty in the colonies for the senior commanders to fail to recognize the gravity of Riedesel's caution.

Then Burgoyne again stood.

"We are grateful to the baron for his thoughtful and most carefully reasoned appraisal of our current collective circumstance," the commanding general said.

Burgoyne glanced around the table. "All right, gentlemen, please feel free to offer me your own best advice. Should we attack – and when? Or should we now contemplate a pullback to Ticonderoga for the winter? Simon, your thoughts first, if you would be so kind."

Burgoyne sat down again as Simon Fraser rose. A decisive man of action by nature, Fraser was never at ease when addressing groups.

"War inevitably lacks certainty," he said. "The baron has made good points. His logic cannot be denied. But we beat them decisively on the field five days ago. They could not deny us the ground we now hold, nor do they possess the power to wrest it from us. We earned that ground with blood and sweat, and victory for us is at hand. I am reluctant to abandon it when it is so near. I, too, urge attack – and soon. Let us be done with this as quickly as we can manage."

Then, before he sat back down, Fraser gazed into the faces of his comrades. More quietly, he then said, "It must be noted that there is glory to be had here, gentlemen – a matchless opportunity to serve our king and country in a noteworthy fashion that can greatly benefit all our careers and fortunes. Circumstance – and, of course, the perception and vision of our commanding general – has left us engaged in a matter of great moment. One must not shrink from opportunity. Despite uncertainties, we must not shrink from this one."

As Fraser sank back into his chair, Burgoyne favored him with an approving smile. Fraser's thinking quite cleared mirrored that of the commanding general.

"General Phillips?" Burgoyne said.

Will Phillips stood, straight and tall. "We have ample powder and shot for our big guns. Victory requires nothing more now than courage, discipline and resolve. We've come too far now to abandon this quest. General Fraser's appraisal is quite correct; glory is within our grasp."

One by one the senior commanders stood and expressed similar sentiments while Burgoyne listened impassively and while Frederika translated their comments into her husband's ear. When Burgoyne's senior commanders finished with their remarks, the noblemen were heard from – the youthful Earl of Balcarres, the still recovering Lord Acland and several others. When all had finished, a process that took nearly a half hour, Burgoyne again rose.

"Gentlemen," he said, "I am most grateful for the conscientious observations of all at this table. His Majesty is remarkably well served by each and every man present. Permit me now to offer my own thoughts on the momentous matter so thoughtfully presented by the baron."

Burgoyne paused for effect. "We must win, gentlemen, and win we shall. Could we win on our own – without help from General Clinton from the south? It is my considered appraisal that we could, but we should not risk our army unnecessarily with a rash frontal assault without aid from Clinton. We shall require all the strength we can muster next spring when we sweep eastward through New England and bring this vile rebellion completely to heel.

"Moreover, it is my judgment that if we now abandon this campaign for the winter we might well endanger General Clinton's command. The rebel army now before us would then be free to turn its attention southward, to where Clinton is now fighting his way north along the Hudson to join us. General Clinton could then find himself and his force of two thousand with renewed rebel resistance at his back and a much superior force bearing down upon him from the north. Under such a circumstance, his losses could be considerable, and the result could be that New York City itself, with the entire royal fleet in its harbor, could be threatened. New York City is the fulcrum of this continent, gentlemen, and such a risk to its security is unacceptable.

"It is therefore my decision that we shall persevere here until we receive word from Clinton that he has reached a juncture to our south to serve as the anvil to our hammer. We shall then launch our attack upon the rebel fortifications at Bemis Heights and be done with this preliminary business once and for all. We shall then winter in Albany, with abundant food and ample shelter against the hardships of the elements, and sweep eastward in the spring to put an end to this whole bloody business of revolution once and for all."

Around the table, the senior commanders nodded and grunted their assent to the commanding general's decision. Clerke proposed a toast to the success of the campaign. At their end of the table, Frederika von Riedesel leaned over to her husband and translated Burgoyne's speech.

"You tried, Freddie," she whispered in his ear.

The baron frowned and was silent for a long moment.

Then he said, "Ya, my duty I have now performed."

Franklin. 1777

His own city of Philadelphia was a fresh, surging, shining town of twenty-five thousand souls. It glittered with freshly kilned pink brick, gleaming new glass and skillfully hewn cobblestones on its narrow streets along the Delaware River shoreline. Franklin had always liked Philadelphia much more than he liked New York, which was smaller, about a century older, still very much a Dutch community in both feel and tone and already down at the heels a bit. The rowdy port town of New York City possessed none of the elegant character of London, where Franklin had lived for so many years as the representative to the king's court of several colonial governments. And none of those three cities could compare, in Franklin's mind, with Paris, the jewel of the European continent and, in the American commissioner's view, the home of the world's most beautiful women.

Despite his seventy-one years, Franklin had never lost his taste for women – unless he considered his wife, Deborah, who had remained at home in Philadelphia after her husband had amassed a gigantic fortune as a printer and publisher and had involved himself in political matters both in the colonies and in Europe. Involvement in international politics was a step Franklin had taken largely to escape Deborah's increasingly chilly companionship. However successful, men inevitably make mistakes in the course of life, Franklin had often observed to friends, and the only appropriate course of action was to rectify those mistakes. Or, if a man was in a position to do so – as Franklin was — to flee from their consequences as gracefully as possible.

Franklin was entertaining the ladies this evening in the salon of a fine mansion on the fringes of the Bois de Boulogne. The grand house was the home of a lovely French widow, Madame Helvetius, a youngish woman of noble Austrian blood and considerable influence in the court of Louis XVI. As a world celebrity of major dimension and as one of the representatives of the new American government, Franklin made a point of accepting every invitation from every powerful person in Paris — and, especially, from the lovely and lonely widows, wives, sisters and daughters of powerful men, whom he made a special point of captivating with his carefully developed wit, wisdom and humor. He paid special attention to the exceedingly lush Madame Helvetius, who referred to him affectionately as "Cher Papa" and who found neither Franklin's pedestrian personal appearance nor the yawning gap in their ages an impediment to a fairly torrid love affair.

In contrast to his comrade as the other American commissioner to France – stodgy, humorless, perpetually irritable John Adams

— Benjamin Franklin was a sly, skilled, practiced drawing room performer. He was well aware that every smile, every tinkle of delighted laughter from a lovely lady in such a setting, increased his odds of getting what he wanted from the king – and, if he was lucky, from the lady as well. His captivating monologues had brought him huge success in both regards during his years in London, where he'd enjoyed both considerable influence at the court of King George and a gratifying, years-long love affair with his buxom landlady, Margaret Stevenson – not to mention a simultaneous romance with Margaret's daughter, Polly. Franklin had deeply regretted his forced departure from London as the colonial rebellion loomed large, but life in Paris had its compensations, of which Madame Helvetius was only one.

Franklin was recounting one of his immensely entertaining – and utterly imaginary — stories of American frontier life to the several ladies in the low-cut silken European gowns he found so attractive. Franklin was in mid-sentence when he spotted the Comte de Vergennes enter the spacious, crowded room. A stern-looking woman of fifty or so was on the comte's arm. Franklin immediately rose to his feet, excused himself from his tittering audience and made his way to where the French foreign minister was being greeted by Franklin's French mistress.

"Oh, Cher Papa," Madame Helvetius said as Franklin approached. "Surely you know the Comte and Countess de Vergennes."

"I do, indeed, my love," Franklin said. "Countess, my great pleasure at seeing you once again."

"Enchanted, Dr. Franklin," the woman said with conspicuous disinterest.

"I wonder," Franklin said to her, "if you would permit me a few moments of the comte's time. I have some private news of some consequence for him and for the king."

"As you will," the countess said. "I am well aware that Charles' time is never his own – and most assuredly not mine," she added icily.

A few moments later, in the private evening shade of the mansion's elegant garden, far from the crowd of party-goers and over glasses of fine French cognac, Franklin said to Vergennes, "Life does have its burdens, does it not, my dear Comte?"

"Some burdens weigh more heavily than others," Vergennes said wearily. "You are a married man, I take it, Dr. Franklin?"

"A widower," Franklin said. "My wife died a dozen years ago, while I was assigned to the court of King George. We had been apart for some years at that point. Duty to country, as you know, can make small allowance for personal concerns."

Vergennes smiled wryly. "Duty has its distinct virtues, which is why I devote most of my attention to mine. I presume that you want to inform me of Burgoyne's progress southward."

"I do. I presume that you already may know this, but I received a dispatch two days ago. It's nearly six weeks old now, of course, but it was highly encouraging in tone. Burgoyne has crossed to the west bank of the Hudson with a force much reduced by his travails after leaving Ticonderoga. His red men have deserted him, as have most of his Tory troops. He suffered a rather stunning defeat in the Hampshire Grants that reduced his force of Germans. Meanwhile, our forces at Saratoga are growing stronger by the day with vigorous volunteers. It's quite cheerful news, my dear Comte. It bodes exceedingly well for the future of our fledgling republic."

Vergennes sipped at his cognac. "You are aware, Dr. Franklin, that your largely untrained volunteer forces are up against what is probably the finest military commander The English can field against you. You are aware that many of his troops are battle-hardened from bitter conflicts both in Canada and Boston, not to mention the battlefield experiences of his senior staff in Europe. That's especially true of the Germans, by the way. And your commander there, General Gates, is not terribly well regarded, except by your General Washington. Moreover, that regard seems based primarily on the friendship that exists between the wives of the two men rather than on a cool, considered appraisal of General Gates' capabilities. You must explain to me how, in light of such odds against your troops in the New York colony, you can retain such ferocious optimism about the outcome of the impending clash."

Franklin shrugged. "We're fighting for our homes and our proud new nation. They're fighting for glory and pay. That difference offers us a huge advantage, my dear Comte. That's why we shall win and they shall lose. That's why victory at Saratoga is at hand for us, and the French government can assure our ultimate victory in this conflict with sufficient aid in our time of need."

Vergennes was silent for a long moment. Then he said, "As I told you before, Dr. Franklin, provide me with a rebel victory at Saratoga, and I'll do my utmost to provide you with the aid and weaponry you've requested. You must, you understand, send me to my king with ammunition sufficient to make a credible case."

Franklin nodded in satisfaction. This was a stronger commitment than any he'd yet received from the foreign minister. "Then I have your assurance that, if we win at Saratoga, you'll take our case to King Louis?"

"You do, Dr. Franklin. I am, after all, a Frenchman. The sheer romance of your struggle has undeniable appeal to my Gallic soul. Tell me, if you lose, will you return to North America or might you remain here in Paris? Madame Helvetius seems quite taken with you – as does all of Paris, actually."

"Anne-Louise and I have discussed marriage," Franklin said quietly, "but the madame would never leave France, and once my country is free of threat I must return home to nurse it through its infancy. We'll need a functional central government, which we do not have now. We'll need a thoughtful constitution. Once these birth pains we're now experiencing are overcome – hopefully, with the aid of France, my dear Comte – our new nation will need the same slap on the rump that all newborns require. I must then return to Philadelphia to provide that impetus."

"Too bad," Vergennes said. "You are obviously quite at home here amid the comforts of Paris, Dr. Franklin."

"I am," Franklin admitted. "For a man born and raised on the frontier—"

"—You may spare me that fiction, Dr. Franklin," the foreign minister said with a smile. "I'm well aware that it captivates the ladies, but we both know that you're a sophisticated, worldly man of the city who appreciates the many pleasures of Paris. I've noted that your French is excellent in private conversations with me, however halting and countrified you manage to make yourself sound in our language during salon conversations with the ladies as they titter."

Franklin smiled ruefully. "Yes, well, entertaining ladies is God's work, is it not?"

"Most assuredly," the French foreign minister agreed. "This would be a fine place, Dr. Franklin, in which to finish out a well-spent life under the tender ministrations of the glorious Madame Helvetius. All of us would welcome your permanent companionship."

"Well," Franklin said with a slight smile, "perhaps we'll lose after all."

"Yes," the French foreign minister said, sipping his cognac. "I rather imagine that you will."

Clinton. 1777

From a rocky, tree-studded mountain slope on the west side of the Hudson River, his boots perched on uneven ground perhaps three-quarters of a mile from the action, General Sir Henry Clinton peered intently through his brass-coated spyglass. Through the lens, he could see the rebel forces scurrying around both inside and outside the stockade of fresh logs that had been erected at the edge of a sharp cliff above the water. They were now abandoning the rude structure as a mass formation of Clinton's troops moved in from the south through a thick cloud of bluish-gray powder smoke from their Brown Bess muskets. Clinton could hear the English drums beating out their relentless rhythm of death. So, clearly, could the rebels.

"They certainly began running quickly enough," Clinton said to his aide, a red-cheeked young colonel from Sussex named Nichols. "Wise of them, actually. As we were told, they have no cannon on this side. Everything they have, such as it is, is aimed at the river."

"Yes, Sir Henry," Nichols said. "They're apparently fleeing down those cliffs to the river to escape us. I imagine they have boats down there on the river bank to transport them to the other shore. Should I dispatch some troops to stop them at the water?"

Clinton returned the spyglass to its leather case suspended around the general's neck. "Let the blighters go – those who can escape, at any rate. God knows that I have little need of more prisoners to nursemaid. I simply need this pathway cleared, and we seem to be well along with that task, Colonel. Any word from the other fort further north?"

"A courier arrived a few moments ago," Nichols said. "There has been some hard contact with the enemy, but that fort is being abandoned as well."

Clinton nodded in satisfaction. "Excellent. Then in a few hours we can camp for the night and then continue on to the north. This is how you do it, Colonel. Brawn is useful; brains are critical."

Clinton's brawn was represented by the thousands of men under his command in this operation. It was represented by the sixty transport vessels from the royal navy fleet in New York Harbor. It was represented, too, by a squadron of English warships bristling with cannon and commanded by a battle-hardened commodore. Sir Henry Clinton had come to the Hudson River highlands well prepared for whatever he might encounter.

The highlands constituted a key strategic position on the river forty miles north of New York Harbor. At this spot on the Hudson stood walls of sheer, vertical rock rising up starkly on either side of the water. The Highlands soared to two hundred feet over the river's surface at a narrow, perilous point of passage for vessels below. Here the rebels had begun to erect two forts, still only half built. The forts were situated on the western shore about seven miles apart. Spanning the river, barring passage of any vessel, hung an impregnable barrier of logs and chain linking the two shorelines. Clinton had understood from the beginning that any attempt to sever the chain barrier under cannon fire raining down from the forts above could result in huge losses of both English vessels and troops. That's where the brains had come in.

After surveying maps and consulting with Tory leaders familiar with the terrain, Clinton had come to understand, too, that the makeshift forts were uniquely vulnerable to attack from the land – just as Ticonderoga had been vulnerable to Burgoyne in the spring. It was into this strategy that Clinton had thrown his efforts to break through this obstacle to reach Burgoyne's forces. Once past the highlands, with these feeble log forts reduced to rubble and the rebels on the run, Clinton still faced a northward journey of more than a hundred miles before he could reach Saratoga.

The rebels were headquartered at Peekskill, an old Dutch village on the river's eastern bank just south of the Highlands. Their commander was Army of the United States General Israel Putnam, a crusty, capable Indian fighter from the French and Indian War who was skilled in forest tactics. Putnam commanded all the rebel forces around the forts. Tory spies had informed Clinton that Putnam had been forced to send troops to a hard-pressed Washington outside Philadelphia, leaving Putnam badly undermanned here along the river. Leaving New York City, Clinton had known that the English now faced no more than fifteen hundred rebel troops at this location, mostly poorly trained volunteer militiamen. It had been Clinton's plan from the beginning to anchor his ships south of the highlands, to land his troops both on the western bank to threaten the forts and to land a second force on the eastern bank to threaten Putnam directly. Clinton would then march his western bank invaders up and down through the rugged, heavily wooded mountains south of the forts and attack the rebels from the rear on dry ground. Once the forts were subdued, the chain and log barrier could be severed and Clinton's flotilla could continue on its way north. The strategy seemed to be working flawlessly, and Clinton was pleased.

Clinton had gotten off from New York City more slowly than he would have liked. Before he could move to aid Burgoyne, he'd been obligated to see to the city's defenses, his first priority, and he'd been unhappy with his troop strength there. Howe had denuded the New York command to staff his assault on Philadelphia. He'd left Clinton with a perimeter of nearly a hundred miles to defend and a defensive force depleted by smallpox and other ailments. That meant that Clinton had been forced to delay his thrust up the Hudson for the arrival of more troops from Europe. Finally, as September began to fade, the transport vessels had arrived in New York Harbor containing three thousand troops. They, too, were ravaged by illness, but more than half of them were healthy enough for immediate duty. Once those troops were properly deployed along the New York City perimeter, Clinton had been able, finally, to muster an expeditionary force and sail north.

The rebels had struggled to defend the paths through the mountains behind the forts and to their south, but they had been no match for massed English musket fire and brutal bayonet charges. Now the English would destroy the log and chain barrier, occupy both forts for the night and move on in the morning. Clinton was now in a fine mood – unusual for him, as Colonel Nichols was well aware

"This has gone remarkably well, Sir," Nichols said.

"Indeed," Clinton replied. "We should get off a courier to General Burgoyne in the morning before we again set sail."

That evening, in a tiny cabin inside the southernmost fort, Clinton sat at a table in candlelight and received a full report of the day's action. Each fort had been captured. The chain and log boom across the river had been destroyed, and Clinton's losses were minor – no more than forty dead and one hundred and fifty wounded, although a key English officer had been killed in the assault. The English had killed or captured more than three hundred rebels.

An eminently successful day, Clinton thought.

He was still thinking that when the courier arrived late in the evening. Nichols brought the general the message that Howe had sent from Philadelphia. As Clinton read Howe's missive all good humor vanished. Nichols could see that in his commander's face.

"Bad news, Sir?" the aide asked.

"Excellent news for Lord Howe," Clinton said quietly. "He has defeated Washington's army at a place called Brandywine and is about to take Philadelphia with no further resistance. But his message is bad news for General Burgoyne. Lord Howe insists that I send him more troops. He specifically wants the seventeenth dragoons, the sixty-third, twenty-sixth and seventh regiments and several battalions of the Germans as well. He orders that these reinforcements be sent to him without delay. "Without delay,' Colonel. That's the key phrase here."

In his head, Nichols counted up the forces Howe demanded. "If we send Lord Howe that many men, General, then we can't properly defend New York City without the troops we have with us here."

"Precisely," Clinton said quietly. "This order is utterly unambiguous. Lord Howe demands specific regiments and their immediate dispatch to his side at Philadelphia."

"Then we must turn around and return to New York City?"

"I see no other course of action available to us," Clinton muttered. "We'll return to New York City tomorrow morning. Get a courier off to General Burgoyne at dawn. In fact, get off two couriers. The ground between here and Saratoga will be crawling with Putnam's men. I'll write the messages tonight."

When Nichols had left, Clinton gathered together quill pen, ink and paper. He brought out his encoding template as well. For a long moment as the candle's flame danced in the shadows of the tiny hut, General Sir Henry Clinton composed his thoughts. How candid should I be? he wondered. But, of course, the question was more or less academic, he supposed. As the rebellion had ground on, the rebels had become more sophisticated about the English communications system. Now most English military couriers no longer carried lengthy, coded messages folded into the heels of boots, which invariably were searched thoroughly when a courier was captured. Instead, the couriers swallowed tight, terse messages contained in hollow musket balls of silver. Clinton would have only a few sentences in which to explain to Burgoyne that Clinton would not be arriving at Saratoga and why. Given that reality, and the accompanying reality that the couriers probably would be captured in any event as they moved into the rebel-held region to the north, Clinton decided to ignore the decoding template and, instead, to compose only what Burgoyne needed to know — and what the rebels, if they captured the couriers and intercepted the messages, would know already. Clinton dipped the quill in the ink and wrote:

Cannot join you. Politics intrudes. Good fortune. H.C.

That summed it up nicely, Clinton supposed.

Babette. 1777

She didn't know what had awakened her. Perhaps it had been the steady drumbeat of autumn rain on the thick slate roof of Schuyler's mansion. It might have been the shiver sent involuntarily through her body by the moist, piercing chill of the October air. Whatever it was, Babette had come awake and almost instantly alert in the gigantic bed in Schuyler's sprawling master suite. She realized despite the darkness that Jack was not in bed with her, as he had been when they'd drifted off to sleep after a particularly intense round of fevered lovemaking. Jack had seemed almost desperate to have her the night before as they'd sunk beneath the thick down comforter. Babette had been surprised at his urgency — almost desperation, she'd noted — and she'd accommodated the commanding general in all that he'd asked of her, as was both her habit and her joy.

The depth of her love for this handsome, older man with his gentle manners and complete, confident command of all the world around him sometimes simply awed Babette, when she took time to weigh the matter in her mind. Jack Burgoyne was both her passion and her dream come true – a miracle that had come to her as a totally unexpected gift after years of deep, private despair with Peter. And now Jack, mysteriously, was missing from their bed. Babette crawled out from beneath the covers, nude and shivering in the cold, and wrapped herself in a soft, thick woman's robe she'd found in the bedroom closet when the English has taken over this place. A candle flickered in its pewter holder near the door. Babette took it, padded barefoot down the stairs and found Jack sitting as still as a statue in one of two tall, richly upholstered wing chairs in a small, shadowy sitting room on the mansion's first floor. His own candle flickered weakly on the small table between the chairs. As she entered the room, Babette spied him in the shadows, sipping from a glass of wine.

"Jack," Babette said softly, "are you all right?"

In the shadows, she could see him stir. He put down the glass next to the candle, stood and walked to her in three steps across the small room. Then Burgoyne wrapped his arms around her and pressed her tightly to him. He, too, wore only a thick, rich robe from Schuyler's closet. The patroon had burned his fields and slaughtered his livestock in deference to the English invasion, but he'd been kind enough in his southward flight to Albany to leave behind many personal items.

"I'm merely engaging in some thought, my love," Burgoyne said softly. "The burden of command sometimes requires moments of private reflection. Here, sit down next to me."

Babette sat in the other wing chair. Burgoyne was an early riser but a sound sleeper. If he was up this many hours before dawn, Babette knew, he was troubled.

"It's what the baron said, isn't it?" she said.

Burgoyne shrugged, "Our poor baron was more or less shouted down, was he not?"

"He was," Babette agreed. "You disagreed with him in front of the others, but you were listening to what he had to say, I think."

"Listening is a critical component of leading. I learned that early on as a soldier. Yes, I heard the good baron clearly enough even though my officers dismissed him. There's a natural antipathy, you know, between us English and the Germans, even though we're paired by His Majesty in this noble effort. Simon displays that distaste for them constantly. So does General Phillips. Riedesel is a good soldier, though – a professional, a man to be taken seriously on all occasions."

"And ..." Babette said.

Burgoyne smiled in the shadows. "The baron is essentially correct. An attack now, before General Clinton arrives and with us so weakened at this juncture, would be distinctly perilous. So, too, however, would be a retreat back to Ticonderoga, and it's this danger that he appreciates insufficiently, in my view. A healthy army of men in good condition can march fifteen miles a day — even an army heavily laden with cannon and ox carts, as we are. But I have eight hundred wounded men in those hospital tents out there, and food supplies are dwindling for my troops in the cold mud surrounding this house."

"You can find more food, can't you?"

"I have money enough remaining in the war chest to buy more, but from whom would I buy it now? The countryside has risen up against us, thanks to the antics of our red brethren. A retreat, I judge, would be more dangerous than attack. An early snowstorm on the way back to Ticonderoga could halt us in our tracks. Even if we didn't freeze to death in place, I can assure you that a winter of hunger at Ticonderoga – near starvation, at the very least – would constitute more than an ordeal. The lake will freeze. No supplies could reach us from Canada for many months."

Babette pondered her lover's words. "We did not march fifteen miles a day on our journey to this place."

"Indeed, we did not. The terrain was challenging and the resistance stiffer than I'd imagined. A retreat over the same route would involve similar challenges, I fear."

"And we stayed in one place for many days on a number of occasions, Jack," she said. "Any many nights, too."

"We did," he agreed, nodding. "I deemed it crucial for you to spend as much time as possible socializing with the ladies and learning their ways. As I've told you many times, London is a uniquely class-conscious environment – a place where those who hope to rise must learn to effectively mimic the manners of those born their betters.

You are a keen observer and an apt pupil, my love – quite quick to learn. Your manners are now nothing less than superb. You will fit in quite nicely in London salons – once we overcome this final obstacle in our path, that is."

For a long moment, Babette remained silent. Then she said, "I should hate to entertain the possibility that my education imperiled your mission, Jack."

Burgoyne said quietly, "Your education – your diligent preparation to stand proudly on my arm in London against all those of more fortunate birth and gentler upbringing – is my mission, my love. All that I might gain from the success of the Grand Strategy would have no meaning for me were you not beside me to share both the rewards and the glory."

Burgoyne sipped from his wine glass. "Before all that can happen, however, we must win here at Saratoga. We then must regain our strength as we winter in Albany and complete our mission to put down this rebellion in the spring. I but await General Clinton's arrival to accomplish that chore."

"Have you heard from him?" she asked.

"Not since he set out from New York City. The problem is that time is fast fading on me now. I must, within just a few days, either retreat or move against the rebels. It appears now that I will be forced to launch a final assault with Clinton or, if fortune so decrees, without him."

"Why does he not come? Babette demanded. "Why has he delayed so long?"

Burgoyne took her small hand in his large one. "I have a dangerous opponent in London, my love. I have no doubt that Lord North's colonial minister – operating with Lord North's tacit acquiescence or, perhaps, even his ignorance – has taken what steps he could devise to deprive me of General Clinton's support in this venture."

"Why would anyone do that? Don't the powers in London want to put down the rebellion?"

"Of course they do, but they most assuredly do not want to see that noble goal accomplished by me or through my plan. The colonial minister wants for himself whatever credit will accrue to whoever wins this war for the king."

"And generals like Clinton would be complicit in a thing like that?" Babette demanded. "Soldiers like yourself would cooperate in a plan to actually lose a battle to the rebels?"

Burgoyne glanced at the face of his mistress. Her expression in the shadows was one of open horror.

"Not Clinton, no," he said. "Lord Howe, however, is a different matter. The Royal Army is rife with politics – filled with high officers who bought and paid for their commissions and regiments. That was how I began, after all – with command of an entire regiment raised with the money of my father-in-law. The Earl of Derby felt that his daughter's low-born husband — of whom he did not approve, incidentally, until Charlotte and I produced a child — should hold a proper station in life."

Babette was silent for a moment. Then she said, "You never told me that before."

Burgoyne shrugged. "I take little pride in it, but it is how I began. I then earned my further advancement through diligence and proper development of all the qualities a senior officer should display. From that point I earned my way through deeds, my love, as I hope now to earn advancement to the king's ministry as well. Lord Howe would surely cooperate in preventing my possible elevation to the cabinet and, especially, to the post of prime minister. All it would take would be a private, written message to Lord Howe from the colonial minister communicating — in appropriately veiled terms, of course – that my failure in this campaign would be well received in London."

Babette shook her head in sheer amazement. "And they would actually do that?"

"Indeed they would. I fear that my London enemies are vast and powerful – as, my dear, are the enemies of all who would achieve in any circumstance. We are the finest army the world has ever known, but this is our great weakness – the venality of our generals and the treachery of our politicians."

"Then I despise all politicians," Babette said quietly.

Burgoyne laughed softly in the candlelight. "As a member of Parliament, I share your distaste for us. Still, if we are successful here at Saratoga and in our efforts next spring, opposition to me will evaporate. Many such failed plots were mounted against the elevation of Lord North himself, and all to no avail. So it is with advancement to any position of power and influence – except, of course, to an inherited title and wealth. Dame Fortune denied me that. I cannot believe that she also would deny me this as well. After all, fortune brought me you, did she not?"

"You brought me to you," Babette said evenly. "I am in love with

Jack Burgoyne the man much more than I'm in love with General John Burgoyne the politician."

The commanding general leaned forward in his chair, bent over and gently kissed the fingers of his beautiful mistress. Burgoyne gazed upon the face of the woman who'd moved into the spot in his heart that Charlotte had occupied for so many years. Charlotte no longer existed except as a memory, but the love that Burgoyne had borne for her still did, and he was grateful that he'd found a suitable outlet for it.

Holding Babette's hand, he said, "The man, the general and the politician are, my love, utterly indistinguishable at this late date."

Gates. 1777

Horatio Gates stood just inside the tree line, with an escort of two dozen Hampshire Grants militiamen huddling — as was the commanding general — behind the boles of trees blazing with vivid fall colors. Through his rimless spectacles, Gates carefully surveyed the scene to the north across the vast open field of Freeman's farm, the scene of so much violent bloodshed only a week before. From less than a mile away, Gates could see the English line – could examine minutely their tents and their fortifications. He could see, too, their cannon, aimed at the open ground and no doubt crammed with grapeshot to discourage any mad rush by rebel infantry.

Gates respected those big guns. He envied Burgoyne his vast store of powder and shot, but Gates' decades as a commissary officer – his knowledge of how much fighting men needed to eat each and every day to function effectively in a combat environment – told him that the English had to be low on food now. They'd been harvesting wheat from farm fields to the north, he knew, but he'd received no reports of any notable English success in foraging. Farmers like Schuyler had burned their fields and moved their livestock to distant points to deny them to the English. Gates was acutely aware that the shortage of food would drive strategy for the English now – that and the looming threat of the coming winter. With food supplies available to him from the south, Gates could hold his position indefinitely; Burgoyne, Gates was certain, was now running out of time.

They have to come soon, the commanding general thought. They must come to us or they must retreat. And if they retreat we'll have them.

Gates shivered beneath his cloak in the bitter breeze off the field. His fingers were stiff and cold, but he was warmed by the prospect of harrying the English all the way back to Ticonderoga – of picking off their marching troops in vast numbers from the forest, of perhaps even cutting off the road to them as they fled north. The worst that could happen if the English pulled back, Gates knew, was that Burgoyne would be taking them back to freeze for the winter in the huge stone fort without sufficient food. If they retreated to Ticonderoga, Gates suspected, he might even be able to mount cannon, as Burgoyne had against St. Clair, on the mountains surrounding the fort on its land side and spend the winter slowly destroying the entire English force as it huddled for many months inside the fort to escape the brutal snow and ice that was coming. He had them now, Gates knew, if he could stave off the fresh attack he strongly suspected had to be coming fairly soon.

Gates was thinking of the attack when he became aware that Wilkinson was at his side. The general's aide had made his way, as had Gates and his escort, stealthily through the woods to this vantage point near the English lines.

"I have good news, Sir," Wilkinson whispered. "Two hundred more volunteers have arrived in camp this morning. These new ones come from the Mohawk Valley, and they've brought in a canoe full of powder and shot."

"That is good news," Gates whispered back in agreement. "Have half the powder and all the shot distributed to Morgan's men. They'll make the best use of it. The rest of the powder should go to our artillery. They'll need it when the English advance, as I suspect they'll be doing soon enough."

"You don't believe, then, that they'll pull back to Ticonderoga?"

"I do not," Gates said. "I well recall Burgoyne from European campaigns, even though he might not recall me. The man had a well-earned reputation as an inveterate gambler – a devoted gamester, Colonel – with horses, with cards, with dice. He will roll the dice here, I'm certain. The lure of a gain so immense will be too beguiling for him to abandon. And when he does roll those dice, we must resist him with all our force and valor. What is our strength now with these latest recruits?"

"My best assessment is nearly ten thousand troops, General. The notices you sent to every village throughout the northern colonies about the Jane McCrea affair have been most successful in attracting militamen, but many are unarmed and most of them are utterly untrained."

Gates said, "Then they can fight with hatchets and axes and hammers and other farm implements, Colonel. They can fight with pitchforks. They can fight with knives and forks and spoons, if necessary. We can stop the English here. We can do what General Washington could not do in the middle colonies. We can win a victory here over the Royal Army if we just hold fast behind our lines and stoutly withstand their assault."

"Yes, Sir," Wilkinson said. "If we can do that, we can win."

Gates said, "General Washington tried to take Morgan's men from me, you know."

"I did not know that, Sir," Wilkinson said.

"Oh, yes," Gates said. "After his loss at Brandywine, he sent me a message demanding Morgan's Rangers. I appealed to Congress, and the order was set aside. There is, it seems, an insufficient appreciation on General Washington's part of the gravity of this portion of the conflict. I say that only to you, Colonel. It must not be repeated."

"Of course not, Sir," Wilkinson said. "I would advise, however, as is my duty, that General Washington would not be an enemy for anyone of prudence to make."

Gates nodded. "I agree most heartily. I know the man well and respect him greatly. We are friends and neighbors in Virginia, and our wives are quite close. But I could not give him Morgan, Colonel. I need Morgan too badly here."

"I agree, Sir," Wilkinson said. "Might I suggest as well that we need General Arnold, too. He's just sitting in his tent drinking day and night, General Gates. I submit that General Arnold in the field would be a crucial asset once the assault is launched by the enemy."

"So he would," Gates said, "if he could be trusted. I know you served as General Arnold's aide and that you hold him in high regard, Colonel, but you must accept that Arnold is unduly rash, insubordinate and intemperate in his approach to all of life – especially to his duty as a soldier. In the Royal Army, he would long ago have been cashiered out of the service – if he hadn't been hanged, that is. I cannot have in the field a senior commander whom I cannot trust to obey my orders. I have advised General Arnold to request that Congress reassign him. He maintains that he has done so. I'm not certain, however, that he has been sober enough even to write that letter."

"I don't know if he has," Wilkinson admitted.

Quietly, from behind his tree, Gates peered out at the enemy lines across the field.

"In any event," the commanding general said, "my concern at the moment is not what General Arnold does or might do. It's what Gentleman Johnny Burgoyne will do."

Fraser. 1777

It was Simon Fraser's habit, before he retired to his tent at night, to move among his men around their campfires in the charred fields outside Philip Schuyler's abandoned mansion. He would chat with them, inquire after their needs, commiserate with them about the hardships of the campaign, discuss with them the successes the expedition had thusfar enjoyed. Fraser would share their bawdy jokes and slap their backs in good fellowship. It was a personal, paternalistic leadership style that stood in stark contrast to Will Phillips' stern, aloof manner and the stiff, formal detachment that Riedesel maintained from the men he'd brought with him from Germany. Burgoyne, too, maintained a certain distance from the troops, as was only proper since it was necessary for the commanding general to be viewed by the rank and file as an Olympian, almost godlike figure incapable of error or ordinary human frailty.

Fraser, however, understood that at least one member of the senior staff had to be both approachable and accessible so, if for no other reason, he could serve as the commanding general's eyes and ears among the troops. It was a role that Fraser, gregarious and outgoing by nature, carried off with a heartfelt authenticity. He'd just completed his nightly rounds of the campfires and was heading toward his tent to retire when he spied Burgoyne amid a knot of soldiers on the high bluff in front of the mansion that overlooked the river. Fraser immediately changed direction and headed Burgoyne's way, his boots squishing in the mud as a rumble of thunder rolled over the west bank of the Hudson. In the growing darkness, he found the commanding general giving personal direction to the deployment of several rocket launchers.

"What have we here?" Fraser asked as he approached.

"I'm putting up some rockets for General Clinton," Burgoyne said. "If he's near and he spots them, he'll surely respond. Keep your eye fixed on the southern sky, Simon."

The powder-filled rockets, once their fuses were lit, launched under their own power from long, slim steel tubes erected on steel tripods. As weapons they were fairly benign. The English could launch them into a cluster of enemies who might be frightened by their flash and noise, but aside from the occasional burns they inflicted as they blossomed into fiery display in such circumstances they tended to do little real damage. Rockets did, however, serve as effective nighttime signals, and this was Burgoyne's intention this evening. Over the next twenty minutes, the two generals watched the heavens to the south as one rocket a minute was launched into the black sky over the river. Each rocket soared high, exploded in a flash of blinding light and a showery umbrella of sparks that danced among the thick autumn clouds and then faded into the chilled, October blackness. For a long moment after each rocket was fired, Burgoyne and Fraser stood silently and scanned the sky to the south for an answering signal from Clinton. The southern sky remained dark.

After the final rocket did its dance among the threatening clouds, Burgoyne turned to his friend.

"Simon," the commanding general said, "please order an extra ration of rum for the troops as they retire. I want them to sleep soundly tonight and to be well rested in the morning."

Fraser nodded. "You've decided, then?"

Burgoyne smiled slightly in the dim light. "My good friend, when have you ever known me to exhibit indecisiveness?"

"There'll be no Clinton, it seems," Fraser warned.

Burgoyne nodded. "And no shared glory, either. All the glory will be ours alone."

Frederika. 1777

It was the baroness's habit, every morning, to bring her young daughters to Burgoyne's dining room for the enormous breakfasts prepared daily for senior officers by the commanding generals' staff of continental chefs. The von Riedesels' quarters in an old, deserted farmhouse north of the Schuyler mansion were comfortable enough – the baroness had occupied much more meager quarters in other campaigns over the years, to be sure – but the food at these morning gatherings of the general staff and their ladies was matchless. Frederika insisted that whatever other hardships the campaign might involve, her children had to be properly nourished.

At the great table in Schuyler's dining room, the children and the senior officers' ladies dined each morning on fluffy omelets and biscuits, poached capon and thick slices of roast pork, all buried beneath rich, buttery French sauces. She missed the fine German breakfast sausages she so loved back home, but the baroness well understood that the generally superb quality of food in this campaign was a decided luxury on such expeditions. Her primary interests were the faithful support of her husband and the care and feeding of their children. So, every morning, the Riedesels arrived at the mansion in their calash, and she watched with satisfaction as the girls stuffed themselves at the long, elegant table in Schuyler's dining room.

On this particular morning, the von Riedesels arrived simultaneously with Lord Acland and Lady Harriet, who had been brought to the mansion behind a driver in an ox-cart with their affable Newfoundland, Jack, sitting between them and panting jovially. The couples greeted one another warmly at the mansion's front porch. The baron and Lord Acland exchanged pleasantries in French as the Riedesel children bounded from the calash and began gleefully frolicking on the grass with the huge, gentle dog.

"Zey love zat beast," the baroness said with a smile as she watched the girls play.

"Everyone loves our dear Jack," Lady Harriet responded. "He's such a jolly old fellow."

"Your husband seems well-recovered now," the baroness said.

"Yes," Lady Harriet said. "The burns still cause him pain when he tries to sleep, but he can move about freely now, and during the day he ignores whatever discomfort he might feel. Men can do that, I suppose."

"Ya," the baroness said. "Ze good ones, at least."

As the two couples entered the elegant house, they were greeted at the door by a genial, smiling Sir Francis Clerke.

"Ladies," he said cheerily, "General Burgoyne is meeting with his officers in the drawing room, where breakfast will be served to them separately. Please proceed to the dining room where, delightfully, you'll find you have rather more room at the table this morning."

"Thank you so much, Sir Francis," Lady Harriet said as Clerke moved back to the front door to greet another arriving couple.

"That's unusual," Lady Harriet said in a low voice to the baroness.

"Ya," Frederika said, gazing about. "Somezing is afoot zis morning."

At the dining room table, they found Babette locked in conversation over breakfast with several other women who normally were paired with senior officers. The baroness took the chair immediately to Babette's left.

"Goot morning, Madame," Frederika said.

"Good morning to you, Baroness."

"So?" Frederika asked. She saw no need for a more detailed question.

Babette only shrugged, which Frederika found to be a uniquely annoying Gallic gesture.

She knows, the baroness thought to herself. We'll all know soon enough, apparently.

When Freddie emerged from the drawing room, Frederika was waiting for him in the hallway. He didn't bother to await his wife's inquiry. The baron told her in German, "We're moving forward this morning. He wants to probe their left – to assess if there's a chance to turn them there and obtain a passage behind them."

"A reconnaissance, then?" she said.

"And in some force," the baron said, placing his uniform hat on his head. "We'll take fifteen hundred men and four cannon – and a party of the remaining savages as well. I'm going with him. So are Fraser and Phillips. The other senior commanders will remain here – Specht and Hamilton and the rest. If General Burgoyne smells blood, then we'll bring up the forty-five hundred effectives we're leaving behind here to guard the camp and what remains of our supplies."

"This is what you advised?" she asked.

"Well," Freddie said, "you were there. I advised that we do something. Now he's doing it. What this will turn out to be we'll have to see."

Frederika nodded. "I think he will smell blood this morning," she said quietly.

Freddie smiled slightly. "Ya, but whose blood?"

After breakfast, the baroness loaded the children into her calash and transported them back to the old farmhouse. Along the way north on the river road that wound along the grey-green water, the calash found itself in the midst of a crowd of Indians flooding southward from their camp at the northern end of the English encampment. Frederika noted that the half-naked warriors were decked out in paint and bristling with bows, arrows, knives, hatchets and even a few muskets decorated with turkey feathers. As they marched southward, they chanted a single word over and over.

"What are the savages saying, Mama?" one of the girls asked.

"Driver," the baroness called out to the German grenadier who handled the reins, "what is that word they keep shouting?"

The driver turned his head and called over his shoulder as the band of warriors passed by," They're rousing themselves for battle, Madame. They're calling out their word for war, over and over."

Frederika sank back against the calash's leather seat and wrapped her arms around her little daughters. Ya, she thought. Today will be a day for war.

Burgoyne. 1777

The English had erected two sturdy log fortifications at Freeman's farm – one commanded by the youthful Earl of Balcarres and the other, farther west, manned by German mercenaries under the command of one of Riedesel's most valued officers, the stern and businesslike Lt. Col. Nicholas von Breymann. During their brief lives, each redoubt had come to be referred to in the ranks of the royal forces by the name of its commander. Burgoyne, emerging from the woods into a small clearing behind his advance guard of Indian warriors and with his troops arranged about him in battle formation, had appropriated the forces of each redoubt as he led his reconnoitering force through the forest somewhat west of Breymann's position . The commanding general sat atop his white horse with Sir Francis Clerke at his side on a far less showy mount. Once past Breymann's redoubt, Burgoyne called a halt to the advance while he surveyed the scene.

"Are we halting here, Sir?" Clerke asked.

"Only momentarily I hope, Sir Francis. We must give the savages time to range ahead and test the obstacles before us. We learned in the last clash how useful such a tactic can be. If the savages encounter no meaningful resistance, then we'll move forward again. That's our purpose here, after all – determining how much opposition we might meet if we decided to advance in genuine force along this route."

"Very good, Sir," Clerke said, gazing about at the heavily wooded terrain all around him. "From here, I can see none of our forces, I fear."

"Oh, they're there," Burgoyne said, peering directly ahead at the thick forest. "We should be spread out now, through forest and field, in a battle line roughly a fifth of a mile long. I have General Fraser off there to the right with the twenty-fourth – along with Balcarres and his light infantry. The baron is directly ahead in the center with

Breymann's grenadiers, and Lord Acland is to our left with our own grenadiers."

As Burgoyne spoke, General Phillips, on horseback and surrounded by a squad of mounted cavalrymen to serve as couriers to the various commands, emerged from the forest at the commanding general's rear.

"The big guns are positioned, Sir," Phillips said. "I have two twelve-pounders and two six-pounders up ahead with the baron. Lord Acland on the left has access to the cannon we have positioned on the line there. General Fraser, you should know, rejected my offer of cannon on the right. He says they'll only slow him up when we move forward."

Burgoyne chuckled. "Simon always favors mobility over firepower – especially when probing unfamiliar territory. Commanders of advance troops always tend to think that way, General Phillips."

"Yes," Phillips said stiffly. "He told me that cannon only slowed up the Germans at Bennington, much to their regret."

"Much to the regret of us all," Burgoyne said. "That, however, was yesterday, gentlemen. This is today, and fortune seems to be smiling on us this morning. The sun is shining, and I hear no musket fire from the front."

"No," Phillips said, gazing up ahead at the silent forest across the clearing. "The rebels seem to be more heavily concentrated to our left today. Lord Acland is most likely to encounter them first, I would presume. Shall I send out couriers to order a renewal of the advance?"

"If you would be so kind," Burgoyne said, his mount prancing nervously beneath him. "Instruct the commanders to confer with me once we halt again beyond this stand of forest now before us. And now forward, gentlemen — into what I'm confident will be the loving embrace of Dame Fortune."

Amid the twittering of birds and in the growing warmth of the autumn sun, the English advance continued through thick forest until the woods gave way to a broad expanse of farm field with split rail fencing bordering a wooded hillside on the west and heavy woods to the east on the plateau above the river. Near the forest from which the royal forces emerged stood two small huts. As Burgoyne's senior officers gathered around him, the left and right flanks of the reconnaissance force formed a strong line along the edge of the woods, which struck Burgoyne as ideal ground for the deadly snipers the English had encountered in their first such sally against the rebel lines.

"Good morning, gentlemen," Burgoyne said. "What have you seen?"

"Nothing thus far, Sir," said Lord Acland. "The woods are empty."

Fraser and the baron nodded in assent. Burgoyne turned and gazed across the vast carpet of wheat waving in the field before them.

"Well," the commanding general said, "if we're encountering no rebels, we've at least been fortunate enough to encounter some food. Sir Francis, have a detachment begin to harvest some of this wheat to take back to the Schuyler estate. Meanwhile, I would prefer a better view of everything. Whoever has a spyglass, come with me. We're climbing up on the roof of that hut over there to look around. Where are we, precisely? Doe this location have a name?"

Fraser said, "The maps designate this place as part of Bemis Heights, Jack. Some chap named Bemis owns a tavern down on the river road over there. I would imagine that he's closed for now."

"What a profound pity," said Sir Francis Clerke.

Wilkinson. 1777

Leaving his mount firmly tied to a tree bole at the edge of the woods, Wilkinson made his way carefully through the stand of thick forest. After several hundred yards, he spied daylight through the trees to the west and slowed his pace markedly. Dropping to his knees, Wilkinson crawled the rest of the way, until he could see clearly across the farm field beyond the trees. Several hundred yards to the west, he finally spied what a few of the militiamen had told him of as they'd rushed into the Army of the United States headquarters a half hour before. Wilkinson watched as red-coated English troops slashed away at wheat in the fields. At the same time he saw a combination of German grenadiers in dark blue coats and high metal helmets and German foot soldiers in their coats of forest green standing guard at the edge of the forest to the north. Beyond the English troops laboring in the field, Wilkinson could see a small knot of uniformed men milling about on the roof of a tiny hut beyond them. Wilkinson unlimbered his spyglass, placed it to his eye and twisted its focus ring until the image was sharp.

"My God," he whispered aloud to himself.

Through the glass, Wilkinson could see four English officers moving around on the roof. From their uniform colors and insignia, he recognized a tall, straight English general in his dark blue artillery coat, a chubby general in German green and two men in red coats, each with a spyglass. The one with the burgundy sash and the hat with the curling plume, he surmised, had to be Burgoyne himself. The commanding English general was again in the field, just as the militiamen had assured Wilkinson. If one of Morgan's rangers had been nearby with his long-range Pennsylvania rifle, Burgoyne would have been a perfect target on the roof of that farm hut. Wilkinson cursed himself for failing to grab one of Morgan's deadly marksmen before he'd sprinted from Gates' headquarters and galloped west to substantiate the militiamen's report.

Wilkinson studied the scene for a long moment. The English and German troops had dropped to the ground, sitting with their bayonet-tipped muskets across their laps as they kept watch on the woods and on their English fellows conducting the wheat harvest. The royal forces faced a broad expanse of open ground and were surrounded on each side and to the rear by heavy tree cover. The officers atop the hut were using spyglasses to minutely examine the terrain to the southeast, where Army of the United States forces were solidly dug in behind the woods and effectively hidden by trees. Through the glass, Wilkinson took several minutes to carefully study the man he presumed to be Burgoyne. Yes, the English commanding general looked very much as Wilkinson had imagined him – tall, well-set up, as dashing in appearance as any stage actor, as Wilkinson had heard. Then Wilkinson replaced the spyglass in its leather case and began to crawl back through the woods to where he'd left his horse. General Gates had to know about this, and Wilkinson felt a surge of excitement at being able to bring his commander this momentous news.

Burgoyne is within our grasp, he thought.

Horatio Gates was bent over maps when Wilkinson arrived back at headquarters. Patiently, the commanding general listened to his aide's report. Wilkinson's eyes glittered with excitement. Gates received the news without expression.

"What is the nature of their ground?" Gates finally asked. "And what is your opinion, Colonel?"

Momentarily, Wilkinson found himself taken aback. The commanding general had never before asked for Wilkinson's opinion on any topic. The young officer quickly described the terrain.

"They're foraging, Sir," he added, "but I do not divine that to be their true purpose – not with General Burgoyne in the field. I believe, General Gates, that their main goal is to reconnoiter your left and that they offer us battle."

"And … " Gates said.

"Their front is open. Their flanks rest upon woods from which they may be attacked effectively, especially by Morgan's Rangers. It is my opinion, Sir, that if they want battle, we should indulge them."

"Well then," Gates said quietly, "order on Morgan to begin the game."

Wilkinson found Morgan at a campfire, downing dark tea with Tim Murphy and several other of his men. Like Murphy, the other rangers were Irishers speaking with thick brogues. When Morgan had formed his group in Virginia several years earlier, he'd displayed a marked preference for woodsmen with clear marksmen's eyes and the genetic hatred of the English that coursed through Irish veins.

"Draw me a map," Morgan snapped to Wilkinson, who used the point of his saber blade in the dirt to reconstruct the scene he'd observed.

"They're open in the front here," Wilkinson said, "And the woods are on their flanks here. There's good, high ground over here to the west beyond a rail fence."

Morgan studied the lines scratched into the dirt next to the campfire. Then he said, "We can hit them cleanly from all sides. I can move my rangers around behind them through the woods to gain that high ground to the west. If General Poor leads his New Hampshiremen to attack their left, we can worry them with ranger fire from the right, and General Learned can come at them with his New Yorkers and Bay Colony men across that wheat field to attack their center. He should hold back, though, until the attacks on the flanks are underway. We'll need a vast mob of men to do this properly, Colonel – especially for that assault on the center by Learned."

"We're not sure of their total strength," Wilkinson cautioned.

"Hell," Morgan snarled, "we must have nine or ten thousand men in this camp today. They've flooded in like a tidal wave since that first engagement."

"Many green militiamen, though," Wilkinson said. "Many of them have no weapons but farm implements."

"You sound like General Gates," Morgan said. "Hold back, hold back, hold back. Well, today he says go forward, and forward we shall go. Whatever the English strength in this sally of theirs, they can't match our numbers."

Wilkinson hesitated. Gates' order had mentioned only Morgan, not Poor and Learned and their various regiments. If Wilkinson approved this plan of Morgan's, he knew, he would be doing it on his own. He would be a colonel transmitting to generals an order far more sweeping than the one that actually had been issued by the commanding general.

"We have teeth enough today to tear them apart," Morgan said, pressing, "and they've just placed their head in our jaws."

For a long moment, Wilkinson pondered the situation. He felt his heart thumping furiously, like a cannonade within his chest. Then he said, "I'll deliver word to Learned and Poor."

Wilkinson bounded atop his mount and galloped off. Morgan turned to Murphy.

"Round up the rangers, Tim," Colonel Daniel Morgan said grimly. "Today will be a day for killing."

Lord Acland. 1777

The first casualties of the day occurred on the English left, in the forces commanded by Major John Dyke Acland. Lord Acland, still in constant pain from the burns he'd sustained in the fire in his tent, heard the musket fire rattle out of the woods and turned just as several of his grenadiers fell next to the tree line. In just a heartbeat, the rebels were roaring out of the woods – no uniforms, of course. The rabble was clad in buckskin and homespun with many wielding nothing more than scythes, sickles and pitchforks. The grenadiers formed up as they'd been trained to do and loosed several blasts of musket fire as the shrieking mob ran forth from the trees. Then the English bayonets were brought to bear, and Acland was on his horse, saber in hand, shouting orders over the din and thrusting, stabbing, slashing into the mob as the powder smoke rose and billowed around him.

Until he went down.

Riedesel, 1777

On the roof of the hut, Baron von Riedesel caught the sound of the firing off to his left. He turned and saw clearly as the surging rebel mob swept over the English left flank only a few hundred yards to the east. Through the smoke, Freddie watched Acland's horse, with Acland aboard, go down.

"Mein Gott," the baron said aloud, bounding off the roof with an agility that belied his bulk and then clambering atop his own mount. He glanced up as Burgoyne, Fraser and Phillips scrambled off the roof. Riedesel began to speak, but as he did he became aware of a similar uproar on the right, as leather-clad men with long guns and tomahawks, hundreds of them, came rushing down the wooded hillside and tore into Fraser's troops.

The numbers, Riedesel thought. Where did they get so many?

"I am going to my troops," he shouted to Burgoyne in French. "The center must hold."

"And just in time, my good baron," Burgoyne said, pointing out toward the wheat field.

Riedesel turned in his saddle. From the far side of the field, several hundred yards away, he saw a surging flood of uniformed rebel forces bursting from the trees and racing toward the English and German troops through the waving wheat. For a long moment, Riedesel sat in his saddle, watching wave upon wave of men emerge from the trees at a dead run toward the English forces. Long accustomed to glancing quickly at an enemy force in the field and estimating its strength, the baron immediately assessed the strength of the rebel mob in mid charge.

Thousands, he concluded. Mein Gott.

Phillips. 1777

The first of Phillips' cannon blasts sent a storm of grapeshot across the field. He could hear the sound of those bits of nail and chain as they whipped through the stalks of wheat toward their targets. Beyond the smoke from the big guns, Phillips could hear screams and grunts of agony from out in front. When the smoke cleared in the wind wafting through the wheat, he noted with satisfaction that a wide gap had been torn through the ranks of the mob sprinting through the wheat.

"Reload," Phillips bellowed. "Fire at will."

Burgoyne. 1777

The left flank was gone, Burgoyne realized – gone in more or less an instant. Acland was down. The grenadiers had inflicted enormous damage on the rabble with both musket fire and bayonets, but now, as they struggled to reload their Brown Bess muskets, the English grenadiers were being slaughtered at close range with farm tools, knives and simple clubs. The rebels had swarmed over the English cannon, slaughtering both the gunners and their horses. The situation on the right was little better. Fraser, on his gray horse and using his saber to great effect both to kill and direct troops, had rallied his men and was holding back the rebel charge through iron discipline and the use of withering fire, but rebel sharpshooters were diminishing his ranks at a disturbing rate. Burgoyne estimated that several hundred of his men were down already on both the left and the right. In just a few minutes, the entire English line was under terrific pressure with devastating casualties and no visible reduction in the forces charging at them or in their fury.

Burgoyne watched it all from the center, from behind Riedesel's stoic German grenadiers and Phillips' booming cannon. The battle had been underway now for roughly half an hour. Already the carnage was nothing less than spectacular on both sides, but the direction here was now clear to the commanding general, and it was hardly encouraging. He turned to Sir Francis Clerke, who rode beside him only a few feet away at all times.

"Spread the order, Sir Francis," Burgoyne called out over the din. "We're retreating back to the fortifications."

"What about our cannon, Sir?" Clerke called out.

"We should save the big guns if we can," Burgoyne shouted, "but the rebel bastards have earned them, and it's the army itself I must save now."

Burgoyne watched as Clerke galloped off to spread the order. As his aide faded into the forest, Burgoyne touched his spurs to his own mount and, to his surprise, felt the glorious white animal collapse soundlessly beneath him.

He's been shot, Burgoyne realized in shock as he fell from his saddle into the brown autumn grass.

Varick. 1777

In the late morning, soaked through after a night of rum and rowdy resentment, Benedict Arnold had banished his aide, Dirk Varick, from the general's tent and had drifted off to sleep in his canvas cot. Several hours later, he awakened to the dull, insistent sound of booming guns to the north and west. Arnold emerged from his tent, still fogged in with sleep as Varick, red-eyed, came galloping through the camp and pulled up, his coal-black horse snorting and spraying sweat, in front of the general.

"What's happening?" Arnold demanded."I've just been at headquarters," Varick said, pointing.

"The English have attacked over there. Learned and Poor have engaged them – and Morgan, of course. There's fierce fighting, I'm told."

For a long moment, Arnold stood unmoving, listening to the

sound of cannon fire in the distance. He was unshaven and rumpled. And, Varick could tell, he was thinking.

"Where's Gates?" he demanded.

"In his headquarters, receiving reports."

"Not in the field, then," Arnold said. "No, never in the field – not that one. I'm going to the scene of the battle, Dirk."

"You can't, Sir," Varick said quickly. "You've been ordered to remain in your tent."

"Like hell," Arnold said, turning and ducking into the tent. In just a few moments, he emerged hatless but otherwise in full uniform, fastening his sword belt. "I need your horse."

A milling crowd of men was gathering around the tent, Varick realized. Most of them were new recruits, freshly arrived militiamen from throughout the region already excited by the sound of fighting off in the distance and anxious for a glance at the fabled General Benedict Arnold.

"Sir ..." Varick began.

Which was when Arnold reached up, grabbed his arm and pulled Varick unceremoniously from the saddle. As Varick hit the ground, rolling, and then regained his feet, Arnold pushed past him and swung up on the big black beast.

"You musn't, Sir," Varick said.

"No, Dirk," Arnold said, his bright blue eyes glittering. "I must, you see. I simply must."

With that, Arnold dug his spurs into the horse's flanks. Startled, the animal half-reared, and then Arnold was off, galloping across the camp, jumping the animal over campfires as cheering militiamen chased after him, entranced by the spectacle. On foot now, Varick followed the mob, which grew with every bound the black horse made in the tight spaces between the tents. A few hundred yards from his own tent, Arnold pulled the animal to a rapid halt next to a barrel of rum. He drew his saber, smashed the hilt into the top of the barrel, splitting open the top, and then held out his hand for a dipper. One of the militiamen eagerly supplied one. Arnold drew forth a dipper of rum and shot it down. He followed that with another and then another as the militiamen cheered wildly. Then, from atop his horse, Arnold threw the dipper to the ground and flourished his saber.

"There's a battle out there, men," he called out to the militiamen. "Our comrades need help. I'm going stand with them. Who goes with me?"

Immediately, the camp was alive with cheers and shouts and shaking fists filled with axes and knives and, here and there, an occasional musket. With a broad grin on his face, Arnold pointed his saber skyward.

"Victory or death!" he roared out.

Then he dug his heels into the black horse, wheeled the wide-eyed animal about and galloped off to the sound of the guns, followed by hundreds of cheering, shouting militiamen.

Wide-eyed, Varick watched the entire spectacle from the edge of the crowd and found himself in just a moment standing alone in that section of the sprawling camp. Dirk Varick knew what he had to do, though – what his duty demanded of him now, as much as performing that duty troubled him.

Slowly, and on foot, Varick set off for Gates' headquarters to inform the commanding general that Benedict Arnold, against direct orders from Gates himself, had just entered the field of battle. Victory or death, Varick thought, shaking his head as he strode through the empty camp. Arnold really doesn't care which.

Wilkinson. 1777

Wilkinson, having notified Poor and Learned of orders to attack and assisting them in getting their troops in motion, arrived back at Gates' headquarters just as Varick was exiting the little building.

"Be careful," Varick warned. "I just told him that General Arnold has joined the battle. He's furious."

Wilkinson entered the building to find Gates red-faced and sputtering.

"Did you hear?" Gates demanded.

"Yes, Sir, I did."

"Find Arnold," Gates ordered angrily. "Bring him back to camp and have him slapped in chains. I'll deal with the mutinous son of a whore as soon as this is over."

Wilkinson nodded in measured silence, saluted and made his way outside to his horse. In less than ten minutes he was at the scene of the conflict, where he'd first spotted the English incursion. The scene had changed markedly. Men milled about the field and in the woods on either side of the wheat field. Corpses were strewn about everywhere – German, English, Army of the United States regulars, militiamen. At a glance, Wilkinson could see hundreds of men crumpled on the ground, most of them unmoving. The cries of the wounded nearly drowned out the cheers of Poor and Learned's forces, who were jubilant over managing to drive the English back. He found one of Poor's colonels joyously straddling the barrel of a brass English twelve-pound gun, a prize of the clash.

"Have you seen General Arnold?" Wilkinson demanded.

"Back there, through the woods," the colonel said, laughing. "We're chasing the sons of bitches all the way back to Canada, and Arnold is leading the chase."

Carefully, Wilkinson guided his horse through the tangle of bodies in red and blue and German green and in homespun and buckskin, too. The carnage was breathtaking. Wilkinson came upon a red-haired rebel army field surgeon wandering the field in an attempt to aid the wounded. The man's face was alight with joy. He held up hands soaked in red for the commanding general's aide to see.

"Look, Wilkinson," the surgeon said. "I've dipped my hands in English blood."

Wilkinson shook his head and guided his mount around the gore-drenched surgeon. All around the field he could see militiamen bending over enemy corpses stripping them of weapons and trophies. Closer to the woods, he spotted two of the New Hampshiremen he knew laughing uproariously beneath the tall metal helmets they'd recovered from dead Germans. As he passed near one youthful militiaman digging through the pockets of a prone English officer with blood-soaked legs, Wilkinson heard the fallen soldier say weakly, "Protect me, Sir, against this boy."

Wilkinson fixed his eyes on the militiaman, who turned out to be a boy of no more than fifteen. The youth held a knife in his hand, poised for killing.

"You would murder this man?" Wilkinson demanded.

The young man's eyes were ablaze with unadulterated hatred. "My older brother surrendered at the Battle of Brooklyn. The English bayoneted him as he held his hands aloft."

"We'll not do that here," Wilkinson said, pointing toward the tree line to the north. "Be off with you. The battle is that way."

For just a moment, the boy hesitated. Wilkinson swung down from his horse, and the youth jumped to his feet and scampered away. Wilkinson knelt down beside the wounded English soldier.

"What's your rank?" Wilkinson asked.

"I'm a major," Lord Acland replied. "I had the honor to command the grenadiers."

"Where are you hit?"

"In both legs. The first wound came in the battle as my horse went down beneath me; the second as I lay wounded. I was dragged back here by the woods by Captain Simpson of our thirty-first, but he's a stout man, and he wearied and was finally obliged to abandon me. I asked my retreating men as they passed to rescue me. I offered fifty guineas to the man who would do it, and a grenadier tried, but the fire was too heavy, and he fled, too. And now you've saved me. That boy would have slit my throat with great glee."

With enormous effort, and with the aid of a nearby militiaman he impressed into service, Wilkinson finally managed to get Lord Acland off the ground and into the saddle of Wilkinson's horse. Blood bubbled over the top of the English officer's knee-high boots.

"Get him back to our field hospital," Wilkinson ordered the militiaman. "Your face is now in my memory. If this officer comes to harm, I'll find you, have no doubt. And keep him away from that demented red-haired surgeon."

As the militiaman led the horse away, with Lord Acland slumped over in the saddle, Wilkinson entered the woods at the northern end of the field. Beyond the trees, he could hear the rattle of musketry and the occasional blast of English cannon. In this place there was blood aplenty. Up ahead, there would be even more blood. And it was up there, Wilkinson knew, that he would find Benedict Arnold.

Burgoyne. 1777

The retreat was as orderly as possible, under the circumstances.

Once Burgoyne had freed him leg from the weight of his dead horse, he stood up to discover that the coat of his field uniform had been ripped by two musket balls, one of which had torn through the lower edge of his waistcoat, only an inch from his guts. He'd apparently been the target of several marksmen firing more or less in unison, and he surmised that the shots had gone off target simply because the first one had struck his horse in the skull and the commanding general had gone down so quickly with the sudden collapse of his mount.

At the very center of the English forces, Burgoyne immediately commandeered another horse from a junior officer and rallied his panicky troops. Bolstered by the very sight of their commanding general riding high among them and fighting at their side, the red-coated troops managed to mount several bloody and brutal bayonet charges that slowed the oncoming mob markedly, but Burgoyne saw several of his men go down to attacks with axes and shovels. The sheer numbers of the rabble were too much, he realized. Slowly, and despite their well-earned status as the finest, most intensely trained hand-to-hand fighters on Earth, the outnumbered English were forced to give ground.

Still, though, with Burgoyne in personal command and with Riedesel assisting with his Germans, the English center was holding in hard-pressed retreat. Burgoyne knew that he no longer had a left wing, so he ordered Reidesel to move his troops to that side in hope of maintaining some semblance of a functional battle line. He could not let the rebels get behind him and press his troops from both front and back. Burgoyne had absolute faith in both Riedesel's ability and stoic willingness to hold the left wing or to die trying, as had Lord Acland.

The question is, Burgoyne asked himself as he fell back through the woods with his men, do I still have a right wing?

Fraser. 1777

"Spread out! Spread out!" Simon Fraser was roaring. "Don't let them get around that end."

Having received no orders whatever from Burgoyne, Fraser had assessed the situation and had begun a disciplined withdrawal back to the redoubts beyond the woods behind him. English musket volleys were keeping the rebel mob at bay as Fraser's men moved backward through the trees. Periodically, as his troops steadily retreated through the thick clouds of musket smoke, Fraser would dash forward on his gray gelding, shouting and waving his saber, to order a counterattack with bayonets to slow the progress of the rebel army. He was struggling to maintain the line as, at the same time, he was forced to concentrate his forces here and there to prevent an open rout.

Several slugs had nicked his gray gelding. The creature was as battle-hardened as any other soldier, but the horse's nerves were now nearly gone. Fraser was keeping the animal under control only with immense difficulty.

"Get down off that beast, Sir," one of Fraser's captains begged him as the gray gelding reared on its hind legs. "You're too high — too fine a target for those bloody marksmen."

Fraser pulled hard on the horse's reins, digging the bit into the animal's mouth.

"The men must see me, Captain," Fraser called out as he calmed his skittish mount. "They must receive no message of fear from their commander."

Morgan. 1777

Just into the woods to the south of Fraser's troops, Dan Morgan located a clear, narrow pathway through the trees. From two hundred yards away, he could see the English slowly backing off under heavy fire from both Morgan's Rangers and, up fairly close, Dearborn's light infantry. Racing around the English ranks back and forth and shouting orders, Morgan could clearly see, was a ruggedly built officer on a gray horse. From the red-coated officer's age and general bearing, Morgan knew he had isolated a senior commander.

"Tim!" Morgan called out. In just a heartbeat, Tim Murphy was at his side.

"You called, Colonel darlin'?" Murphy said.

Morgan pointed through the pathway in the trees. "There's a brave man up there on a gray horse. Kill him for me, please."

Murphy peered along the path Morgan had indicated. Then, wordlessly, he grabbed a nearby low-hanging branch, swung into a tree and clambered like a monkey to a height of fifteen feet in the air. Morgan watched as Murphy positioned himself solidly against the tree bole, sighted his rifle and fired quickly. Morgan glanced back through the trees.

"You missed him," Morgan called out. "Drop your rifle down. I'll reload for you. Meanwhile, try a real rifle, Tim."

Murphy dropped his weapon. Morgan caught it easily in one hand while he bent at the knees and launched his own rifle upward with his other hand. Murphy leaned out of the tree and deftly caught the weapon by the barrel. He pulled his commander's rifle in close and settled back into a secure firing position.

"He's an annoying target, that one, jumping around on that horse as he is," Murphy called down to his commander.

"Take a moment to aim this time," Morgan advised.

Murphy did.

Arnold. 1777

At the very front of a cheering, shouting squad of hundreds of rebel soldiers, Arnold emerged from the forest on his big, black horse. Before him — across a field of thick, green grass — stood a sturdy log fortification. Dozens of blue-coated German mercenaries, their high brass helmets glittering in the sun, were flooding across the field for the shelter of the logs. At one end of the fortification, Arnold could see, stood a tall German officer, waving his sword and calling to the men to take positions behind the redoubt and to fire back at the pursuing rebels.

Arnold pulled his horse to a halt. He turned in the saddle as the cheering, shouting militiamen gathered around him from the surrounding forest. The general gazed down upon his impromptu army – at the command given him not by Gates but by Arnold's in-born gift for rousing men to violent action with only scant regard for their own mortality.

"There they are," Benedict Arnold bellowed out. "They're digging in to stop us here. Will we let them do that?"

Crowded around the rearing, plunging horse and its rider at the edge of the woods, the militiamen roared out their refusal to permit the German guns to halt their advance. Arnold sat tall in his saddle and pointed his saber directly at the log redoubt across the field.

"Then follow me!" he roared, digging his spurs deep into the horse's flanks.

Breymann. 1777

Nearly an hour before, from his command at the log redoubt, Lt. Colonel Nicholas von Breymann had heard the guns up ahead begin their deadly serenade. He'd known instantly that Burgoyne's reconnaissance force had encountered rebels. When retreating German grenadiers began filtering through the woods from the front in a trickle he'd realized that the engagement was going badly. When the trickle had become a flood — as the bloody, battered, terrified men had emerged from the forest carrying their wounded on their backs — Breymann had debriefed them as they'd reached his position and had settled them into combat position behind the shelter of the logs.

"Reload," he'd ordered. "We'll hold them here. They won't get past us now, will they?"

The men were badly shaken, Breymann realized. The combat beyond the woods had been sudden, brief and, apparently, unspeakably brutal. Each retreating grenadier knew he was lucky to be alive, as so many of his comrades no longer were. It was his job, Breymann understood, to put some steel back into their Teutonic spines and to hold this position at all costs. He worked to accomplish this chore through the resourcefulness that both his training and experience had imposed upon him – through a combination of cheering words, sympathy, support and authority. These men were soldiers, after all. Their sworn duty was to win, or to die trying. One reason a soldier fought well, he understood, was the certain knowledge that failing to do so would result in harsh discipline later.

As a commander, Breymann knew, one of his obligations was to be more terrifying to his men than any enemy could possibly be.

So, when the fleeing grenadiers were safely behind the barricade and the pursuing rebels emerged behind them from the woods, Breymann stormed among the still-shocked, exhausted German troops, waving his saber and furiously challenging them to behave like men. In a burst of sharp, shouted commands, he reminded them of their training, appealed to their pride as German soldiers, invoked their sacred duty to their prince back in Brunswick and threatened them with certain execution if they failed to stand bravely against the oncoming enemy. Breymann continued his ceaseless rant as the rebel officer across the field launched his black horse directly at the redoubt followed by that screaming, shrieking mob of farmers and shopkeepers at his rear.

"Aim and fire!" Breymann roared. "Aim and fire!"

They did. The redoubt was five feet tall – high enough to protect its defenders from incoming musket fire but still low enough for his men to stand behind it and employ their own weaponry to good effect. When the survivors of the rebel charge reached the redoubt – and Breymann could tell from the very numbers of the enemy that his men could not kill them all as they rushed across the field directly at the Germans – then the grenadiers would meet them with bayonets as a single, impregnable wall of sharp, merciless steel.

"We can stop them," Breymann called out as the firing from the redoubt began. "We can stop them here – for God and our prince."

The smoke from the German muskets instantly filled and obscured the space in front of the log fortification. The men reloaded and fired in teams as Breymann peered into the cloud, struggling to see the enemy, whose wild cries he could hear growing ever louder. Then, from the billowing smoke just a few yards in front of the fortification, came a man with a hatchet, who hurled himself over the top log, through several defenders and onto the ground inside the log barrier. As the man scrambled to his feet with his ax poised for mayhem, Breymann whirled and thrust the point of his saber into the man's middle. As the enemy fell with a scream, Breymann whirled and saw other attackers clearing the barricade to be met by German bayonets. But he also saw his grenadiers beginning to break. Some were dropping their muskets and turning to run. Breymann knew instantly what he had to do to hold this position. He stepped back several paces from the log wall. When the next grenadier turned to run Breymann drove the point of his saber into the man's guts. The German soldier collapsed in a shrieking heap on the grass. Breymann glared at his troops.

"Stand and fight, you damned cowards," the colonel roared out. "Stand at the wall and do your duty or die here, at my hand."

Which was when a German grenadier, standing only a few feet from Breymann, raised his freshly reloaded musket and fired it directly into his commander's rage-filled face.

Burgoyne. 1777

The battle line was broken now, Burgoyne could tell. From the back of the chestnut mare he'd commandeered, he could see through the thick fog of powder smoke that Riedesel's force on the left was fleeing.in disorder, with men dragging wounded comrades and firing back into the smoke before them only sporadically. To the right, he could see Fraser's advance troops moving steadily backward, firing and reloading in calm, controlled fashion, but retreating nonetheless. Burgoyne's own center was badly pressed. The rebel fire was coming through the smoke with regularity and to disturbing effect.

"Back to the barricades," he called out to his troops as he rode back and forth furiously along the line at the center. "Back to the barricades and to our big guns."

At the far right end of the center line, Burgoyne found a captain of Fraser's command. The man was dragging his right leg as he shouted commands to his men to reload and fire, reload and fire, reload and fire.

"Where's General Fraser?" Burgoyne demanded.

"Wounded, Sir," the captain shouted back over the din of gunfire. "He's been taken back."

Burgoyne continued to the right. With Fraser out of commission, the commanding general knew that he now had more than a thousand yards of line to maintain on his own. This wasn't quite a rout yet, but it was close enough. Burgoyne was certain, however, that if he could reform his line behind the log redoubts and earthworks and cannon emplacements to the rear, he then would enjoy a chance to halt the rebel advance at that location.

For the next twenty minutes, firing off commands to junior officers as he rode back and forth along the line hunched down over his horse's neck, Burgoyne managed to lead his men out of the woods, across the field of thick grass and back to the fortified line. Once they had achieved that position, Burgoyne jumped the horse over an earthen breastwork and directed the troops to put up a steady stream of fire into the smoke that obscured the line. At the same time, he galloped along the line behind the fortifications ordering the discharge of grapeshot into the smoke, blast after blast of it. At one gun, he found Phillips, coated in black powder soot but otherwise unharmed as he supervised the weapon's repositioning.

"Simon Fraser has been wounded, Will," Phillips told him.

"I've heard," Burgoyne said. "Have you seen Sir Francis?"

"I have not, Sir."

"Take over the right wing, please, General Phillips. The cannoneers can do their duty without further immediate direction by a general officer."

"Very good, Sir," Phillips said, immediately moving off to the right without further comment.

As the last of the surviving English forces reached the barricades, clambered over them and the overall firing diminished, Burgoyne could see the smoke begin to lift in the steady breeze off the river beyond the trees to the east. On the far side of the field, he saw knots of rebel fighters in their mishmash of colors emerge from the trees and halt as they instinctively appraised the width of the field and the bristle of English guns beyond. Firing on each side began to sputter out.

In just a moment, an eerie silence hung over the open field where wispy clouds of gun smoke swirled in the breeze. Here, Burgoyne knew from experience, was where courage often failed. Here was when men stood on one side of an open killing ground and pondered the prospect of racing headlong into massed enemy fire – into a world where skill and courage and right and wrong had no meaning, where all that counted was sheer, blind luck. This where officers earned their keep — leading men into the sheer madness of a charge into opposing fire through cajoling, cheering, bullying and, if necessary, begging.

While their blood was hot now, these were largely green, untrained troops he faced, Burgoyne knew. In no major engagement with the English thus far – not in Boston, and certainly not in New York City — had the rebel officers distinguished themselves. Like the men they led, the officers were mostly shopkeepers and farmers to whom warfare was new and distinctly terrifying. If today's rebel momentum was to be stopped, Burgoyne understood, it would be here, where the rebels would find themselves matched against the might of the Royal Army on open ground. It was possible, he knew, that no charge would come – that the officers could not convince their inexperienced troops to rush headlong into massed English firepower. To lead them enthusiastically into such an ordeal, he knew, would require a unique officer who commanded the full regard and confidence of his men – who led not merely by words and intimidation but by magnetism of personality and stark personal courage.

Burgoyne was astonished at the rebel numbers, though, as they continued to emerge from the forest in group after group. There were thousands of them, Burgoyne could tell — far too many, the commanding general realized, for his dug-in troops to kill more than a fraction of them as they rushed across the few hundred yards separating them from the English guns. Most of the enemy, he knew, would reach the English fortifications. When that happened the fighting would be hand to hand, as it had been near the huts in the engagement's initial moments. His troops were good at that, Burgoyne knew, but they would be outnumbered by at least four to one once the rebel troops reached these barricades.

For a long moment, the opposing forces assessed one another in relative silence across the field of grass that separated them. On the English side, officers marched back and forth behind the lines urging their troops to stand ready and hold steady. Brown Bess muskets were being frantically reloaded. Burgoyne could hear the cannoneers at work, driving home powder and grapeshot in advance of the anticipated charge. On the far side of the field, he knew, rebel officers were unlimbering their sabers and doing what they could to bolster the nerves of their troops. When the charge came – if it came — the junior officers would be the first into the teeth of English weaponry, the courage of their example prompting their troops to follow into the heavy fire that would spit out like dragon's breath from the English emplacements.

They might not do it, Burgoyne thought. These are not real soldiers. They might not charge after all.

As he gazed across the field, waiting to see if the charge actually materialized, Burgoyne glanced to his right. Down the opposing line, just outside the thick woods, Burgoyne spotted a bareheaded Army of the United States officer on a black horse suddenly emerge from a large knot of rebels at the tree line and, without the slightest hesitation, spur his mount into the field, waving his saber above his head. Completely by himself, the officer dug his heels repeatedly into his mount and began a furious gallop directly at Breymann's redoubt at the far right of the line. Instantly, Burgoyne heard a blast of German grapeshot loosed in the madman's direction. Heavy musket fire began to emerge from the redoubt. Yet the officer continued his individual charge through a virtual bee's swarm of lead as the men he'd left behind rose up in a ferocious shout and began to run after him, directly into the enemy fire from the log fortification.

That'll do it, Burgoyne thought to himself.

The commanding English general stood in his stirrups and shouted out, "Here they come, men. Stand fast for God and country and the king!"

Wilkinson. 1777

James Wilkinson was mystified as he worked his way through the woods and heard the firing and the riotous shouting ahead suddenly subside. For just a moment, saber in hand, he stopped and listened. Above the eerie silence, all he could hear were the moans of the wounded at the edge of the woods behind him.

What's this? Wilkinson wondered.

Then, with immense caution, the youthful colonel bent low at the waist and carefully made his way forward through the corpses amid the trees until he spotted daylight ahead. Then he saw the movement of men, his own troops, up ahead, and Wilkinson stepped up his pace to arrive at the rear of the rebel battle line just as a great cheer sounded slightly off to his left. Wilkinson elbowed his way into the mob and fought his way to the front just in time to see Arnold on a wild-eyed black horse galloping across the field directly at the English line followed by a cheering, shouting mob of several hundred blue-and-buff clad infantrymen and militiamen in buckskin and homespun. All along the rebel line on either side of him Wilkinson heard sudden cheers and battle cries burst from thousands of throats. Then, in a great wave of noise, the rebel troops were launching themselves into a ferocious charge across the expanse of field as the English line exploded into a thunderclap of musket and cannon fire. Wilkinson found himself swept along with the mob, and he fought to move to his left – to where he'd seen Arnold leading the charge.

By the time Wilkinson had worked his way to the left of the charging rebel line and could gain some visibility in front of the redoubt, he had a clear view of Arnold's horse going down in a blast of fire from the log walls. His leg pinned on the ground beneath the dead horse – the very leg, Wilkinson knew, that Arnold had broken in combat the previous year at Quebec — Arnold immediately sat up and continued to wave his sword and urge his men forward. Despite the gunfire, from only forty or so yards away Wilkinson could hear Arnold's clear voice call out, "Don't kill that fellow there. He only did his duty when he shot me."

As Wilkinson watched, the rebels flooded past the wounded general pinned beneath his dead horse and swarmed across the log barrier into the redoubt. From beyond the log wall, Wilkinson could hear shouts and screams and the sound of exploding muskets and the clink of steel against steel. Wilkinson was almost at Arnold's side as some of the men returned from the log emplacement and pulled the general from beneath his dead horse. Arnold's leg was bathed in blood, Wilkinson could see, and hung loosely, clearly broken once again and also sporting a conspicuous hole through the top of the boot through which blood flowed freely. As rebel forces reached the English line all up and down the field, perhaps a dozen blue-clad regulars and militiamen, delirious with victory at the redoubt, lifted Arnold's prone form on their shoulders and, amid cheers and cries of triumph, began to carry him back from the log wall across the field and toward the hospital tent back in the rebel camp. It was at that moment that Wilkinson caught Arnold's eye. General Arnold responded by raising his sword arm in Wilkinson's direction.

"We've won this, Wilkinson," a grinning, bleeding Benedict Arnold called out above the din of war. "Tell Granny Gates that the true warriors have won the day out here without him."

Frederika. 1777

A small, rather intimate dinner party had been planned for that evening at the tiny farmhouse the Riedesels occupied to the north of Bemis Heights. The baroness had looked forward to the company that evening of Simon Fraser, the Aclands and several senior German officers and their wives. She also had looked forward to being spared the company of Burgoyne's lady, whom the baroness still regarded with cool, artfully disguised contempt.

She had known, however, as soon as the big guns had begun booming to the south that the dinner party would not materialize. Instead, she'd ordered her servants to clear the table of china and silverware and to send word to the field hospital that her house was available as a hospital adjunct. A short time later, the Irish surgeon with whom she'd worked after the first battle arrived with an ox cart full of wounded English and German soldiers who stank of blood and dysentery. The baroness sent her children out to play behind the house and immediately immersed herself in her work as the surgeon's assistant. She and her maids were soon joined by Lady Harriet, conspicuously pregnant but in an old dress and eager to help. That's what they were doing when a bleeding Simon Fraser arrived in an ox cart. The baroness helped carry the general inside and aided in stretching him out on the dining room table. In just a moment, the Irish surgeon was at Fraser's side, examining him as other men of lesser rank moaned and bled elsewhere in the tiny building.

"How bad is my wound?" The ashen-faced Simon Fraser got out.

The surgeon bent over, ripped open the general's tunic, removed the makeshift bandage covering the wound and examined Fraser's bare, bloodied torso as the room grew dark and the maids lit candles from the kitchen fire. "The ball entered just below the breastbone and lodged near your spine, Sir."

Fraser was silent for a long moment. Then he said, "Tell me, to the best of your ability and judgment, if you believe that my wound is mortal."

The surgeon stood upright and gazed down at the general. "I regret, Sir, to inform you that it is. The ball penetrated your intestines. Infection is inevitable. You cannot possibly live more than another twenty-four hours."

Fraser remained expressionless, as did the surgeon, but the baroness immediately turned away from the table with tears gushing down her cheeks. Lady Harriet took Frederika in her arms and led her into the kitchen.

"He's my favorite," the baroness choked out, "my favorite of all of zem."

"Perhaps the surgeon is wrong," Lady Harriet said.

Frederika shook her head. "He is right. I haff seen such vounds before."

From the other room, she heard Fraser calmly tell the surgeon, "Inform General Burgoyne of my condition. Have paper and pen brought to me. I will leave a will and burial instructions."

"Very good, Sir," the surgeon said.

Frederika sniffled and used her knuckles to dry her eyes. Then she turned and went back into the dining room to stand at Fraser's side. She took the general's hand in hers. Fraser gazed up at her.

"I'm not yet in pain, Baroness" the general said quietly. "Others here are suffering more. I can hear them about me."

"Did you see my Freddie?" the baroness asked.

"I did. He fought nobly and well and was unharmed when last I laid eyes upon him. Your husband is a fine soldier, Baroness – a man to be proud of."

"As are you, Simon," she said, clutching his hand tightly in her grasp.

"If I'm still able, I'll write this down when they bring me pen and paper, but tell Jack that I wish to be buried on that high bluff overlooking the river. He'll know the one. Tell him, too, that he must speak to my wife when he returns to England. She must know that my final thoughts were of her."

Frederika nodded. "I vill be certain zat he knows zat, but you vill see him."

Fraser nodded weakly. "If he lives. The commanding general was in the thick of the battle, Baroness, and Jack would go down fighting before he would surrender."

In another hour, as a feverish Fraser lay on his back on the dining room table scribbling his will and a few letters, other ox carts arrived, wounded men were treated and died and, finally, the Baron von Riedesel arrived by horseback in the darkness. In front of the farmhouse overflowing with wounded, Frederika hugged him tightly and silently as Lady Harriet appeared in the doorway.

"My John?" she asked the baron in French.

Riedesel delayed his response for only a moment. Then he said, "I saw him fall, Madame."

Lady Harriet's lovely face contorted in a grimace of grief just as the surgeon inside called for aid. Without another word, she turned and disappeared inside.

"A defeat, then?" Frederika asked in German.

Riedesel nodded. "We lost a thousand men, Breymann among them. The English are blaming him for the loss – because the capture of his redoubt on the right led to the collapse of the line. We are safe for now behind new fortified lines south of the estate, but this campaign is over."

"General Burgoyne?"

"Here he comes now," Freddie said, motioning over his shoulder as Burgoyne and a party of English officers emerged from the darkness on horseback.

Burgoyne swung down from his mount. "Simon?" he said.

"Inside," the baroness said. "In ze dining room."

Hurriedly, Burgoyne disappeared into the darkened house.

Wilkinson. 1777

Wilkinson delayed in returning to Gates' headquarters to inform the commanding general of Arnold's feat at Breymann's redoubt. He suspected strongly that Arnold's success would infuriate Gates, and he knew that the commanding general would be occupied receiving reports from the battlefield. Moreover, Wilkinson wanted to observe the battle's aftermath. He'd arrived on the scene too late to participate in any serious way in the final charge but not too late to walk to the English emplacements, from which Burgoyne's troops had been routed, and to watch the rebel forces in riotous celebration as they stood by their captured cannon and over the corpses of English and German defenders. Militiamen and blue-clad army regulars alike stripped the enemy bodies of trophies. In several cases that Wilkinson witnessed, they dispatched wounded and helpless English and German soldiers with the enemies' own feared and hated bayonets.

As darkness fell, Wilkinson could hear the sound of gunfire from the woods as the Royal Army forces, fleeing for their lives now, escaped through the forest to the north and to the safety of more heavily fortified lines beyond the great ravine that bordered the southern edge of Schuyler's Saratoga estate. He also watched the wagons rolling onto the battlefield from the rebel encampment bearing barrels of rum for the rowdy, delighted rebel forces to consume while they quite literally danced on the corpses of the enemy. It was, at once, a triumphant and macabre scene. Wilkinson was certain that for the rest of his life he would recall it as a moment of both fulfillment and horror, the stuff of both dreams and nightmares for the balance of his days.

When darkness fully descended on the scene and as campfires sprung up along what had been the fortified English battle line, Wilkinson left the battlefield and returned to the small cabin behind the lines that served as Gates' candlelit headquarters. All around the tiny building rebel soldiers and militiamen were drinking and celebrating with raucous enthusiasm. As Wilkinson entered Gates' headquarters, he was surprised to find the commanding general sitting in a chair beside his bed, which was occupied by a prone English officer bleeding heavily from gut wound. Wilkinson instantly recognized the wound as the type that virtually always led to a brief and fatal infection.

"Did you find Arnold?" Gates demanded.

"He was wounded as he led the final charge, Sir. He was being carried to the hospital when I last saw him."

Gates was expressionless. "A fatal wound, do you suppose?" the commanding general asked – almost hopefully, Wilkinson couldn't help but notice.

"It was his leg, General Gates. He'll likely survive. Who is this here?"

"Meet your counterpart, Colonel. This is General Burgoyne's chief aide, Sir Francis Clerke. He was brought down by that man of Morgan's – Murphy, his name is? We were discussing matters of gravity when you came in. Do tell Colonel Wilkinson what you were saying to me, Sir Francis."

Clerke nodded weakly. "I was saying that it's not too late for you to surrender. I'm certain that General Burgoyne would be generous in his terms. His only goal is to repatriate loyal subjects of the king. The simple signing of a renewed oath of loyalty to the Crown and an agreement to disband would, I'm certain, be all that would be required of you or any of your troops."

Gates rose from his chair. "Please excuse us, Sir Francis."

Gates put his hand on Wilkinson's shoulder and guided him through the door to the tiny front porch of the building.

"Is he serious, Sir?" Wilkinson asked.

"He is, indeed," Gates said. "I had him brought to me when I was informed of his identity, but he has no information of any use to us at this juncture, and he annoys me mightily. The man is growing delirious, I fear. He keeps muttering gibberish about the thunder of captains or some such nonsense. Have someone come and take him to the hospital tent. He'll be dead before dawn at any rate. Have you an estimate of our losses?"

"I do, Sir. My estimate is one hundred and fifty dead and perhaps another two hundred wounded or taken prisoner – although they didn't stop to take many prisoners as they fled the field."

"Good. I imagine that their losses were a good deal higher. Have our cannon moved north during the night. We'll begin bombarding them up at General Schuyler's estate at dawn. And send heavy forces across the river tonight to cross back over north of the estate and occupy the river road above the Schuyler estate. We'll need to bottle up the English there to force a surrender in the next day or so. They can't have much left in the way of provisions."

"Very good, General Gates," Wilkinson said.

"Get me a full list of the English and German officers we've taken prisoner. We need to begin a prisoner exchange tomorrow morning."

"I'll have that information in your hands within an hour."

"But first get this impudent son of a bitch out of my sight," Gates said.

Wilkinson nodded wordlessly and saluted. He was privately astounded at Gates' petty pique and venality at the very moment of his triumph.

"Too bad about Arnold," Gates said as he went back into the headquarters building.

For a long moment, Wilkinson stood alone in the darkness outside the headquarters building, wondering just what the general had meant by that final comment – whether Gates was saddened over Arnold's wound or over Arnold's glory in leading the final charge or over the news that Arnold probably would survive his injury.

All three, Wilkinson finally concluded.

Babette. 1777

She'd spent the night in the hospital tents along the estate's southern border near the ravine. Babette had watched as horribly wounded soldiers, one by one, had died in agony as she'd nursed them, struggled to comfort them in their final moments and failed. The sheer numbers of the wounded had left her numb – that and the brutal severity of the injuries that had left so many of them screaming on the hospital cots as they'd departed this world. The scene in the hospital tents had been appalling beyond anything Babette could ever have imagined. The sheer scale of the carnage had unnerved her badly.

She'd finally returned to the mansion in pre-dawn darkness soaked in blood and exhausted, both physically and emotionally. Babette had stripped off the bloody clothing, scrubbed her naked body from the wash basin in the vast bedroom and climbed into bed alone and shivering in the icy blackness. Just before the sun rose, Burgoyne had entered the shadowy room. Babette had leaped from the bed and embraced him and wept bitterly both from the strain of her ordeal and with joy that Jack was still alive, although the holes in his coat and waistcoat from musket balls sent a chill down her spine. Burgoyne was contained and controlled, as always, but the dry, confident humor was utterly absent from his demeanor.

"Simon just died," he told her. "I was with him all night, receiving all my reports there. We'd moved him from the table in the dining room into the baron's bed. We'd spent the night talking about all our days together – all the good and arduous moments we'd shared over the years. I shall very much miss that sunny, laudable man."

In the shadows of the bedroom, as the sun crept over the eastern horizon and began to illuminate the room, Burgoyne held Babette in his arms in bed. Despite their weariness, neither could sleep. Burgoyne described the battle for her and expressed his concern for Lord Acland and Sir Francis, who had not been located among the surviving English forces and whom he assumed had been killed or taken prisoner. Babette told Burgoyne of the woman she had nursed – a camp follower who had accompanied her man, a foot soldier in the twenty-fourth regiment, into battle. The woman had, in her furious grief after her lover had been killed by a rebel sharpshooter, taken his place at a cannon.

"She'd lost her right arm," Babette said. "If no infection sets in, she should live, but the horror of it, Jack – the sheer horror of it all."

"It's war, my love – war at its ugliest."

"What shall we do now?"

"Bury our dead, nurse our wounded and run – if we can, that is. I soon must arise to organize matters. We must reach Ticonderoga before the snow flies, and the going will be slow with all these wounded. I'll be forced to leave most of them to the care of the rebels, I fear. First, though, we must bury Simon. There's a place near here that he wanted for a gravesite. My friend will get his final wish. Whatever else might happen, that will occur."

She pressed close to him in the bed.

"Oh, Jack," she said, "it's all so awful."

"Yes," Burgoyne said quietly. "It is that."

Burgoyne. 1777

Dodging sniper fire in periodic bursts of heavy rain and preparing his battered, bloodied army to move northward, the English commanding general spent much of the following day wondering why Gates did not launch a ferocious attack, as Burgoyne most certainly would have done in Gates' place. The rebels had moved disturbingly close to his southern lines, Burgoyne knew. The two sides exchanged cannon fire all day. General Phillips displayed some dazzling skill with his beloved big guns in keeping the rebel forces at bay. Thick and regular bursts of grapeshot through the trees along the Schuyler estate's southern border kept the fire from rebel sharpshooters down to a manageable level as the English army packed up, although it did not prevent the rebels from establishing several cannon emplacements at the edge of the farm fields west of the estate. In mid afternoon Burgoyne received the message he'd expected from Gates – a ritual demand for surrender along with a request to establish a prisoner exchange. It was in that message that Burgoyne received word that Sir Francis Clerke had died in a rebel hospital tent and that Lord Acland remained alive, although badly wounded in each leg. He personally transmitted that information to the conspicuously pregnant Lady Harriet as she labored among the English wounded in the hospital tents.

"I must go to him," Lady Harriet said calmly. "I can nurse John back to health as can no other."

"I'll make the necessary arrangements with General Gates for you to cross the lines safely." Burgoyne told her. "We shall be desolate without your matchless company, Lady Harriet, but the news that Lord Acland survives is most gratifying."

"To me it is," she said.

Late in the day, after Simon Fraser's corpse had been properly washed and garbed in his dress uniform, Burgoyne led his senior staff and the body to the top of the bluff along the Hudson to bury the fallen general in a grave dug that day by foot soldiers. Because the burial site that Fraser had selected was in full view of a rebel artillery position across the farm fields to the west behind the mansion, the ladies of the company were forbidden to attend the ceremony. Instead, they watched from the sweeping porch of Schuyler's mansion some distance away. The young chaplain, the Rev. Edward Brudenell, performed the lengthy service for the burial of the dead in its entirety. As he did, the rebel battery to the west of the estate opened fire. The shots were going over the burial party and to either side. Brudenell continued his reading, coolly ignoring the shots as they fell around the group, although dirt from the falling ordinance pelted him with speckles of mud.

"They lack the necessary skill with the gun to zero in on us properly," Phillips told Burgoyne. "By the time they get the distance, we'll be finished here."

"I hope you're correct," Burgoyne said as Brudenell finished his reading. Then the commanding general stepped forward. Fraser had asked that only officers from his personal staff attend the ceremony, but Burgoyne had added his senior commanders to the party. Reidesel stood off to one side, understanding only a few words of the English prayer. Phillips stood next to Burgoyne. The Earl of Balcarres and several other senior officers stood respectfully hatless in the drizzle from the leaden skies above.

"Simon Fraser was my friend and comrade," Burgoyne said to the group in a strong, level voice. "A braver, more able man never walked this Earth. General Fraser's life was too brief, but it serves as a noble, matchless, shining example to us all of selfless dedication to duty and of compassion for each of God's creatures, regardless of station in life. For the rest of my days, I shall miss his companionship. His memory will forever serve as my lantern on days of darkness. Farewell to you, Simon. I am confident that we shall meet again."

As Burgoyne spoke, the cannon fire from the rebel emplacement intensified, but Phillips immediately realized from the sound that the enemy guns were now firing only empty bursts. No bombardment was now issuing from the barrels of the rebel cannon.

"They've finally realized what we're doing here on this bluff," he told Burgoyne. "Instead of shelling us now, they're now firing a salute to the fallen general."

"Good for them," Burgoyne said. "A touch of unexpected gallantry from the enemy. Simon would approve, I suspect. Well, come, General. We've considerable work to be about now that the sun is falling."

"We're retreating tonight, then?" Phillips said.

"At dawn," Burgoyne told him. "We'll complete our preparations, dine properly one last time and then move out. It's not as though we have a choice."

Frederika. 1777

Standing on the sweeping porch of Schuyler's grand house, the baroness had been badly shaken when rebel cannon had begun bombarding the scene of Fraser's funeral. As the shot had rained down on the site, she'd watched her husband standing off to one side as the chaplain had read the prayers. Throughout the ceremony, Freddie had stood at rigid attention in the drizzle, acting as though cannon fire were not being directed at the site while Frederika had leaned against a pillar, in abject terror, expecting at any moment to see the entire party obliterated by an explosive shell. When the ceremony ended, the party of senior officers at the gravesite conferred with Burgoyne then broke up to go about their duties. The baroness immediately sprinted down from the porch and intercepted Riedesel as he moved off in the direction of his troops. Frederika rushed up to him and hugged him ferociously.

"Are you all right, Freddie?" she asked anxiously. "You were not injured?"

"No one was injured," he said. "There are far too many of them, this rabble, but they cannot fire big guns with any skill. Now that this is done, however, I must attend to the preparations for our retreat. It is the commanding general's plan that we depart at daybreak. He will not leave the rebels our cannon, and he believes that the river road is too soft with mud for us to move north with the big guns before that time."

"You disagree, I take it," Frederika said.

"When you fight, you fight," von Riedesel said, "and when you run, you run. We should move out under cover of darkness; the hell with the cannon. We need to get far enough north and free of this rebel fire to erect a bridge back across this river or we will never be able to make it back to Ticonderoga. Oh, and one more delay is on his mind. Before we leave, he plans another supper for us all tonight. You must dress for dinner, my darling. We are socializing again this evening."

In the growing darkness, Riedesel could just barely see his wife's face turn bright red. He heard her mutter a uniquely foul Germanic curse common among the ranks of his troops. Despite his own irritation, Riedesel laughed.

"Ah," he said, smiling through his own grim humor, "a soldier's lady after all."

"He is doing it for her," Frederika hissed out. "Her delicate nerves must be eased. Madame's distress must be allayed. He cares more for her needs than for the needs of the entire army. It has been this way from the very start, Freddie. This whore he picked up in Quebec has clouded his judgment from the beginning."

"I cannot dispute that conclusion. Nor, my beloved one, would I ever risk disagreeing with you when are so angry."

"He must be spoken to," Frederika said.

"I remind you that he remains the commanding general," the baron said in a tone of voice that Frederika both recognized and had learned to take seriously. "He commands; we do our duty and follow. Now, return to our quarters and dress yourself properly for this occasion. I shall meet you at this manor house in two hours."

"Freddie ..." the baroness began.

But the baron had already turned on his heel and was marching briskly into the camp. Silently, Frederika watched her husband disappear into the sea of tents in the darkening drizzle. She glanced back at Schuyler's mansion. Already, she noted, the great house's windows were ablaze with light from candles in the vast dining hall. Two ox carts jammed with fine food and wines had pulled in front of the mansion and were being unloaded by servants. She could see the assemblage of musicians mounting the steps to the porch with their instruments in hand. Another merry evening, quite clearly, was planned by the commanding general – another interlude of light chatter and songs and champagne for the senior officers and their ladies. Only this time, Frederika realized, the pleasure of the occasion would be marred by a number of empty chairs around Schuyler's huge dining table.

The farmhouse that quartered the baron and baroness, the house in which Simon Fraser had breathed his last just before dawn, stood about a half mile north of the Schuyler mansion. Frederika briskly walked the distance through the night drizzle along the muddy river road. By the time she arrived, she was soaked through, and her mood was as dark as the chilly autumn night. She saw to it that the servants properly fed the children and settled them into bed. Then she entered the room where Fraser had died, scrubbed herself down from the wash basin and spent forty-five minutes dressing carefully and properly composing herself for the evening's events. When the baroness emerged from the farmhouse, she noted that the rain had eased. As she moved to climb into the calash her maids had ordered brought from the barn for Frederika's disposal, she found herself suddenly met in front of the building by several muddy soldiers from the Hesse-Hanau regiments who had emerged from the darkness. They were begging for food.

"Have you nothing to eat in camp?" Frederika demanded.

"No my lady," said one grenadier. "Our regimental stores were exhausted by mid day. Just a few scraps of bread or, if you can spare it, some potatoes or some bits of meat. That's all we ask. Tomorrow, as we retreat, we might be able to forage a bit."

"Go around the back and see the cook," she said. "He crossed the river today and stole some eggs and some chickens to roast. Tell him I said to feed you. Tomorrow, though, you must forage. We will have no more here after tonight."

The men were effusive in their gratitude. They went around behind the small building before Frederika had climbed into the calash, her eyes blazing with anger. The calash deposited her at the mansion just as Lady Harriet was coming down the porch steps from the imposing building. Frederika, who had heard that Lord Acland had been wounded and taken prisoner, intercepted Lady Harriet as the pregnant woman descended the steps.

"Haff you received more vord of your husband?" Frederika said in her heavily accented English.

"He lives," Lady Harriet said. "I'm going to him at dawn in a flatboat accompanied by Reverend Brudenell under a flag of truce. General Burgoyne has had an exchange of letters with General Gates. I'm assured that I will be treated with appropriate courtesy."

"Zen ve vill not see you again," Frederika said. "Ve will be retreating north at dawn. Vill you take your dog vis you to ze enemy camp or do you vant me to take him? My children, zey love zat big, friendly beast."

"There's no need," Lady Harriet said quietly. "Some soldiers killed Jack at nightfall and ate him. I didn't know it had happened until later."

"It is zat bad for ze English, too, zen?" the baroness said.

Lady Harriet nodded. "In a few more days, after they eat the horses and the oxen, they might be killing and eating one another. There is no food left except what's inside this house."

"Zere is food at Ticonderoga," Frederika said.

"If you can get there. For my part, though, I must go to my John. And I must, at all costs, protect this child I carry."

"Ya, at all costs," the baroness said, embracing Lady Harriet tightly.

After watching Lady Harriet vanish into the wet darkness of the camp, Frederika climbed the stairs to the sweeping porch and strode into the house. As she entered the dining hall, she could hear the musicians at the far end of the room tuning their instruments. The smell of roasting meat and vegetables circulated through the room from the cooking sheds at the rear of the building. Freddie was nowhere to be found, but General Phillips, the Earl of Balcarres and several other senior commanders were already at the table, drinking wine and talking seriously. Their ladies, including Babette, were congregated in a corner of the room, glorious in their glimmering gowns and jewelry.

"Vere is General Burgoyne?" Frederika asked Phillips.

"In that room across the hall there," the artillery officer

replied. "He's reading a message from General Gates. He'll be out momentarily, I'm sure, Baroness."

Without another word, Frederika turned and walked to the closed door. She didn't bother to knock. She opened the door and found Burgoyne at a desk reading a document.

"Good evening, Baroness," Burgoyne said, glancing up.

Frederika closed the door behind her. She sat down in the chair facing the desk. For a long moment, as Burgoyne put down the document he had been reading and surveyed the situation, Frederika said nothing. Then Burgoyne said, "I presume there is a matter you wish to discuss with me, Baroness."

"Ze men are hungry," she said.

Burgoyne nodded. "I'm acutely aware of that circumstance. I am hopeful that our foragers will have good fortune tomorrow as we move north, and my war chest still contains a considerable sum for the purchase of provisions if we can find someone to sell to us."

"Zey are hungry now," Frederika said quietly. "My husband's troops are begging food. Ze English troops ate Lady Harriet's dog. Ve cannot do zis, General. Ve cannot feast and drink tonight as brave men starve in ze cold rain outside. Zis is not right."

Burgoyne sat back in his chair, eying the baroness silently.

"I know zis is not my place," Frederika said, somewhat more awkward now. "My apologies, General. I am a woman who sometimes speaks her mind too freely, I know. But ve are here, in zis circumstance, because ve took too much time coming down from ze lake. Ve spent too many evenings in zis fashion. Zere vas no need."

"I had a need," Burgoyne replied quietly.

Frederika leaned forward in her chair. Her eyes narrowed. "She had a need. Her needs outweighed ze needs of all others. Zey outweighed the needs of zis campaign. Now zey outweigh ze needs of our brave and ravaged troops."

For a long moment, Burgoyne did not reply. He merely leaned back in his own chair. Frederika watched his face. Burgoyne remained expressionless. Then, suddenly, he stood. Instantly, Frederika also rose.

"I appreciate your candor, Baroness," Burgoyne said quietly. "The wife and daughter of generals has reminded another general of his duty. For this you have my eternal gratitude."

Burgoyne rounded the desk, threw open the door and marched purposefully across the broad hallway and into the dining hall.

"General Phillips," Burgoyne called out as he entered the room.

Instantly, both Phillips and Balcarres scrambled to their feet. "Sir?" Phillips said.

"How close are we to being able to get under way?" Burgoyne asked as the music died at the far end of the room.

"We're waiting until dawn, Sir," Phillips said, "but, if you prefer, we could be fully under way in the darkness in just three hours."

"Very well," Burgoyne said. "We shall begin the march to Ticonderoga in three hours, then. There will be no dinner in this house this evening, gentlemen. Instead, order the chefs to distribute what they have prepared and all remaining provisions equitably to the troops – including the wine and the champagne."

"Very good, Sir," Phillips said.

"One more thing," Burgoyne said. "In case the rebels attempt to molest us, establish a line of cannon at the edge of the woods to the north of this building to cover our retreat up the river road."

"That will be difficult, Sir," Phillips said. "The mansion will block our view of the road and the fields to the south."

"That's a problem easily solved," Burgoyne said quietly. "Just before we begin the march to Ticonderoga, we'll burn this house to its foundations."

Babette.1777

Babette was startled. She listened to Burgoyne's announcement with surprise. The moment he finished speaking he headed back to the small office he'd established across the hall from the dining hall. As Babette passed the baroness in the hallway she was fairly certain that she'd recognized the faintest hint of satisfaction on Frederika's face. Babette followed Burgoyne through the door and closed it as he resumed his seat at the desk.

"We're leaving in only three hours?" she asked.

Burgoyne nodded. "You must pack immediately, my love. Have my valet pack my bags and leave a fresh field uniform on the bed for me."

"But why so quickly?"

Burgoyne gazed up at her. "The men are starving. We must get about the retreat so we can find food for them."

"But why burn this house, Jack? It's such a lovely place. Where will we sleep tomorrow night?"

"The troops are not only hungry, they're also freezing in this abominable weather. I plan to build them a large fire to warm their bones in advance of our departure. I have here on my desk a letter from General Gates demanding our surrender – our capitulation, he calls it. If I reject this demand, and I shall, then the rebels will quite soon attack – probably tomorrow, in fact. We cannot stay here a moment longer. Now, as I instructed, go pack."

Babette rounded the desk, bent over and embraced the commanding general. To her surprise, she found him stiff and unresponsive. Confused, Babette released him and gazed thoughtfully into his face. In the flickering candlelight from the desk, Burgoyne was impassive.

"I'll be ready quickly, Jack," she told him quietly.

She wasn't, however. In the sprawling bedroom she'd shared with John Burgoyne, Babette packed carefully – folding her gowns meticulously and painstakingly stashing her jewels in one small bag she could carry in one hand — and then piled the bags near the door as Burgoyne's valet packed up the commanding general's clothing and equipment in silence.

"When the general is ready, carry the bags downstairs," she told the valet as Burgoyne entered the room.

"Wait outside on the porch," he told her. "I'll be down in a moment."

Again, Babette tried to embrace him, but she could feel the coldness there. She had never seen Jack like this before. It unnerved her. She descended the curving staircase and emerged on the porch to find Lady Harriet and handsome young Reverend Brudenell standing just outside, near the door, wrapped in heavy cloaks against the severe night chill. She greeted them warmly.

"General Burgoyne just gave us a safe passage document," Brudenell said. "We're going now, before this army departs this place and the rebels rush after you. We'll go by torchlight down the river in the flatboat."

"If the rebels don't fire on us," Lady Harriet added.

Brudenell took her hand. "God will be with us, Lady Harriet," he said.

Babette embraced Lady Harriet and waved as an ox cart transported them away from the house and down to the river where the flatboats were pulled up on the shore. From the porch Babette could, through the darkness, see and hear the sheer madness in the camp just to the south of the mansion. The frenzy – the shouting of the sergeants, the sight of tents being struck – was always the same when the army began to move. Tonight, though, the enterprise struck Babette as even more frantic than usual. She was watching the flurry of activity when, simultaneously, an ox cart driven by an solemn-looking, middle-aged Indian pulled in front of the porch and Burgoyne emerged from the front door dressed in a clean but rather worn field uniform.

"This is for you, my love," Burgoyne told her, gesturing toward the ox-cart. "Climb aboard and meet your driver. His name is Keuka. He's a member of the Seneca nation. Colonel Skene assures me that, unlike so many of our red brethren, he's a highly reliable man."

Babette was confused. "Then I won't be traveling in the calash with the baroness?"

"You will not," Burgoyne told her quietly. "The baroness and the other ladies will be traveling with this army as we attempt to reach the rather questionable safety of Ticonderoga. Keuka speaks no English, but you can communicate with him, more or less, in French. He will be taking you further north along the river road and then across more rugged roads, I fear, through the mountains back into Canada. This, my love, is where we must part."

Babette's eyes widened in pure shock. She felt a thrill of … well, she wasn't precisely sure how to characterize the emotion, settle into the pit of her stomach. She began, "Oh, Jack …"

By then, however, Burgoyne had swept her up in his arms and was pressing his lips to hers. It was a familiar sensation, one she treasured, and then he was stepping away from her, his large hands still encasing her small ones. He said, "It's finished. You must have grasped that by now. It's possible that this army might reach Ticonderoga – although, frankly, I have my doubts. And, if we do, the hardship of the winter there, even assuming that we can prevent the fort from being captured, would be too arduous for you to be subjected to."

The realization of what was happening sinking in on her, Babette began to weep. Again, Burgoyne drew her to him and held her tightly in the darkness.

"You'll be safe," he told her. "In that cart is a sturdy sack containing much of what remained in this army's war chest. It's solid gold English coin to ensure that you can provide for yourself — and in rather grand style, actually — for the rest of your days. If I'm forced to surrender, as I suspect I shall be rather soon, the rebels would only confiscate that money to purchase weaponry to use against English troops. I fully expect when I return to London to be cashiered out of the army and possibly even ejected from Commons, but no one will blame me for the loss of the war chest."

"I can't leave you, Jack," Babette choked out between her sobs.

"You must, Bab," Burgoyne told her simply. "This is how our dream must end. We now must go on separately – you to a long and happy life and me to disgrace in London. The fates have decreed this ending for us. I shall never forget you, my love. Your face shall be in my final thoughts, and your memory shall reside in my heart forever."

Babette was inconsolable. "But what shall I do without you, Jack?"

For the briefest of moments, a slight, ironic smile played around the corners of Burgoyne's lips. Finally, he said, "Well, you might consider returning to your husband. At the moment, his prospects would appear to be considerably brighter than my own."

It took Burgoyne a few more moments to get the sobbing Babette into the cart. Weeping uncontrollably, she was hunched over on the bench seat next to the Indian as the cart pulled away from the porch in the darkness. Well north of the estate, just before the ox cart made the final turn into utter blackness of the river road, Babette turned in her seat and glanced back. On the river, as a small speck of light against the inky surface of the water, she could see the torch-lit flatboat bearing Lady Harriet and the Reverend Brudenell south to the rebel camp. Closer and off slightly to her right as she observed the torchlight receding on the river, Philip Schuyler's elegant country mansion, thoroughly doused in coal oil by now, erupted into a gigantic ball of fire.

Babette watched through her tears as the flames soared and danced upward into the cold night sky over Saratoga.

Burgoyne. 1777

Marching northward in the relentless drizzle along the Hudson's western bank, Burgoyne found himself, as he'd feared, unable to secure sufficient food for his men. In just a few days, they had slaughtered and eaten virtually all of the oxen and most of the horses — activities conducted under relentless and dependably deadly rebel sharpshooter fire from the rear. That same rebel fire resulted in several failed English attempts to erect another bridge back across the Hudson. English cannon were abandoned along the route and employed by the rebels to disturbing effect as Burgoyne drove his remaining troops north. Dysentery ravaged the troops, both English and German. When Burgoyne learned from the few remaining Indian scouts that Fort Edward had been wrested from the small contingent of troops Burgoyne had left there and secured by rebel forces, he realized that even if he could somehow manage to construct a bridge and move his badly battered army back across the river, the path of Ticonderoga had been effectively blocked. That was when he called his officers together.

"Gentlemen," the commanding general said after describing their situation to his subordinates, "I seek your guidance and your best judgment. What course of action do you recommend to me?"

The verdict for surrender was unanimous. Early that afternoon, on

October 16, 1777, Burgoyne sent a courier with a message to Horatio Gates. The rebel commanding general responded with a courier of his own. At Burgoyne's request the surrender document would be labeled a "convention" rather than a "capitulation." The formal surrender would occur the next day. In his letter, Gates specified arrangements and details. The following morning, Burgoyne and his senior officers, resplendent in their dress uniforms, stood outside the commanding general's pavilion-like tent as James Wilkinson rode up flanked by two Army of the United States cavalrymen beneath a white flag. Wilkinson recognized Burgoyne instantly from the glimpse he'd caught of the English commanding general standing on the roof of that hut at Bemis Heights. Wilkinson saluted and introduced himself.

"You're to be my escort, I presume," Burgoyne said.

"I am, Sir," Wilkinson said. "You and your senior staff are to accompany me to General Gates."

The party mounted up. Phillips and Riedesel rode side by side flanked by their staffs. Burgoyne and Wilkinson took the lead. The route the English officers pursued in following Wilkinson took them for a brief period along the river. Burgoyne glanced out over the water to his left.

"Tell me, Colonel," Burgoyne said, "do you think the river might be fordable at this point?"

"Indeed, General Burgoyne," Wilkinson said, "but as you surely understand there are American troops on the far side."

"Yes," Burgoyne said from his saddle. "I've seen them as we've marched northward – and for far too long, actually."

Just north of the rebel camp, as the party of horsemen crossed a wide meadow, the sun emerged from the clouds and beamed down on the scene. Burgoyne glanced around at the meadow flanked by trees garish and gaudy in their October splendor. Gates, his senior officers and a crowd of hundreds of civilians met the party at the edge of the rebel camp. Burgoyne swung down from his mount, examining Granny Gates in his plain blue field uniform in contrast to the showy red, blue, white and gold of Burgoyne's attire. Wilkinson, as he had been instructed, conducted formal introductions. Burgoyne struggled to recall Gates' face from their mutual service in Europe, but he'd apparently taken little note of the commissary man in those bygone days. Horatio Gates was a complete stranger to him. Burgoyne removed his plumed hat and bowed.

He said, "The fortunes of war, General Gates, have made me your prisoner."

Gates saluted. Then he said, "I shall always be ready to bear testimony that it has not been through any fault of Your Excellency."

The surrender document Gates had prepared was simple and to the point. Both Gates and Burgoyne signed it beneath a sweeping tent canopy. It called for the English and German troops to lay down their guns, which they did in regimented fashion after marching in formation into the rebel camp behind their officers. The surrender document required all English and German troops to sign a separate document pledging that they would never again fight against the government of United States of America. They also had to agree to be marched to Boston, where they would be dispatched back to Europe on English ships at English expense. The ceremony concluded with the obligatory surrender of Burgoyne's sword to Gates and a fair amount of surprisingly brisk marching by English and German troops in the meadow to the north of the rebel camp to a concert of English military band music. Burgoyne had ordered his bandmaster to perform a century-old martial tune entitled The World Turned Upside Down, which struck the English commanding general as ironically appropriate for the occasion.

Most of the regular Army of the United States troops had been ordered to stay away from the ceremony to avoid the possibility of friction with Burgoyne's troops, but an exception was made for a uniformed band that played Yankee Doodle as the English and German troops marched in the meadow. As they marched relieved of their weaponry, some of Burgoyne's men carried pets that the invaders had obtained during the campaign – a number of now domesticated raccoons and foxes as well a tame deer on a leash and even a young black bear roughly the size, shape and color of the Aclands' now departed Newfoundland. The invading troops were followed across the field by hundreds of their women, camp followers who had made the journey with their lovers down from Canada and were now witnessing the ignominious end of this campaign.

Burgoyne knew that many of his troops — and Riedesel's, too, he imagined — would never arrive in Boston. Instead, they would peel off with their women and build new lives in this new country where so many of their comrades had left their blood and bones. Despite Gates' order that the American troops largely stay away from the proceedings, militia members flagrantly ignored Gates' instructions and stood silently examining the survivors of Burgoyne's command as they marched in the field. The militiamen were going home once this business was finished, and they all wanted to look into the faces of the men they had defeated.

Once the formalities were concluded, Burgoyne and his senior officers were to dine with Gates. At one point, Burgoyne stepped outside the tent where the document had been signed for a breath of fresh air. He was surprised to find the Baroness von Riedesel standing outside the tent.

"Is Freddie inside?" she asked in French.

"He is," Burgoyne said. "I would hope, my good Baroness, that your apprehensions are relieved. Your husband and your children are now out of danger – as are all those who have been in my charge for these long, trying months."

For a moment, Frederika's eyes dropped to the ground. Then she looked up and said, "I hope, General, that I shall be forgiven for my outburst at the mansion the night we left. It was not my place—"

"—it was most assuredly your place, Madame," Burgoyne broke in. "I had been distressingly remiss in my duties. No one else had the courage to point that out to me. You displayed such courage, Baroness, just as you have displayed such enviable courage throughout this entire adventure. Your husband, the baron, is to be commended highly in his choice of wives."

Frederika blushed. "You flatter me, General Burgoyne, and no woman is ever immune to such blandishments. You should know that there is a man here who seeks your acquaintance. He met me and my children when we arrived in our calash and showed us great graciousness when I had expected only scorn from these rebels."

Frederika motioned over her shoulder with her thumb. "He stands there, by that tent."

Burgoyne glanced over the shoulder of baroness. Perhaps fifty feet away, beside a row of tents, stood a tall, lean, hawk-faced man wrapped in a long, black cloak.

"Excuse me, please, Baroness," Burgoyne said, curious. He marched toward the man, who met him halfway.

"I'm Philip Schuyler," the man told Burgoyne as he extended his hand.

Burgoyne grasped Schuyler's hand firmly. "I'm afraid, General Schuyler, that I had to burn your grand house at Saratoga."

Schuyler shrugged. "I'll erect another. It'll constitute no great hardship. This is a proud and prosperous land we're building here."

Franklin. 1777

The last time Benjamin Franklin had worn the blue velvet suit, the one he'd had meticulously constructed to fit his bulky form at an exclusive Saville Row tailor shop, had been in the well of the House of Commons just after news had broken in Parliament that those demented colonials had signed a declaration of independence in Philadelphia. At the end of that long, rancorous response in Commons to that unforgivable act of defiance by the government Franklin represented in London, the colonial representative had been ejected from those stately surroundings and had, shortly thereafter, arrived in Paris as one of the American commissioners to the French court. From that moment forward, Franklin had worn old, modest clothing trimmed in fur, perfecting his fraudulent image as a frontiersman. He had missed wearing his treasured blue velvet suit.

Today, though, as he stood in front of his great house in the Paris suburb of Passy watching the gilded coach drawn by four gleaming white horses come through the gate, Franklin stood resplendent in his favorite garment. As the carriage pulled in front of him and the footman scurried down from his seat to open the door for Franklin, the American commissioner heard the voice of the Comte de Vergennes from inside the coach.

"I see you have found a new tailor, Doctor Franklin," said the French foreign minister.

Franklin clambered into the coach and took the seat opposite Vergennes, who was clad in an elegant coat of embroidered silk – the sort of foppish garment the French tended to favor.

"I know that today's meeting with King Louis is no more than a formality," Franklin said, "but I thought that the king deserves the respect of my finest attire for the signing of this treaty. This is crucial for us, my dear Comte. With this welcome aid from the French government, we can most assuredly hold on to the nation we've created."

Vergennes smiled broadly as the coach got underway for the royal palace at Versailles.

"Doctor Franklin," the French foreign minister said, "how could you ever have doubted our faith in your ultimate success?"

Frederick and George. 1781

Darkness shrouded the hill and the vast tent in which Lord North and King George III had spent a long, exhausting day in deep discussion. Frederick had been minutely thorough in his presentation, omitting no detail he felt the king might deem even remotely relevant. As he completed his recitation, Frederick sank back into his chair. His voice was gone now. So was his spirit.

"You understand," the king said slowly, "that I must now accept your resignation as my first minister. There is no other recourse."

"Of course," Frederick said softly.

"It will be only a formality. After Yorktown, your government cannot stand in any event. I'm merely avoiding the unpleasantness of attempting to have the Crown stand by you during what would be certain to be a vigorous assault in Parliament. You do understand my position, I trust."

"I do, indeed, your Majesty."

"I'm thinking of supporting Lord Rockingham as first minister. Tell me, Frederick, would that selection meet with your approval?"

Lord North laughed aloud. "A Rockingham government would not long stand, I fear."

"No," the king said. "In all likelihood, it will fall soon enough. This entire business with the colonies has left us in a rather nettlesome position. The empire will not soon recover from this loss."

"We live in troublesome times, your Majesty," Lord North said. "The world is changing on us."

"Too bad, really," said King George III. "I rather liked the world as it was."

"Yes," Frederick Lord North said, "and as it will never be again."

Epilogue

• After a time as an honored guest at Philip Schuyler's Albany mansion, John Burgoyne returned to England to patter his way through hearings in Parliament on his defeat, to resign from the army and to reinvent himself as an eminently successful London playwright. His most unforgettable stage character was the uniquely beautiful and irresistible Lady Bab Lardoon, who made her appearance in a long-running play entitled The Maid of the Oaks. In his late fifties and sixties, Burgoyne's political career flourished again while he fathered four children with a lovely young opera singer whom he never married. Upon his sudden death at age seventy, he was buried in a place of honor in Westminster Abbey, a hero of the English Empire despite the disastrous defeat of his army at Saratoga.

• Lord John Acland and Lady Harriet stayed with Burgoyne at Schuyler's mansion and returned with him to London. After his arrival in England, Acland died of injuries sustained in a duel provoked by derogatory remarks about the courage of the English forces at Saratoga. Lady Harriet remarried. Her new husband was the Reverend Edward Brudenell.

• Philip Schuyler went on to become a U. S. senator and a bitter political opponent of John Adams, who became the nation's first one-term President.

• Horatio Gates was transferred to South Carolina. There he lost a key battle with English forces and was relieved of his command after fleeing the scene of combat on a race horse.

• Benedict Arnold was incensed by, among other things, the fact